ONE FOOT IN EDEN

The above engraving by John Bewick is taken from *The Looking-Glass for the Mind*
(London: E. Newberry, 1792).

ONE FOOT IN EDEN

MODES OF PASTORAL IN ROMANTIC POETRY

Lore Metzger

UNIVERSITY OF NORTH CAROLINA PRESS

CHAPEL HILL AND LONDON

Library of Congress Cataloging-in-Publication Data

Metzger, Lore, 1925–
One foot in Eden.

Bibliography: p.
Includes index.
1. English poetry—19th century—History and
criticism. 2. Romanticism—England. 3. Pastoral
poetry, English—History and criticism.
I. Title.
PR590.M48   1986   821'.7'09145   85-16462
ISBN 0-8078-1678-7

The publication of this work was made possible in part through
a grant from the National Endowment for the Humanities, a
federal agency whose mission is to award grants to support
education, scholarship, media programming, libraries, and
museums, in order to bring the results of cultural activities
to a broad, general public.

Designed by Neil Morgan

In memory of Rosalie L. Colie

One foot in Eden still, I stand
And look across the other land.
The world's great day is growing late,
Yet strange these fields that we have planted
So long with crops of love and hate.
Time's handiworks by time are haunted,
And nothing now can separate
The corn and tares compactly grown.
The armorial weed in stillness bound
About the stalk; these are our own.
Evil and good stand thick around
In the fields of charity and sin
Where we shall lead our harvest in.

Yet still from Eden springs the root
As clean as on the starting day.
Time takes the foliage and the fruit
And burns the archetypal leaf
To shapes of terror and of grief
Scattered along the winter way.
But famished field and blackened tree
Bear flowers in Eden never known.
Blossoms of grief and charity
Bloom in these darkened fields alone.
What had Eden ever to say
Of hope and faith and pity and love
Until was buried all its day
And memory found its treasure trove?
Strange blessings never in Paradise
Fall from these beclouded skies.

Edwin Muir, *One Foot in Eden*

CONTENTS

PREFACE

"A genre endures," Claudio Guillén says, "insofar as it continues to be a problem-solving model, a standing invitation to the matching of matter and form" (386). Of all classical poetic genres, only epic has had greater influence than pastoral (Curtius 187). It is the thesis of this book that pastoral was revitalized as an influential "problem-solving model" by major English Romantic poets after a century of lifeless and trivial productions in this genre. My purpose is not to provide an exhaustive overview of Romantic pastoral, but to offer a closeup of key poems that reveal the spectrum of Romantic permutations of pastoral tradition. Romantic pastoral poems are frequently traditional while being avant-garde, classical while being romantic.

Surprisingly little has been written on Romantic pastoral, compared to the plethora of critical commentary on Renaissance poetry in this genre. With the exceptions of Wagenknecht and Lindenberger, critics have been much more concerned with natural supernaturalism, the Romantic sublime, or, more conventionally, Romantic nature imagery. Most recently, a study of Wordsworth's influence on the nineteenth and twentieth centuries confines itself to "nature poems that are at one and the same time 'human nature poems'" (Keith 4) but has nothing to say about pastoral as a special kind of "human nature poem."

Perspectives on landscapes and poetics of pastoral overlap, no doubt, but they are not identical. Romantic pastoral embodies some key features of the pastoral tradition that are not found in other nature poetry in the same dense configuration, which is why Wordsworth's *Ruined Cottage* is not a pastoral narrative but *Michael* is.

Pastoral is most readily identified by both its microstructure and its macrostructure. Its microstructure has as its centerpiece a stylized landscape, a *locus amoenus*, which is typically a quiet arbor surrounded by shady trees, perfumed by spring flowers, animated by a gentle breeze, and enlivened by a bubbling spring or stream. Whether the inhabitant of the pleasance is a shepherd or some nonbucolic refugee from the world beyond the bower, he is an independent soul who shares his seclusion with a chosen few, with whom he enjoys amicable contests. This pastoral microcosm readily assimilates allusions to a golden age, paradise, Eden, or Arcadia. These are the pastoral equivalents of the recurring motifs by which we readily identify epics—challenges to single combat, a heavenly forged shield, councils in heaven, descents into the underworld. Neither epic nor pastoral can be reduced to its formulaic conventions, which serve the purpose of quickly signaling to the reader that an epic or pastoral scenario is in progress. As in all memorable epics, in memorable pastoral poems the formulaic language releases fresh meanings by synecdochically meshing with the poems' macrostructure. Explicitly or implicitly, the macrostructure embodies some of the following antitheses: between nature and art, country and city, *otium* and *negotium*, retirement and active life, leisure and work, summer and winter, happiness and melancholy, energy and acedia, past and present, communality and alienation.

It is true, however, as Paul Alpers has recently noted, that there is no agreement on a definition of pastoral among the most important modern critics on the subject, from Empson to Poggioli, from Kermode to Raymond Williams. Most critics' versions of pastoral are indeed based on different criteria, with some privileging the psychological or sociological, and others privileging the formal or thematic. Alpers's own definition centers on Kenneth Burke's rhetorical concept of a "representative anecdote" that functions as both a reflection and a deflection of reality. Alpers argues that taking the lives of shepherds as the representative anecdote of pastoral enables the critic to analyze specific instances of pastoral discourse while also following the course of the literary genre that "evolves by transforming the structures and the stock of conventions provided by its previous instances" ("What Is Pastoral?" 442), just as Virgil's *First Eclogue* transforms Theocritus's representative anecdote. Alpers's formula succeeds in highlighting the intertextuality of pastoral poetry across different historical periods and the self-conscious use of convention that explicitly or implicitly convenes an absent predecessor ("Convening and Convention" 277–97). It fails, however, to explore what aspects of reality these convenings and conventions re-present and what aspects they inevitably omit, nor does it account for how the re-presented reality is enmeshed in the specific historical moment in which the text is situated.

In examining how individual Romantic poets use pastoral conventions as a resource and a recourse, I have profited from Alpers's as well as from other modern theories of pastoral, but I have found none as heuristically productive as Friedrich Schiller's. Schiller offers a critical perspective that is at once aesthetic and moral, hermeneutic and normative, historical and theoretical. Lukács calls Schiller "the precursor of Hegel in aesthetics" in that "the sense of important social determinants of bourgeois life is basic to his aesthetic categories; in that he accepts without reservation the existence of these social determinants and their aesthetic reflection, and by studying them works out the specific characteristics of modern literature" (*Age of Goethe* 123). It is precisely because Schiller's typology of poetry frees itself from classical authority and orients itself by modern literary practice, challenged by contemporary political events, that his distinction between elegy (regressive, nostalgic) and idyll (progressive, projecting a goal of human perfectibility) serves to define modes of Romantic pastoral—its desires, tensions, and failures.

In my study of permutations of pastoral in English Romantic poetry in the light of Schiller's modes, I have tried to bear in mind Raymond Williams's caveat (developed in his contrast between country and city) that "at every point we need to put these ideas to the historical realities: at times to be confirmed, at times denied. But also . . . we need to put the historical realities to the ideas, for at times these express, not only in disguise and displacement but in effective mediation or in offered and sometimes effective transcendence, human interests and purposes for which there is no other immediately available vocabulary" (*Country and City* 291). English poets from Wordsworth to Shelley resorted to the pastoral repertoire of *topoi*, themes, and representative anecdotes for articulating their belief in the ideals of the French Revolution while also affirming that these goals were attainable without revolution. (Blake was a notable exception in his advocacy of revolution in and through his poetry.) That is to say: pastoral most frequently functions in English Romantic poetry to articulate radical ends of social reform attenuated by an insistence on conservative means. Romantic pastoral typically foregrounds the belief in the perfectibility of the individual as the means of transforming society into a model of communality. This belief assumes as a given the paradox that the stable institutions of society can be preserved intact while ultimately revolutionary results can be achieved by the transformation of the individual consciousness. Romantic pastoral on the whole reinforces and is reinforced by the Romantic commitment to imagination (even when it is skeptical about its efficacy) as the means of connecting the actual and the possible, object and subject, present and future.

My study is of course indebted to many scholars, especially to the brilliant work on Renaissance pastoral by Rosalie L. Colie and on Romantic rhetoric by Paul de Man. In learning to take the measure of Schiller's myriad-faceted thought, I owe a special debt to the exemplary scholarship of Elizabeth M. Wilkinson and Leonard A. Willoughby. To both I am also indebted for many years of generous encouragement and advice. Among others who have also encouraged and advised me at crucial points, I wish particularly to thank Martine Brownley, Frederick Garber, Ernst and Ilse Gombrich, Marjorie Kaufman, Helen and Patrick McCarthy, and Jean Sudrann. I am grateful to Lee Ann Lloyd for the calm professionalism with which she has coped with my revisions in preparing the final version of my manuscript.

Two chapters of the book have previously appeared under the same titles but in less comprehensive versions: Chapter 5 ("Wordsworth's Pastoral Covenant") in *Modern Language Quarterly* 37 (1976) and Chapter 6 ("Coleridge in Sicily: A Pastoral Interlude in *The Prelude*") in *Genre* 11 (1978).

KEY TO ABBREVIATIONS

AL   Schiller, Friedrich. *On the Aesthetic Education of Man, in a Series of Letters.* Edited and translated with an introduction, commentary, and glossary of terms by Elizabeth M. Wilkinson and Leonard A. Willoughby. Oxford: Clarendon Press, 1967.

BL   Coleridge, Samuel Taylor. *Biographia Literaria.* Edited by James Engell and W. Jackson Bate. Vol. 7 (in 2 parts) of *The Collected Works of Samuel Taylor Coleridge.* Edited by Kathleen Coburn. London: Routledge & Kegan Paul; Princeton: Princeton University Press, 1983.

BL (1907)   Coleridge, Samuel Taylor. *Biographia Literaria.* Edited with his Aesthetical Essays by John Shawcross. 2 vols. Oxford: Oxford University Press, 1907.

CL   Coleridge, Samuel Taylor. *Collected Letters.* Edited by Earl Leslie Griggs. 6 vols. Oxford: Clarendon Press, 1956–71.

CN   Coleridge, Samuel Taylor. *The Notebooks.* Edited by Kathleen Coburn. 3 vols. to date. London: Routledge & Kegan Paul, 1957–.

EY — Wordsworth, William. *Letters of William and Dorothy Wordsworth: The Early Years, 1787–1805.* Edited by Ernest de Selincourt. 2nd edition revised by Chester L. Shaver. Oxford: Clarendon Press, 1967.

Forman — Keats, John. *The Poetical Works and Other Writings.* Edited by H. Buxton Forman. Revised by M. Buxton Forman. 8 vols. Hampstead Edition. 1938–39. Reprint, New York: Phaeton Press, 1970.

GA — Goethe, Johann Wolfgang. *Gedenkausgabe der Werke, Briefe und Gespräche.* Edited by Ernst Beutler. 27 vols. Zürich: Artemis Verlag, 1948–71.

Gow — *Theocritus.* Edited with a translation and commentary by A. S. F. Gow. 2 vols. Cambridge: Cambridge University Press, 1950.

Home — Wordsworth, William. *Home at Grasmere.* Edited by Beth Darlington. *The Cornell Wordsworth.* Edited by Stephen Parrish. Ithaca: Cornell University Press, 1977.

MY — Wordsworth, William. *The Letters of William and Dorothy Wordsworth: The Middle Years, Part 1, 1806–1811.* Edited by Ernest de Selincourt. 2nd edition revised by Mary Moorman. Oxford: Clarendon Press, 1969. *Part 2, 1812–1820.* Edited by Ernest de Selincourt. 2nd edition revised by Mary Moorman and Alan G. Hill. Oxford: Clarendon Press, 1970.

NA — Schiller, Friedrich. *Werke. Nationalausgabe.* Edited by Julius Petersen, Gerhard Fricke, Lieselotte Blumenthal, and Benno von Wiese. 17 vols. to date. Weimar: Hermann Böhlaus Nachfolger, 1943–. (Note: I have modernized the spelling in quoting from this edition. All translations are my own.)

Norton Prelude Wordsworth, William. *The Prelude, 1799, 1805, 1850.* Edited by Jonathan Wordsworth, M. H. Abrams, and Stephen Gill. New York: Norton, 1979.

Oxford Shelley Shelley, Percy Bysshe. *Poetical Works.* Edited by Thomas Hutchinson. London: Oxford University Press, 1967.

Prelude Wordsworth, William. *The Prelude.* Edited by Ernest de Selincourt. 2nd edition revised by Helen Darbishire. Oxford: Clarendon Press, 1959. (Note: All references are to the 1805 text unless otherwise noted.)

1799 Prelude Wordsworth, William. *The Prelude, 1798–1799.* Edited by Stephen Parrish. *The Cornell Wordsworth.* Edited by Stephen Parrish. Ithaca: Cornell University Press, 1977.

PW Wordsworth, William. *The Poetical Works.* Edited by Ernest de Selincourt and Helen Darbishire. 5 vols. Oxford: Clarendon Press, 1940–49.

Reiman Shelley, Percy Bysshe. *Shelley's Poetry and Prose: Authoritative Texts and Criticism.* Edited by Donald H. Reiman and Sharon B. Powers. New York: Norton, 1977. (Note: All citations from Shelley are from this edition unless otherwise noted.)

Shedd Coleridge, Samuel Taylor. *The Complete Works.* Edited by W. G. T. Shedd. 7 vols. New York: Harper, 1853.

ONE FOOT IN EDEN

THE CALL FOR A MODERN PASTORAL

"Shepherds were the men who pleas'd me first," Wordsworth recalled in *The Prelude*, claiming for these shepherds a greater vivifying influence in the world of his time than could be exerted by those mythical herdsmen of the golden age of Saturn or those of the Arcadian tradition transmitted by the ancient poets (8:182–85). Thus at the beginning of the nineteenth century, Wordsworth carried on the centuries-old debate over whether pastoral should imitate golden-age shepherds, as the neoclassic critics maintained, or whether it should imitate real English shepherds, as the rationalistic school insisted.[1]

Typically the neoclassic position in the dispute over pastoral dovetails with the appeal to classical authority in the larger quarrel between ancients and moderns. The two disputes are clearly joined by Pope, who subscribes to the "rules" for pastoral that are derived from the practice of Theocritus and Virgil. "Among moderns," he points out in his "Discourse on Pastoral," "their success has been the greatest who have most endeavour'd to make these ancients their pattern." Thus in his own pastorals he proposes to confine himself to those subjects "which the Critics upon *Theocritus* and *Virgil* will allow to be fit for pastoral" (1:32).

Rationalist critics disputed this rule for pastoral poets, prescribing that they take the ancients as their "pattern" and claiming greater merit for the modern pastoral of Ambrose Philips than for Pope's classical imitations. Philips had challenged the rule for golden-age shepherds by writing of English rustics in an English landscape, as well as by suggesting that Spenser was as worthy a pastoral model as Theocritus or Virgil. Concurring with this view, Addison praised Philips's departure from neoclassic pattern: "One would have thought it impossible for this kind of poetry to have subsisted without fawns and satyrs, wood-nymphs and water-nymphs, with all the tribe of rural deities. But we see he has given a new life and a more natural beauty to this way of writing by substituting in the place of those antiquated fables, the superstitious mythology which prevails among the shepherds of our own country" (Congleton 86).

As this debate dragged on through the eighteenth century—a century more remarkable for uninspired pastoral criticism than for inspired pastoral poetry—critics frequently mingled neoclassic and rationalist criteria, demanding *both* classical myths and realistic imitation of life, or else demanding golden-age shepherds living in Arcadian tranquility *and* wishing to see these ideals verified by contemporary experience.[2] Of course, such requirements were not easily met, especially in an England whose smoke-belching factories were encroaching on the green countryside. Not surprisingly, a reviewer of Gessner's popular idylls in 1789 pointed to Switzerland as unsurpassed in Europe for nourishing the poet's imagination with "rural images": "Where peace, innocence, and contentment reign, there may one realize the pleasing fictions of the golden age, and trace out with facility and truth, the simple manners of a pastoral life."[3] But what of countries where "peace, innocence, and contentment" do not reign? According to this line of reasoning, such countries cannot produce pastoral poetry. Even as sophisticated a critic as Hazlitt adopted this simplistic position. In his lecture on Thomson and Cowper, he pointed out that "we have few good pastorals in the language. Our manners are not Arcadian; our climate is not an eternal spring; our age is not the age of gold. We have no pastoral-writers equal to Theocritus, nor any landscapes like those of Claude Lorraine" (5:98). After decades of such tedious debates, such confusion of art and its subject matter, at least one critic, Nathan Drake, drew the obvious conclusion: "If rural life no longer present us with shepherds singing and piping for a bowl or a crook, why persist, in violation of all probability, to introduce such characters? If pastoral cannot exist without them, let us cease to compose it" (225). Drake nevertheless hastened to reassure his readers that such a drastic solution was not inevitable. Even if shepherds were no longer competing for prize cups—a scene that he claimed was for Theocritus a matter of "hourly observation"—a new pastoral formula could be devised: "simplicity in diction and sentiment, a happy choice of rural imagery, such incidents and circumstances as may even *now* occur in the country . . . are all that are essential to success." Surprisingly, he did not invoke as his modern model Wordsworth's poems that voiced the "admiration and the love, the life / In common things" (*Prelude* 1:117–18)—the *Lyrical Ballads* was published in the same year as Drake's essay on pastoral poetry—but praised Gessner's *Idyllen* for rivaling the ancients through immortal compositions (225).

This call for a new English pastoral dealing with "common things" was given urgency by poets and critics as the *topos* of the pastoral pleasance began to resonate with the pressing issue born of the French Revolution, to envision a new, ideal community, such as Coleridge's Pantisocracy, an experiment in human perfectibility.[4] Similarly the French Revolution taught Wordsworth to recognize that his native mountain valley represented a prototypical egalitarian community. Although he claimed to be "untaught by thinking or by books / To reason well of polity or law / And nice distinctions, then on every tongue, / Of natural rights and civil" (*Prelude* 9:200–203), his conception of Cumberland village communities comes close to the patriarchal stage of social development that, in his *Discourse on Inequality*, Rousseau called "the happiest and most stable" ("l'époque la plus heureuse et la plus durable") (72). During this stage of *société naissante*, men were content with building their own rustic huts, making their own clothes, and gathering their own food,

employing only simple tools and simple skills, requiring no
government since they neither owned nor coveted any prop-
erty: "As long as they undertook only what a single person
could accomplish, and confined themselves to such crafts as did
not require the joint labor of several hands, they lived free,
healthy, honest, and happy lives . . . and enjoyed the delights of
social intercourse between independent individuals" (73). Pre-
cisely this ideal of Rousseau's emergent society—and not of a
primitive state of nature—reverberates in the expressions of
hope sanctioned by a "France standing on the top of golden
hours, / And human nature seeming born again" (*Prelude* 6:
353–54). Thus the paradise that Wordsworth claims as surpass-
ing all mythical paradises is a village community of independent
fellow-laborers, rather than a prelapsarian Eden or a primitive
tribal group:

> But lovelier far than this the Paradise
> Where I was rear'd; in Nature's primitive gifts
> Favor'd no less, and more to every sense
> Delicious, seeing that the sun and sky,
> The elements and seasons in their change
> Do find their dearest Fellow-labourer there,
> The heart of Man, a district on all sides
> The fragrance breathing of humanity,
> Man free, man working for himself, with choice
> Of time, and place, and object. . . .
>   (*Prelude* 8:144–53)

From such an exemplary life of "simplicity, / And beauty,
and inevitable grace" (8:1157–58), Wordsworth gained such a
strong "prepossession" toward the ideals of the French Revo-
lution that the revolutionary events themselves "seem'd nothing
out of nature's certain course, / A gift that rather was come late
than soon" (*Prelude* 9:252–54).[5] Out of his exploration of the
psychological and social experiences that not only nourished
but also threatened or contradicted his "prepossession" evolved
the import of Wordsworth's greatest pastoral poetry—*Michael,*

Home at Grasmere, and the pastoral interludes in the *Prelude*. All these poetic achievements far outdistanced contemporary English critical descriptions and prescriptions for pastoral. For the theoretical acumen that matches Wordsworth's poetic originality, we must look to the great German poet-critic, Friedrich Schiller, whose treatise *Über naive und sentimentalische Dichtung* Lukács called "the first profound philosophical analysis of the essence of modern art" (*Studies in European Realism* 200).

Schiller, like Wordsworth, was a seismograph for the political and social forces of his time. Far from retreating from the momentous events of the 1790s, his writings on aesthetic questions were quickened by the political tumult following the French Revolution. He firmly believed that the humanist had a role to play in counteracting the public's absorption in the daily sensational news of dissension and violence: he could correct the excitement of the moment by directing attention to the connection between the present and lasting human concerns. Schiller was moreover convinced, as he wrote to the Countess von Schimmelmann in November 1795, that "the highest philosophy, like the highest morality and the highest politics, culminates in a poetic idea. It is the poetic spirit that prescribes [*vorzeichnet*] the idea for all three and their perfection lies in approaching this ideal" (*NA* 28:99). That is to say: for Schiller as for Shelley, poets not only represent the world as it is but also, and more importantly, mirror the "gigantic shadows which futurity casts upon the present. . . . Poets are the unacknowledged legislators of the world" (*Critical Prose* 35–36). Schiller had acted out of this conviction in 1794 when he founded a new journal called *Die Horen* (*The Graces*); there, among other contributions, he published in installment form his two major treatises, *On the Aesthetic Education of Man* and *On Naive and Sentimental Poetry*. "At a time when the nearby din of war alarms our country," Schiller wrote in his prospectus for *Die Horen*, "when the clash of political opinions and interests renews this war in nearly all circles and all too frequently drives away the muses and the graces . . . it is as bold as it is salutary to invite the

distracted reader to a totally different kind of colloquy," a collo-
quy aimed at liberating the reader from the narrow, divisive,
and oppressive interests of the present through the higher and
unifying concern with the "purely human" that transcends the
influence of the times (*NA* 22:106). By rigorously shunning
political causes, by zealously eschewing current events, Schiller
promised that his journal would engage in quietly laying the
groundwork for those "better ideas, purer principles, and no-
bler morals, on which all true improvement of the social condi-
tion ultimately depends" (22:107).

Schiller was aware that his utopian idealism was open to ques-
tion. In defending his inquiry into the aesthetic education of
man, he explicitly raised the issue of what it meant to be a
citizen of his age (*Zeitbürger*) as well as a citizen of his state
(*Staatsbürger*) (*AL* 2.2). And he met the issue head on: "Expec-
tantly the gaze of philosopher and man of the world alike is
fixed on the political scene, where now, so it is believed, the very
fate of mankind is being debated. Does it not betray a culpable
indifference to the common weal not to take part in this general
debate?" (2.4). Schiller does not see his insistence on dealing
with timeless and "purely human" questions (*NA* 22:106) as
evading this timely debate. On the contrary, he sees his focus on
moral and aesthetic principles as his way of engaging in the
debate of how to achieve "that most perfect of all the works to
be achieved by the art of man: the construction of true political
freedom" (*AL* 2.1). He argues, further, that the problem of how
to achieve political freedom in practice, in experience, must be
approached through the problem of the aesthetic (2.5).

In seeking to establish the idealistic basis for this enterprise,
Schiller first needed to clarify the interrelation of moral and
aesthetic principles. This was no small task at a time when
aesthetic theory, like political criticism, was remarkable chiefly
for its conceptual confusion. In Germany, no less than in En-
gland, nearly all aesthetic judgments were flawed by what Cole-
ridge termed the "substitution of assertion for argument" (*BL*
2:113). Instead of testing and correcting their feelings about
works of art by appealing to principles, most critics—so Schiller

complained to the Duke of Augustenburg in 1793—tested their aesthetic judgments by appealing to their feelings (*Briefe* 3:249). The following year he again dwelled on the same problem when he told Goethe that if a critic sought to support his judgments through principles, he was embarrased to find that no code of law existed to which he could appeal. He had to choose between remaining silent or becoming both legislator and judge (*GA* 20:24). Clearly Schiller elected the second alternative in writing his literary reviews and critical essays.

Besides suffering from this general legislative confusion and prevailing anarchy in aesthetic judgments, criticism of pastoral poetry suffered even more severely than other literary genres from unresolved contradictions inherent in some eighteenth-century norms. Two widely held views of art and culture were on a collision course. On the one hand, philosophers, theologians, and poets, such as Kant, Herder, and Schiller—to name but the most obvious examples—had come to believe in a theory of human progress, even though they envisioned progress as not necessarily proceeding in a straight line but as involving setbacks or backward spirals as part of the forward thrust toward perfectibility. Goethe once remarked that instead of speaking of the world's progressiveness (*Weltfortschreitung*), we should speak of circumambulation (*Umschreitung*) (*GA* 22: 266). But how was this progress—no matter how roundabout—to be squared with the claim that in the realm of literature norms were fixed once and for all by the classical models? Kant was one of the few thinkers of his time to recognize this difficulty and to solve it by distinguishing between what he saw as continual progress in scientific knowledge and a fixed plane in artistic achievement. In the *Critique of Judgement* he argued that "art stands still at a certain point; a boundary is set beyond which it cannot go, which presumably has been reached long ago and cannot be extended further" (152).

Most literary critics, however, did not draw such a distinction between scientific progress and artistic stasis, or even acknowledge the philosophical problem that Kant thus solved. We have already seen that critical confusion led to the contradictory demands that poets should imitate Theocritus and Virgil but should, at the same time, buttress their Arcadian visions with the realistic depiction of contemporary scenes and individuals. Such a Janus-like posture is well exemplified in Winckelmann's insistence that the only way for moderns to "become great, even, if possible, inimitable [*unnachahmlich*]" is by "imitation [*Nachahmung*] of the ancients" (1:8). This paradoxical compromise between beliefs in modern decline and modern advance brings to mind one of the clichés of the battle between ancients and moderns, that of the modern pygmies attaining new heights of cultural and artistic achievement by standing on the shoulders of the ancient giants.[6] None of the major poets writing at the turn of the eighteenth century cut this Gordian knot by simply declaring the ancient models irrelevant, as some mid-twentieth-century pygmies were to do. Instead, those poet-critics who, like Schiller and the Schlegels, Coleridge and Shelley, continued to admire the classics while radically departing from them, confronted a more difficult problem: how could *both* classic and modern poetry be justly judged, each according to its own value? As Schiller points out, if we deduce the generic norms of poetry exclusively from the practice of the ancient poets, then nothing is easier than to disparage the moderns. But, he adds, nothing is more trivial, either (*NA* 20:439). Instead of pressing for a one-sided victory in this battle, Schiller gives each side its due, examining critically yet sympathetically the basis for a claim for classic perfection on the one hand and for modern perfectibility on the other. Out of this dialectical exploration emerges Schiller's hypothesis of a possible "coalition" of classic and modern. Schiller's concept of pastoral—which undergoes several metamorphoses—plays a crucial part in evolving his synthesis that lies beyond the classic-modern horizons.

But here we are in danger of making Schiller's tratise sound too programmatic. In fact, he fashioned and refashioned his conceptions of classic and modern, as well as his solutions to the contest between the two. Originally, in 1793, he planned an essay dealing exclusively with the concept of the naive. Two

years elapsed, however, before he actually undertook the proj-
ect. By then the naive had become the springboard for three
separate essays that he eventually published as a single treatise,
Über naive und sentimentalische Dichtung.[7] In undertaking the
three essays for his periodical, *Die Horen*, he did not have a
systematic typology of poetry worked out. The first essay had
much less to do with poetry than with psychological and episte-
mological questions concerning man's interest in nature. And
yet, looking back on this essay with the argument of the whole
treatise in mind, we can discern here the groundwork for his
master concept, the dichotomy between naive and sentimen-
tal ways of feeling (*Empfindungsweisen*), ways of relating to the
world.[8] But he allowed the implications of this central di-
chotomy to evolve in circuitous ways without adhering to a
master plan. He told his friend Wilhelm von Humboldt that the
essays dealing with naive and sentimental were related to each
other more through subjective intuition than through deliber-
ate design. To his friend's objection that he should have given
more space to his thoughts on naive poetry, Schiller replied that
when he sent off that first essay to the printer he was unaware
of how much material he had stored up in his mind for the
second one on sentimental poetry (*NA* 28:143–44).

Just as the scope and the proportions of the projected treatise
changed under Schiller's hand in the heat of writing, so did his
emphases and antitheses. Beginning with the question of what
causes us to feel a kind of affection and respect for nature—
whether plants or minerals, animals or children—Schiller wid-
ens the scope of his inquiry to differentiate first between an-
cient and modern ways of feeling about, responding to, nature.
Here his focus narrows down again as he abstracts from these
ways of feeling the more specific contrast between the ways in
which ancient and modern, naive and sentimental poets em-
body in literary works of art their responses to nature. Each
answer gives rise to new questions, often annulling a previous
answer. Schiller's rhetorical strategy in this treatise is the same
as in his *Aesthetic Letters*, aptly characterized by Wilkinson and
Willoughby as an "uncovering" strategy: "Schiller's whole pur-

pose is not to fix the mind, but to keep it moving. And to keep it moving by changing the viewpoint. He takes his reader by the hand and leads him around and around, bringing him now up against a deadlock which will not be resolved until he reaches a different point on the same or on another circle, now to a solution which, as he moves still further around, will reveal within itself problems of even greater complexity. He thus leaves him at the end with an impression, not only of a myriad-faceted problem, but of the multi-dimensionality of the solution he is offering" (lv–lvi).

As Schiller explored different perspectives on ancient/modern, naive/sentimental binary opposites, he enjoyed drawing on his fund of personal experience as poetic creator and creative reader, speaking frequently in the persona of informal essayist rather than that of formal rhetor or philosopher. Not least of the personal experiences challenging his resources of creative reading was his encounter with Goethe, which proved as decisive for his naive/sentimental typology as for his model of wholeness that informed the *Aesthetic Letters*. Schiller's intense preoccupation with Goethe in the summer of 1794 undoubtedly spurred him on finally to begin work on *Naïve and Sentimental Poetry* the following month—writing, as he told Körner, "from the heart and from love" (*NA* 27:46). If the encounter with Goethe acted like an earthquake upon Schiller's whole fund of ideas, it could not fail to jolt his views on ancient and modern poetry.[9] He had been confident, even authoritarian, in his neo-classic pronouncement in his 1791 review of Bürger when he asserted that one of the chief requisites of a poet was the art of idealizing, ennobling, purifying—the art of elevating the individual to the universal (*NA* 22:253). But now, upon more intimate acquaintance with Goethe, Schiller found himself challenged to re-view the comparative merits of an intuitive art created out of manifold particulars and a philosophic art created out of universals. And of course he strained to discover ways of bridging the gap between the two.[10] Previously he had unhesitatingly laid down the law to Bürger to opt for the art of idealization (*Idealisierkunst*) because no one could be a poet without idealizing and ennobling his subject (22:253).

Having confronted the divergence between Goethe's genius and his own, Schiller now needed to rethink what the modern poet's task was: "What path should the poet choose in an age and under conditions like ours?" (28:98). He stated emphatically in his treatise that the most important question confronting aesthetics was "whether and to what extent individuality and ideality can be united in one and the same work of art."[11] The fact that Schiller here poses the question in terms of whether the dualism of ancients and moderns can be overcome through a "coalition" should remove all doubt that he is doing nothing more than defending his own poetic achievement against Goethe's. To say that is not to deny that this personal impulse may have been a driving force for Schiller's speculations; Valéry was surely correct when he observed that "there is no theory that is not a fragment, carefully prepared, of some autobiography" (7:58). But Schiller knew how to distance autobiographic fragments, whether in his poetry or in his prose. Only personal experience detached, even alienated, from the poet can, according to him, communicate universal feelings (22:256). In his *Naive and Sentimental Poetry* he successfully distanced his personal concerns by subsuming them in a larger historical and cultural perspective from which he dialectically explored his typology of naive and sentimental poetry. "Dialectic," according to one of Goethe's maxims, "is the development of the spirit of contradiction [*die Ausbildung des Widersprechungsgeistes*] which is given to human beings in order to learn to differentiate among things" (*GA* 9:650). In Schiller's dialectical inquiry, personal and impersonal concerns, historical and philosophical perspectives, interact productively as Schiller maps the realms of naive and sentimental poetry, discovering their boundaries only to find a vantage point from which such boundaries are barely visible contours in a new configuration. Schiller's argument at every step is exploratory rather than definitive, truly an essay rather than a system.

"As the concept itself implies, poets are always the *guardians* of nature," Schiller wrote near the end of his discussion of the naive. When poets can no longer function as guardians of nature because they have felt the influence of the artificiality of civilization, "they will act as nature's *witnesses* and as its *avengers*. They will either *be* nature or they will *seek* the lost state of nature. From this spring two entirely different modes of poetry [*Dichtungsweisen*] which exhaust poetry's whole domain and take its full measure. All poets who truly are poets will belong either to the *naive* or the *sentimental* category, depending on the nature of the age in which they flourish or on the contingent circumstances that influence their general development and their current disposition [*vorübergehende Gemütsstimmung*]" (*NA* 20:432). Habitual ways of feeling toward nature and of responding to reality determine the two modes of poetry. Schiller repeatedly emphasizes his central concern with the naive and sentimental poets' temper of heart and mind, their responses to the world of experience and to the world of ideas. What may be called the poets' phenomenological horizons determine the options open to them in tackling the task of crafting a model of true humanity.

To reduce Schiller's poetics to his dichotomy between naive and sentimental poetry, however, is to overlook his uncompromising humanism. It is to overlook the relation between the two modes of poetry and his general conception of poetry, which, in a letter to Wilhelm von Humboldt, he expresses through the biological relation of species to genus (*NA* 28:144–45). Poetry in its ideal form "gives to mankind its fullest possible expression" (20:437). Later in his treatise on naive and sentimental poetry Schiller stresses the importance of this general concept of poetry by restating it as the task shared by both naive and sentimental poets if they are worthy of the name *poet* (20:473–74). Clearly Schiller's treatise carries out his announced intention of devoting his journal, *Die Horen*, to gathering together for his readers the particular features of an ideal of humanity that he believed was easily lost sight of in the political upheavals of the day (22:106).

What does Schiller mean by assigning to the poet the task of giving to humanity as complete, as perfect, an expression as possible—"Der Menschheit ihren möglichst vollständigen Ausdruck zu geben" (20:437)? The German *Ausdruck*, like the English *expression*, refers literally to the impression made by pressing a seal into wax. Figurative meanings relevant to Schiller's context include (1) the *act* of representing or manifesting thought, things, feelings, actions in words or symbols; (2) the *manner* or *means* of representing thought, meaning, etc., in language or other media.[12] Does Schiller then mean that it is the poet's task to express human perfection by creating a model of the whole man? Or does he mean the more technical task of finding the best possible poetic means for expressing a model that already exists, such as the model he himself developed in his *Aesthetic Letters*? If he means both—as I think he does—he is stipulating that the poet must combine a philosopher's capacity for formulating moral ideas with the poet's gift for embodying ideas in vivid particulars that are also adequate objective correlatives for his feelings.

If such a coordination of moral and aesthetic activity seems questionable to us, that is a sign of our unwillingness to grant any valid interconnection between the two. When such astute critics as Wimsatt and Brooks are uncomfortable with the moral emphasis of even Aristotle's concept of mimesis, how can Schiller's poetics meet with approval? "Shall we say," ask Wimsatt and Brooks, "that poetry (taken in the educational sense of the *Politics*) assists or parallels the forces of man's moral nature by offering images of the ideal?" A possibility they reject as too close to didacticism. With relief they endorse Butcher's interpretation that Aristotle's phrase "things as they ought to be" must be taken "not in a moral but simply in an aesthetic sense" (28). Spotting only confusion and tautology in the Aristotelian tradition that emphasizes the moral import of the word *ought*, they ask: "Is the thesis about the morality of poetry a truism in the realm of morals, or does it lie actually in the realm of poetics?" (171) Schiller's poetics rejects such disjunctive alternatives and boldly coordinates the two realms. His theory assumes as a given that a poet's—or any other person's—feelings and perceptions ideally are informed by a normative idea of humanity by which he consciously or unconsciously orients his choices and structures his experience. But an intuition of such an idea or ideal does not by itself make a poet, nor does having command of the verbal medium. The poet's task is the creation of an aesthetic form that commensurately reveals an ideal of humanity.[13]

If both naive and sentimental poets share the same basic task, how then do they differ? Schiller's answer is that the naive poet aims at the fullest possible expression of mankind as it actually exists, whereas the sentimental poet aims at the fullest expression of mankind as transfigured into an ideal. In an age of unified sensibility and harmonious integration of the individual in his world—an age like that of ancient Greece—the naive poet can achieve his goal through mimesis of reality, through holding up the mirror of art to the sensuous particulars and living forms of nature. In an age like Schiller's own, however, an age of dissociated sensibility, specialization and fragmentation, the sentimental poet's efforts are directed toward transcending the limits of experience, infusing reality with (in Coleridge's words) "living and life-producing ideas" (*BL* [1907] 2:258), transforming the actual world into intimations of the ideal (*NA* 20:436–37).

Schiller's typology is at once synchronic and diachronic, at once normative and historically descriptive. His purpose is not to trace the historical development of German poetry, but, rather, through key examples to show "the different paths that ancient and modern, naive and sentimental poets follow toward the same goal—that if the former move us by means of nature, individuality, and vital *sensuousness* [*lebendige Sinnlichkeit*], the latter can, by means of ideas and lofty *spirituality* [*Geistigkeit*], exercise an equally great, if not so widespread, power over our minds" (20:458–59).

Schiller's exploration of the two principal paths leading the naive and sentimental poets to the same goal sends him down some notable byways. Or rather, exploring the sentimental poet's road involves repeated bifurcations. For the naive poet, who is also a hypothetical construct, there is a single path, just as there is a single basic mode of feeling. Like all men in Rousseau's hypothetical state of nature, the naive poet exists with senses and reason, receptive and active powers, functioning in undivided unity (*NA* 20:436). Imbued as he is by his harmonious relation to internal and external reality, the naive poet expresses a single, unvarying relation to his poetic object, an all-sufficing reality. He disappears, like the divine creator, behind his works of creation: "He is the work [*das Werk*] and the work is he" (20:433).[14] All the naive poet's works spring from his own indivisible unity. He feels all the forces of humanity active in himself at any given moment and can, out of his own harmonious wholeness, produce an image of highest humanity as it really exists. The sentimental poet's works, however, spring from his drive to recover the unity and harmony he has lost. He is impelled to re-create humanity's wholeness in himself and to give it correlative expression (20:473–74). Whereas the mood of contentment and tranquility characterizes the naive poet, a mood of tension and discord prevails in the sentimental. He is trapped between the realm of experience and the realm of ideas. Since reality no longer offers him the experience of wholeness—either within himself or between himself and the world—that the naive poet enjoys, he strives to impress an ideal import on reality. The feelings he embodies in his poetry can stem only from ideas, from reflection about rather than immediate response to reality. His mode of feeling is well exemplified by Wordsworth's sense that everything he beheld "respired with inward meaning." A walk through the fields in Cambridge could yield such inward meaning:

> A track pursuing not untrod before,
> From deep analogies by thought supplied,
> Or consciousness not to be subdued,
> To every natural form, rock, fruit or flower,
> Even the loose stones that cover the high-way,
> I gave a moral life, I saw them feel,

Or link'd them to some feeling. . . .
(*Prelude* 3:121–27)

Whereas Wordsworth rejoices in the "deep analogies by thought supplied" as a bridge between mind and nature, Schiller sees no such easy reciprocity, no such suitable Wordsworthian marriage, as available to the modern poet. He sees instead the sentimental poet moved by an inescapable conflict between limited reality and limitless ideas. It is both his weakness and his strength that the sentimental poet relates to ideas the reality that sufficed for the naive poet and infuses ideas of which the naive poet had no need into the reality that no longer suffices. He can deal with the realms of the real and the ideal from one of two perspectives: he can either look down on reality as an object of antipathy or look up to the realm of ideas as an object of sympathy and admiration. These two basic perspectives Schiller identifies with the satiric and elegiac modes of feeling (*NA* 20:441). Here we must remember that Schiller repeatedly points out that he intends not to supplant but to supplement traditional generic distinctions.

Since Schiller's contribution to pastoral comes in his critique of the elegiac mode, I shall bypass his discussion of the satiric. Schiller first distinguishes between two kinds of elegiac poetry, both of which may be subsumed under the traditional concept of pastoral. The first kind presents the harmony and innocence of nature, the golden age of freedom and wholeness, as lost in the remote past. Its characteristic mood is melancholic and nostalgic; in short, it is truly elegiac. The second kind, by contrast, presents the pastoral vision not as a source of lament but as a cause for enthusiasm; it depicts not an irrevocably lost Arcadia but the attainable ideal of a future Elysium. Thus Schiller reclaims the *topos* of "soft pastoral" with its images of *locus amoenus* and *otium*, joining it with the "hard pastoral" of an exacting task to be performed, the specific way to an idea to be charted. For this second pastoral mode Schiller reserves the term *idyll*. His concept of idyll evolves, in complex ways, over the course of the entire treatise, continually accruing additional connotations and specifications. Early on, in the midst of his discussion of the concept *naive*, he introduces the idyll and foreshadows its ultimate meaning. In a long direct address Schiller admonishes the "sensitive [*empfindsamen*] friend of nature" to come to terms with the loss of blissful harmony and with the evils of civilization; having done that, he implores him to let nature's perfection become his model of utter calm and childlike innocence. Internalize nature's divine image, he urges, "let it envelop you like a lovely idyll, in which you can always return to yourself from the aberrations of art and artifice, in which you gather courage and new confidence for your course and through which you rekindle in your heart the flames of the ideal that is so easily extinguished in life's storms" (20:428–29).

This is Schiller's first intimation of the idyll as the correlative poetic expression of the ideal of humanity. In this early formulation Schiller is so intent on eradicating all nostalgia for a lost past that he urges the addressed "sensitive friend of nature" to accept even the most questionable oppressions of society in order to strive for an ideal future. Schiller's emphasis on internalizing idyllic wholeness as a sign of the ideal while accepting degrading social conditions leads justifiably to Lukács's accusation that the statement presents what Engels in another context terms "flight from common misery into exalted misery" ("Flucht aus der platten Misere in die überschwengliche Misere"; *Probleme der Ästhetik* 22–23). Schiller proceeds toward a fuller delineation of the idyll by doubling back through four subcategories of sentimental poetry which may be diagrammed as follows:

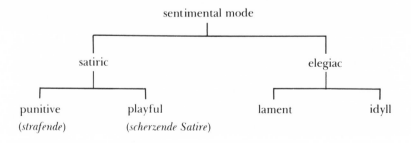

This section includes Schiller's seminal theoretical speculations on the idyllic mode as a future-oriented pastoral and ends with his elevating this mode from a subspecies of elegiac poetry to an independent category that transcends the naive-sentimental dichotomy. Earlier he had claimed that this dichotomy was inescapable, but eventually he arrives at a different perspective that focuses not on the disjunction between naive and sentimental but on their conjunction. This new perspective leads him to discover a dynamic continuity where he had formerly seen an antagonistic clash between the two modes of feeling. He arrives at the insight (which he explains in an important footnote) that the sentimental disposition impels the poet to restore the naive feeling through the reflective understanding. Thus art would be reunited with nature (*NA* 20:473n) in the ideal poem, in what Friedrich Schlegel was to call *Transcendentalpoesie* (2:204).[15]

With the basic tenets of Schiller's flexible typology in mind, let us look more closely at the question of what the consummate idyll transcends. Schiller, as we have seen, criticized the elegiac pastoral for being tainted by civilization and its discontents; tainted, too, by the kind of misanthropic yearning for solitary calm that he saw exemplified in Kleist's poem *Sehnsucht nach Ruhe* (*Longing for Tranquility*), which ends with the line "A true man must live far removed from men" (*NA* 20:454). Like Ovid's *Lamentations* written in exile, Kleist's elegiac yearning for peace and quiet expresses too little energy, too little spirit (*Geist*) to be truly poetic. Against such spiritually and intellectually bankrupt pastoral, Schiller pits his concept of the true pastoral: the idyll as the poetic imperative of projecting a state of blissful innocence as an authentic goal. He reminds us that the choice of subject matter is not a central issue. Writing about bucolic singing contests set in Arcadian pleasances is accidental rather than essential to pastoral. He argues that just because innocence, harmony, peace, and happiness are conditions more readily imagined in a community of shepherds than in an industrial society does not make the subject matter (*Stoff*) the distinguishing criterion of the pastoral mode (20:467). Of course, the

subject must be appropriate to the basic concept of pastoral—
"the poetic representation of innocent and happy mankind"
(20:467). Schiller urges the modern poet to address the task of
imagining a perfect human community not as an Arcadian idyll
but as an ideal compatible with modern civilization, indeed, as
projecting civilization's ultimate goal. The poet's task is to im-
part to this ideal of humanity a sensuous, palpable concreteness
that communicates his dynamic feeling toward the ideal. For the
poet's success—so Schiller wrote to Goethe—depends on both
his inner resources, the fullness of experience that originates in
the unconscious, and on his ability to externalize, to express this
unconscious import completely—to objectivize his "original, ob-
scure but powerful, conception of the whole [*Total-Idee*], which
precedes all technical work," and without which poetry can-
not be produced at all. What distinguishes the true poet from
the non-poet, in Schiller's view, is that in the former "the un-
conscious is united with the conscious [*dem Besonnenen*]" (*GA*
20:852).[16]

Schiller's exhortation that the poet should imagine a para-
disal ideal not retrospectively, as the Arcadian pleasance, but
prospectively, as the Elysian fields, is the single most widely
quoted statement of his essay and the most frequently misinter-
preted. Typically it is read reductively (as, for example, by
the editors of the *Nationalausgabe*) to mean that since Arcadia's
golden age is lost once and for all, man must redeem his origi-
nal sin without eschewing the fruit of the tree of knowledge
(*NA* 21:308). Such an interpretation ignores Schiller's subtle
handling of the moral and aesthetic issues that pastoral poetry
presents. He criticizes golden-age pastoral for its contradiction
between theory and practice, morality and aesthetics, thought
and feeling. It leads us "theoretically backwards while practi-
cally leading us forwards and ennobling us" (20:469). That is to
say: the sentimental poet who dwells on images of an Arcadian
ideal knows that this ideal does not conform to the reality of
modern experience. He has forsaken praxis for theory only to
regress to a childish fantasy. To Schiller this is to misdirect the
modern poet's strength. He cannot serve his own time by taking

his bearings from an idealized past; he can do justice to both theory and practice only by accepting the task of projecting an authentic goal toward which modern man can strive. This task cannot be fulfilled by reducing the ideal of humanity to an exploded dream, no matter how enticingly fashioned in poetic form. Nor can it be fulfilled only by moral dicta, no matter how persuasively debated.

Neither pure aesthetes nor pure moralists belong in Schiller's pantheon of poets. He has no more use for poets who have a palpable design upon us than does Keats. He explicitly criticizes the didacticism in Haller's nature poetry, for example, because the role of the imagination is made subservient to that of the understanding, because the poet's feelings are dominated by moral precepts. By prescribing maxims rather than presenting ideas transmuted into poetic concreteness, the didactic poet violates one of Schiller's cardinal aesthetic principles, that of the poet's and reader's aesthetic freedom. The poet must preserve his freedom vis-à-vis his poetic subject matter and the reader must be left free after his encounter with the fictional world to return to his own world with his feelings and mind in a state of equilibrium, not more disposed toward one specific commitment than another. Schiller firmly condemns the didactic disposition to give the psyche a determinate direction—"dem Gemüt eine bestimmte Tendenz zu geben" (*AL* 22.5).[17] But such exclusion of didactic design from pastoral poetry, as from all poetry, does not preclude the moral import achieved by expressing ideas that act as goals for practical experience, even though they are not themselves verifiable by experience. Schiller argues that since man's actual unity of feeling and reason has disappeared in the state of modern civilization, it can be expressed only as a moral idea. It cannot be affirmed as man's actual condition but can be posited only as a goal to which he can aspire (*NA* 20:437).

To create in poetry a model of humanity's wholeness is no easy task for the modern poet. It is precisely for his failure to make the Sisyphean effort that Schiller criticizes Rousseau, whose idyll of Julie reveals the moral and psychological limitations rather than the full possibilities of human wholeness. His poetic vision is generated by a sick psyche's longing to escape society's discord, rather than by a healthy psyche's striving for moral concord (20:451–52). Elegiac pastoral appeals only to the heart, not to the mind; it can offer only therapeutic tranquilizers, not vital inspiration for the embattled spirit. While a shepherd may appear the embodiment of human nobility to Wordsworth, his way of life would hardly inspire a corporate executive. The bucolic model, according to Schiller, is just sufficiently ideal so that its features lose experiential specificity, and it is just sufficiently concrete so that its intellectual, idealistic import suffers (20:470).

Despite having offered these cogent objections, Schiller is not ready to discard the Arcadian myth. Retrospective elegiac pastoral can, after all, be pressed into service for the creation of the future-oriented, hope-instilling idyll. It can at least provide the building blocks of vivid images drawn from psychological experience, since all people have some memory of paradisal moments and all civilizations have some myths of a golden age (20:468). Thus, for example, much support is to be gained from Milton's depiction of Eden, which Schiller regards as the most beautiful of modern idylls. He praises Milton's magnificent portrayal of Adam and Eve's paradisal innocence: "Here is nature at once noble and inspirited [*geistreich*] . . . here mankind's highest value [*Gehalt*] is embodied in the most graceful form" (20:471).

Although Milton's poetic vision of Edenic existence may be enchanting, its prelapsarian happiness is too confined to become a modern paideia. From Schiller's point of view, man's expulsion from Eden was in fact beneficial. Deploying new weapons in the old nature/art agon that dominated pastoral dialectics from Virgil to Pope, Schiller sees art triumphing over nature through man's capacity for moral choice. Man was fortunately expelled from a paradise of gratified needs, a paradise governed by instinct and ignorance, so that he could some day gain a new paradise governed by reason and freedom. His disobediently eating the fruit of the tree of knowledge marks the first daring step of self-assertion, the beginning of his moral existence. Therefore Schiller calls man's fall the happiest, most decisive event in the history of mankind; for man emerged from nature's tutelage into a moral being, from a happy creature into an unhappy creator.[18] Unhappy because dissatisfaction with his own abuse of moral freedom often leads modern man to regard his freedom as a curse and to long to return to the haven of amoral nature. This state of mind engenders a "double and divergent longing for nature: longing for its *happiness* [*Glückseligkeit*] and longing for its perfection [*Vollkommenheit*]" (20:427–28). Here Schiller identifies two diverse psychic drives that fuel the pastoral quest: the drive for sensuous gratification through indulgence in the pleasure principle, and the drive for intellectual gratification through contemplation of an ideal. Schiller knows that the convergence of the two drives is a near impossibility, that the marriage of feeling and intellect, of experience and theory in a pastoral idyll is improbable in this world. Yet he insists that the sentimental poet must believe in its possibility and never stop striving for it.

Precisely in devising a strategy for uniting what is with what might be, Schiller grants a supporting role to the otherwise discredited elegiac pastoral that feeds nostalgically on the myth of Arcadian simplicity. Such myths provide some concrete images of human perfection and, by virtue of being myths, they help free the poet's and the reader's imagination from the prison-house of the actual world. The Arcadian myth presents an imaginary counterview that, in all its particulars of a pre-industrial and prepolitical egalitarian community, contradicts our experience of competitive and exploitative socioeconomic institutions. Such pastoral fictions can hearten the poet who will gainsay these dark particulars of the modern world, for they are powerful counterfoils to reality. They are (in Coleridge's words) the "Extenders of Consciousness" (*CN* 3:3632). And it was Coleridge who found Schiller's conviction of the mind's liberating force so pertinent that three times he entered in his notebook the lines "Hoch über der Zeit und dem Raume webt / Lebendig der höchste Gedanke."[19] Coleridge and Schiller both shared

Kant's view that the imagination "is very powerful in creating another nature, as it were, out of the material that actual nature gives it" (*Critique of Judgement* 157). This remolding of the material provided by nature, by empirical reality, is precisely the art by which the modern (sentimental) poet excels the ancient (naive). Whereas the naive poet depends totally on the world as he finds it, the sentimental poet, who knows no such dependence, transmutes the deficient material that the temporal world offers him and, by his own inner power, transforms his confined existence into a state of freedom (*NA* 20:476).

Schiller's emphasis on the power of the poetic word to free modern man from the narrow confines of experience has received interesting confirmation in George Steiner's recent work on language. Taking his cue from Ernst Bloch's explorations of the grammar of hope, Steiner reclaims the problem of hypothetical statements from sterile linguistic analysis. "Hypotheticals," he writes, "'imaginaries,' conditionals, the syntax of counter-factuality and contingency may well be the generative centers of human speech" (*After Babel* 215). Unequivocally Steiner asserts—and surely Schiller and Coleridge would have agreed—that language is "the main instrument of man's refusal to accept the world as it is" (217–18). At the turn of the eighteenth century, under the pressure of intensified economic competition and mass production—gross national product is our term, but Romantic poets knew the economic fact—man more than ever needed the resources of language, especially of hypotheticals and conditionals, to revoke experiential reality in order to "dream forward" (in Bloch's phrase) a dream of humane community. That is—to conflate Schiller's and Steiner's theories—man could be said to be most truly human and humane when generating counterfactual ideas, when conceiving alternative realities and freeing himself from his genetically and socially conditioned disposition. Steiner argues convincingly that "through the 'make-up' of language, man is able, in part at least, to exit from his own skin" (225). Through the "make-up" of alternative realities man may have evolved from primitive nature-bound existence into a sophisticated, moral being. Steiner speculates that the decisive step may have been the linguistic development "from ostensive nomination and tautology—if I say that the water-hole is where it is I am, in a sense, stating a tautology—to invention." And he concludes that "the uses of language for 'alternity,' for mis-construction, for illusion and play, are the greatest of man's tools by far. With this stick he has reached out of the cage of instinct to touch the boundaries of the universe and of time" (223–24).

Language's capacity to build up counterfactual worlds is for Schiller a tool not only for prying open nature's "cage of instinct" but also for re-collecting nature's freedom; the freedom, that is, that the sentimental mode of feeling attributes to nature, discovering in nature a symbolic representation of self-sustaining existence—"das freiwillige Dasein, das Bestehen der Dinge durch sich selbst" (*NA* 20:413). Viewed in this light, nature's works appear similar to works of art. Both appear to the beholder's imagination as self-determined and self-subsistent. What gives the work of art its virtual autonomy is, in Schiller's view, its triumphant transmutation of some object—whether nature, a person, a political event, or an emotional crisis—through its artistic medium, on the one hand, which brings with it its own resources and constraints, and, on the other hand, through the artist's unique inner resources. The poet, like all artists, totally re-creates his object so that his meaningful re-creation emerges, despite the linguistic fetters, as free and victorious, appearing before the reader's imagination in its full, living truth.[20] While Schiller stresses the power of aesthetic illusion and play for freeing man from the confines of inner and outer reality, he also recognizes that the artist's work entails a struggle with his subject matter and with his medium. This struggle may result in the semblance of total fantasy or of photographic likeness, but it always involves a complex process of transmutation by which nature, as Coleridge pungently put it, becomes "nature *shakespearianized*"—a symbolic creation in which we can recognize "the Thing itself" while "yet knowing that the Thing is not present to us." The poet has created "that likeness not identity—an exact web, every line of direction miraculously the same, but the one worsted, the other silk" (*CN* 2:2274).

We need to keep in mind this miraculous transformation of the worsted threads of reality into the silk threads of art when we consider pastoral poetry—whether it includes realistic landscapes or idyllic dreams. The spectrum of these transformations, ranging from mirroring naive feeling to projecting idyllic visions, can be illuminated by a current theory of tropes. Reviving the rhetorical tradition of Peter Ramus, some recent linguists, cultural historians, and literary critics have focused on the specific powers of four tropes: metaphor, metonymy, synecdoche, and irony. In the most sweeping hermeneutic deployment of these tropes, Hayden White has aligned them with four world hypotheses derived from Stephen Pepper. White claims that the tropes thus ideologically reinforced act as paradigms generated by language itself. These paradigms are "especially useful for understanding the operations by which the contents of experience which resist description in unambiguous prose representations can be prefiguratively grasped and prepared for conscious apprehension" (34). The tropes join worldviews as follows. Metaphor is paired with the "formist" ideological hypothesis that emphasizes the individual rather than the general truth. Metonymy is "reductive in a Mechanistic manner, while Synecdoche is integrative in the way Organicism is. Metaphor sanctions the prefiguration of the world of experience in object-object terms, Metonymy in part-part terms, and Synecdoche in object-whole terms" (36). White intriguingly calls these three tropes "naive"—they are informed by faith in "language's capacity to grasp the nature of things in figurative terms"—as contrasted with irony, which he calls sentimental in Schiller's sense of "self-conscious" (36–37). Irony provides a "linguistic paradigm of a mode of thought which is radically self-critical with respect not only to a given characterization of the world of experience but also to the very effort to capture adequately the truth of things in language" (37).

White's four master tropes, his four alternative ways of prefiguring experience, can yield some fresh perspectives on Schil-

ler's typology of naive and sentimental poetry. But first we need
to qualify White's claim that metaphor, metonymy, and synec-
doche are naive tropes, whereas irony is sentimental. It is cer-
tainly true that self-consciousness is a prominent feature of
Schiller's sentimental mode, but the radical skepticism that Hay-
den White identifies with irony is not "sentimental" in Schiller's
sense of the term. It is not typical of the way Schiller sees
elegiac, satiric, or idyllic modes of structuring experience. On
the other hand, "irony" in White's sense aptly describes the
aspect of Schiller's own thought process of constantly reviewing
his line of argument. Schiller the theorist does indeed arrive at
self-critical reflections that question the assumptions he has
previously posed as undoubted truths. Ironic moments are part
of Schiller's strategy in developing his typology of poetry, but
irony is not characteristic of any of the types themselves. The
other three tropes—metaphor, metonymy, and synecdoche—fit
better into Schiller's schema. Not all three are naive paradigms,
however, as White asserts; only metaphor appropriately ex-
presses the naive *Empfindungsweise*. (I take White's notion of
tropes as means of prefiguring world hypotheses to be roughly
parallel to Schiller's concept of *Empfindungsweisen* that similarly
emphasizes pre-conscious ways of structuring experience.) The
naive mode of responding to experience is indeed rooted in the
belief that language can adequately mirror reality, and that
reality need only to be named by language in order to figure
forth a meaningful order.

The cultural movement from the naive to the sentimental, as
described by Schiller, is reflected in the progression from meta-
phor to metonymy and synecdoche. Hayden White explains,
"Metaphor is essentially *representational*, Metonymy is *reduction-
ist*, Synecdoche is *integrative*" (34). Applying this progression to
pastoral poetry, we can discern that naive pastoral is representa-
tional while the elegiac sentimental mode is largely reductionist.
Its central image of a community of happy shepherds functions
as metonymy rather than as synecdoche in relation to society at
large. The relationship is not that of microcosm to macrocosm,
but of part to part. The sentimental poet has nostalgically hy-

postatized a pastoral way of life that is viable only for those in the modern world who have seceded from society as a whole. Schiller's idyllic mode, on the other hand, converts this reductive modality of feeling and thinking into an integrative one. In the idyll the *topos* of the happy man takes on an intrinsic relation to man's future; it signals not a mythical paradise but a firmly conceptualized social order. Thus the idyll is indeed centered on the trope of synecdoche that integrates microcosm and macrocosm, image and worldview, into a coherent totality.

The difficulty of transforming a metonymic into a synecdochic mode of apprehending the world can be illustrated by the Romantic poets' symbolic depiction of the child. Wordsworth's child-philosopher is typical of the Romantic attempt to transform a reductive image into an integrative synecdoche. Wordsworth apostrophizes his diminutive paragon:

> Thou, whose exterior semblance doth belie
>   Thy soul's immensity;
> Thou best Philosopher, who yet dost keep
> Thy heritage, thou Eye among the blind,
> That, deaf and silent, read'st the eternal deep,
> Haunted for ever by the eternal mind,—
>   Mighty Prophet! Seer blest!
>   On whom those truths do rest,
> Which we are toiling all our lives to find,
> In darkness lost. . . .
>   (*Intimations of Immortality* 109–18)

Wordsworth's trope for the child—the "Eye among the blind" that discerns truths invisible to the adult—expresses more than a simple connection between part and whole. The trope discloses a way of looking at a series of organic relationships: between child and adult, child and ideal human being, the human and the divine. The trope expands into an integrative cosmic syntax, yet its paradigmatic structure is vulnerable, given Wordsworth's insistence that his poetry portrays the elementary feelings of real people. Not surprisingly, Coleridge asked what made Wordsworth's "magnificent attributes" appropriate to a *child* while making them not "equally suitable to a *bee*, or a *dog*, or a *field of corn* . . . ? The omnipresent Spirit works equally in *them*, as in the child; and the child is equally unconscious of it as they" (*BL* 2:140). Coleridge does not question Wordsworth's synecdochic view of an omnipresent spirit animating all creation. Rather, he questions the adequacy of its symbolic expression in and through the child.

Schiller's view of the child reveals some further problems confronting the Romantic poet who attempts to load the symbol of the child with the freight of a synecdochic cosmic hypothesis. Schiller identifies the Rousseauistic interest in the child with the contemporary fascination with nature: "Our childhood is the only vestige of unmutilated nature that we encounter in our civilized state, and it is therefore small wonder that every trace of external nature leads us back to our childhood" (*NA* 20:430). Schiller is careful to distinguish this feeling from the mawkish taste for "sentimental journeys, gardens, promenades, and other favorite pursuits of this sort" (20:415).[21] He focuses instead on the feeling for natural objects and natural beings that springs from our perceiving them as naive, from which it follows that "nature must appear antithetical to artifice and must put it to shame" (20:413). He points out that our pleasure in the naive—whether it takes the form of flowers or children—is not aesthetic but moral: it is not produced by an immediate intuition of a beautiful form but is mediated through an idea. We love in the naive its unobtrusive creative life, its serene autonomous activity, its eternal unity of being (20:414).

Schiller argues further that our feeling for the naive is strongest when it is inspired by objects that are closely connected with our own lives and that bring home the realization of our own unnaturalness (415–16). Children "are what we *were*; they are what we *should become* once more" (414). Here Schiller epigrammatically elevates the naive quality of the child from metonymy to synecdoche, from representing a vestige of our lost unity of being to projecting an ideal way of life for the future. What enables the child to carry this symbolic import is not its capacity

to be a prophet-seer. In Schiller's argument, it is not what truth
the child sees in the "eternal deep" that is significant, but what
idea the adult sees in the child: unlimited potentiality. "The
child represents *disposition* [*Anlage*] and *intention* [*Bestimmung*];
we represent *fulfillment* [*Erfüllung*], which will always lag far
behind the former" (20:416). Thus Schiller, too, elevates the
child to an ideal. Unlike Wordsworth's, however, his ideal repre-
sents not an attained but an attainable perfection—an ideal that
acts as a challenge and a task. The child symbolizes pure inde-
terminacy (*Bestimmbarkeit*) because he has not yet oriented his
activity toward any specific goals. He is privileged, as Words-
worth said, to try out as mere play some "fragment from his
dream of human life," a wedding or a business transaction,
mere roles to be rehearsed and discarded as the "little Actor
cons another part" (*Immortality Ode* 92, 103). Or consider Schil-
ler's image of a boy at play:

> Spiele, liebliche Unschuld! Noch ist Arkadien um dich,
>   Und die freie Natur folgt nur dem fröhlichen Trieb,
> Noch erschafft sich die üppige Kraft erdichtete
>   Schranken,
>   Und dem willigen Mut fehlt noch die Pflicht und der
>   Zweck.
> Spiele, bald wird die Arbeit kommen, die hagre, die
>   ernste
>   Und der gebietenden Pflicht mangeln die Lust und der
>   Mut.[22]
>   (*Der spielende Knabe* 5–10)

Yet such child's play, which involves no consequences, con-
straints, or obligations, raises the question of how the child can
serve as an adequate model of wholeness for the modern adult,
who must direct his efforts into specialized, determined—
though hopefully not prefabricated—channels. How can the
child's indeterminacy and potentiality provide a guide in the
midst of the kind of progress in an "inventive Age" observed by
Wordsworth's Wanderer? "I have lived to mark," he comments,

A new and unforeseen creation rise
From out the labours of a peaceful Land
Wielding her potent enginery to frame
And to produce, with appetite as keen
As that of war, which rests not night or day,
Industrious to destroy!
            (*The Excursion* 8:89–95)

Given this "progress" at the turn of the eighteenth century, how can a pastoral poet defuse Peacock's satiric charge that a "poet in our times is a semi-barbarian in a civilized community"? Living as he does in the past, his "ideas, thoughts, feelings, associations, are all with barbarous manners, obsolete customs, and exploded superstitions" (170). Is Schiller's myth of the child's "indeterminacy" just another of Peacock's gewgaws or rattles for the "grown babies of the age"? Or can it be argued, on the contrary, that the child for Schiller is a concrete model analogous to the aesthetic experience, which is salutary, even though it does not contribute to the "comforts and utilities of life of which we have witnessed so many and so rapid advances" (Peacock 170)?

Schiller's own penetrating analysis does not retreat from the fact that "if the manifold potentialities in man were ever to be developed, there was no other way but to pit them one against the other. This antagonism of faculties and functions is the great instrument of civilization" (*AL* 6:12), especially of modern civilization, which was increasingly employing capitalist modes of production in all economic sectors. He recognized, even more clearly than Peacock did, that these economic and social developments were threatening great art. In a difference of opinion with Herder in November 1795, Schiller argued that "our civil, political, religious, and scientific life and activity are like prose opposed to poetry. This predominance of prose in our whole existence is, in my opinion, so great and so decisive that instead of mastering it, the poetic spirit will be necessarily infected and hence destroyed by it" (*NA* 28:98). He refers Herder for a fuller explanation of this crisis to the essay on sentimental poets that he was in the process of writing, and he goes on to say that the poetic genius is so seriously threatened by a "coalition" with the real world that his only salvation lies in strict separatism, in his creating an autonomous world undefiled by prosaic reality (28:98). Despite this pessimistic prognosis, Schiller continued to believe that the poetic spirit, like all aesthetic activity, was not useless, even in a time of industrial development that depended on specialized skill. Though threatened with annihilation, the poetic spirit might yet survive as an endangered species, valuable not in practical economic or political affairs but in the intangible psychic economy of the individual. For the value of the aesthetic experience lies in its power to bring back a fruitful state of pure potentiality, pure indeterminacy (*Bestimmbarkeit*) that temporarily restores man's wholeness, letting him step back from his specialized work to his childlike self in whom all potentialities are in "such perfect equilibrium that determinate activity of any kind—judgement or decision no less than overt action—is temporarily inhibited" (Wilkinson and Willoughby 192–93). But this re-creative "co-ordination" of human powers must inevitably yield to a state of "sub-ordination" for adult activity, for all practical, determinate action (193).

I have dwelled at length on Schiller's case for the child as an analogue to aesthetic *Bestimmbarkeit* because it is the philosophic mainspring of his case for the modern poet's task of creating the highest pastoral mode, the idyll. Always aware of the enormous difficulties that this task brings to it, Schiller allows, as I have already pointed out, some merit to those poems that place the ideal of man's wholeness and happiness in the remote past, whether in the infancy of the race or the infancy of the individual. In fact, looking at both the Arcadian ideal and the ideal of the child from the vantage point of Schiller's claim for *Bestimmbarkeit*, we can see that they offer similar hints as to how man in a state of perfect equilibrium within himself and in harmony with his world can be imaginatively specified and poetically realized. Inspired by these two models, Schiller challenges the poet to reach for the supreme achievement of embodying in concrete particulars the image of human nature in its total potentiality, transcending all existing ways of being-in-the-world without, however, transcending the limits of human nature. "For the absolute," Schiller declares, "but only within human limits, is his [the poet's] task and sphere" (*NA* 20:481).

The pastoral poet's task is accordingly to create a model of human wholeness and happiness, a model whose base must rest in the ruinous landscape of modern civilization though its apex might dwell in Edenic utopia. Schiller enjoins the modern poet more than once not to escape the hardship, inequality, and privation that modern society fosters. Pastoral innocence must stand the test of economic and political pressures undreamt of by Theocritus's herdsmen.[23] At the same time, he urges the modern poet to aspire to the highest conceivable poetic mode, the idyll, which he can never fully realize but which he must nevertheless set as his goal. It embodies the ultimate *concordia discors*, the reconciliation of ancient and modern, the meeting ground of infinite aspiration and finite experience, of transcendent beauty and pragmatic choice—a new heaven on earth. Schiller's formulation of this ideal mode must be given in full:

> The concept of this idyll is the concept of a conflict completely resolved both within the individual and within society; it is the concept of a free union of inclination and law, of nature transmuted and refined into the highest human dignity—in short, it is none other than the idea of beauty applied to actual life. Its character thus consists in its total negation of *all opposition between the real and the ideal*, which provided the material for satiric and elegiac poetry, thereby removing all conflict of feeling. (20:472)

What poem could come close to this supreme desideratum? What subject matter could possibly serve as springboard for soaring, like Goethe's Euphorion, into the weightless atmosphere of the ideal, ending, however, not in self-destruction but in self-definition? While he was in the process of completing the last section of *Naive and Sentimental Poetry*, Schiller outlined a plan for just such an idyll in his letter to Wilhelm von Humboldt, in December 1795, projecting it as a continuation of his philosophical poem *Das Reich der Schatten* (later called *Das Ideal und das Leben*). In its poignant dialogue of the mind with itself, *Das Reich der Schatten* prefigures the great meditative lyrics of the English Romantic poets from Coleridge's *Frost at Midnight* to Wordsworth's *Tintern Abbey* and Keats's *Ode to a Nightingale*. Schiller's speaker, like Keats's, stands between two worlds, estranged from both: he looks upward to the ethereal region of the gods, where time assures timeless beauty and serenity; he looks downward at the Keatsian "leaden-eyed despairs" of mortal existence, where time hastens the whirligig of destruction. Even a hero like Hercules cannot escape the painful choices of man's fallen state; even he must carry the burden of pain and labor to the end of his life. Yet in meditating on Hercules's fate, the speaker's vision becomes clairvoyant, penetrating the celestial realm that had earlier seemed barred to all mortals. As he depicts Hercules's apotheosis, his language lifts the reader in a weightless ascent to Olympus. He paints a final tableau: Hercules—now simply called "the transfigured"—in Zeus's realm, being offered the goblet by a smiling Hebe, symbol of reconciliation and rejuvenation (*Reich der Schatten* 177–78).[24]

This final scene of Olympian bliss was to be the point of departure for Schiller's projected idyll, which would celebrate Hercules's marriage to Hebe. Schiller could have found many clues for this marriage in Homer, Hesiod, Pindar, and Euripides, a marriage that reconciles Hercules with Hera, his former tormenter. When Zeus allows Hebe, his daughter by Hera, to marry Hercules, all discord is transformed into concord, and Hercules (according to most versions of the myth) having completed his labors and his suffering, lives happily ever after. "Happy he!" writes Hesiod, "For he has finished his great work and lives amongst the undying gods, untroubled and unaging all his days" (*Theogony* 954–55). Pindar's Tiresias foretells the end to Hercules's trials and battles and foresees "how in time Herakles should have the rest / of eternity in continuous peace," in a life "in the blessed house, and with blossoming Hebe given to be his wife, and domain," praising the "high design of the Gods" (*Nemea* 1:69–70, 73, 75).

Such a scene seems more fitting for a painter like Raphael's pupil Giulio Romano, whose voluptuous wedding feast of Cupid and Psyche adorns a wall of the Sala di Psiche in the Palazzo del Te in Mantua, than for a poet seeking to present a supersensuous model of human wholeness as poetically realized and individualized. Without entering into concrete details, Schiller enthusiastically sketches his vision of Hercules, his joyful sense of release from mortal bonds, a sense of pure light, freedom, and potentiality (*NA* 28:120).

Schiller's eschatological vision of the deified Hercules has a moving personal undertone. It may have moved Goethe, as Thomas Mann speculates, to pay his highest tribute to Schiller under the guise of his tribute to Hercules in the second part of *Faust* (89). Indeed, reading Goethe's lines with Schiller in mind, Thomas Mann's interpretation seems highly plausible. The centaur Chiron, who has known the greatest heroes of his time, responds to Faust's request to speak of Hercules by saying:

> O weh! errege nicht mein Sehnen!
> Ich hatte Phöbus nie gesehn
> Noch Ares, Hermes, wie sie heissen;
> Da sah ich mir vor Augen stehn,
> Was alle Menschen göttlich preisen.
> . . . .
> Den zweiten zeugt nicht Gäa wieder,
> Nicht führt ihn Hebe himmelein;
> Vergebens mühen sich die Lieder,
> Vergebens quälen sie den Stein.[25]
> (*Faust* 2:7382–86, 7391–94)

No tribute to Schiller could be more fitting than this encomium of Hercules, which ironically dwells on art's inadequacy to capture the heroic vision in words or stone. It reminds us that, despite his intoxicating glimpse of a deified Hercules, Schiller was himself unable to translate theory into practice, prose sketch into full-fledged poem. He knew only too well that the artistic deed speaks louder than the conceptual hypothesis. "From concepts," he said, "we can at best predict that a given theme will not be incompatible with its artistic treatment" (*NA* 22:297). Although he told Wilhelm von Humboldt in 1795 that his projected Herculean idyll engaged all his poetic effort (*NA* 28:118), he never mentioned it again. Yet we have no reason to suppose that abstruse research stifled his imagination or that, as Emil Staiger claims, his evocation of Elysium was mere programmatic rhetoric (43). Schiller's theoretical speculations on the nature of the idyllic mode in fact triggered rather than hampered his poetic efforts. As he wrote to Körner in 1794, his ongoing work on naive and sentimental poetry was proving itself a bridge to poetic creativity (*NA* 27:46). Yet he had evidently not solved the problem he so acutely pinpointed when he came to write his *Jungfrau von Orleans*: "One must not let oneself be fettered by a universal concept," he told Goethe, "but must dare to invent a new form for new material [*Stoff*] and keep the generic concept always flexible" (*GA* 20:804).

In his theory of the high pastoral mode, if not in his poetry, Schiller indeed succeeded in keeping the generic concept fluid, exploring it from constantly new angles. As he viewed the idyll's sparkling facets from different perspectives, he must have caught sight of a central difficulty created by his choice of Hercules as subject matter. With all of Hercules's labors and ordeals ended, all obstacles overcome, how could he have informed his vision with the kind of tension and dynamic equipoise that he regarded as essential for achieving any poetic effect? Had he not insisted that the true pastoral idyll must impress on the reader a sense of the "highest unity without reducing multiplicity; must satisfy the psyche [*das Gemüt muss befriedigt werden*] but without arresting all striving" (*NA* 20:473)? And had he not explicitly stated that the idyll must create the dominant impression of utmost calm and tranquility but without lassitude or paralysis (20:472–73)? With his customary incisiveness, Schiller saw the practical difficulty of how to introduce movement into stasis, insisting that without motion [*Bewegung*] and emotion the poet cannot produce a truly poetic effect. Sentimental poetry, he notes, often lacks "the energy that must animate subject matter [*Stoff*] in order to create the truly beautiful" (20:460). In other words, the highest pastoral mode needs to exhibit not only *enargeia* but also *energeia*. While *enargeia*, the verbal achievement of pictorial vividness, is common enough in all varieties of pastoral, *energeia* poses a central challenge: it is "the actualization of potency, the realization of capacity or capability, the achievement in art and rhetoric of the dynamic and purposive life of nature" (Hagstrum 12). Clearly for all serious pastoral poetry the master problem is indeed how to introduce dynamic life into a still center, tension and energy into tranquility and repose, aspiration into fulfillment, theory into praxis, the subjunctive into the indicative mood.

If asked whether anywhere but in utopia pastoral poetry could fulfill these norms, Schiller might answer as he did when he posed a similar question about the Aesthetic State:

> But does such a State of Aesthetic Semblance really exist? And if so, where is it to be found? As a need, it exists in every finely attuned soul; as a realized fact, we are likely to find it, like the pure Church and the pure Republic, only in some few chosen circles, where conduct is governed, not by some soulless imitation of the manners and morals of others, but by the aesthetic nature we have made our own; where men make their way, with undismayed simplicity and tranquil innocence, through even the most involved and complex situations, free alike of the compulsion to infringe the freedom of others in order to assert their own, as of the necessity to shed their Dignity in order to manifest Grace.
>
> (*AL* 27.12)

Whereas Schiller concludes his *Aesthetic Letters* with this resounding affirmation of the possible achievement of aesthetic education by a chosen few, an elect community of finely attuned souls, he does not end his treatise on naive and sentimental poetry with a comparable confirmation of the idyllic mode as the highest achievement attainable by an elect community of poets. Having made the greatest conceivable claims for this mode of pastoral poetry, Schiller ultimately became skeptical of its practical wisdom, even of its theoretical validity. He may have drawn back from the imminent danger of being bewitched by the power of an abstract ideal, the power of the mind freed from the contingencies of concrete choice at a historical moment in society. In any case, he began to voice difficulties standing in the way of his hypothetical ideal of "coalition" between the naive and sentimental modes. He had postulated that sentimental poetry's source of strength was the realm of reason, the realm of the absolute. How could it then be reconciled with the naive, whose province is experience, when only through abstraction from all experience could the poet reach the ideal— that is, only by annihilating the naive mode of feeling (*NA* 28:146)?

Inveterate idealist though he was, Schiller exposed the dangers of transcending experience even more rigorously than those dangers threatening the naive mind that is totally circumscribed by experience. For committed to removing all limits, the sentimental genius may be tempted to cancel the human condition altogether in the process not only of aspiring beyond limited reality in reaching for absolute possibility but also in aspiring beyond the possible itself, indulging in a wild play of the imagination—pure *schwärmen* (20:481). While we may often seek in vain for the spirit (*Geist*) in the creations of the naive genius, in those of the sentimental genius we often look in vain for the object (*Gegenstand*). Both can thus end in mere emptiness: "For an object uninformed by spirit [*Geist*] and the mind playing without an object [*ein Geistesspiel ohne Gegenstand*] both come to nought in the aesthetic judgment" (20:482). Both can become mere caricatures of legitimate modes of feeling. Both the enthusiast and the philistine go to the dogs, as Ernst Bloch's humorous and untranslatable word play suggests: "Der Schwärmer bezieht selbst die Hunde aufs Unendliche, der Spiesser bringt selbst das Unendliche auf den Hund" (2:1235). Schiller's own doubts about the idealist's ability to bring his boundless thoughts to bear on reality were no less devastating at times. Encompassing much in thought yet grasping little, Schiller sees the idealist as losing in insight (*Einsicht*) what he gains in overview (*Übersicht*) (*NA* 20:495).

After constantly reviewing, retesting, and recasting his premises and his deductions, Schiller ends his treatise by warning against the aberrations of the modern, the sentimental, the idealistic *Empfindungsweise* for which he had set out to gain a legitimate place in the canon of poetry. Schiller's theorizing in *Naive and Sentimental Poetry* exhibits the kind of ironic distance that Goethe said was essential if an investigation is to be vital and useful. Insisting that we cannot begin to look at the world attentively without theorizing, Goethe nevertheless cautions that it must be done with full awareness of what theorizing entails, must be done even with irony—which Goethe calls a "daring word"—if it is to avoid the danger of abstraction and achieve the desired dynamic and practical result (*GA* 16:11).

Schiller pursues his theoretical insights into ancient and modern, naive and sentimental poetry with just such self-awareness—he was all too aware that he was dealing with subjects that bordered on dangerous abstractions as well as self-interest—tempered by bold irony and self-criticism. He leaves us an invaluable matrix of structured insights into modes of pastoral poetry as well as a model of undogmatic reasoning about larger aesthetic issues. His own method exemplifies the open-mindedness that he admired in Aristotle's *Poetics*: "This treatise," he told Goethe, "contains many apparent contradictions, which, however, in my view, only increase its value; for they confirm for me that the whole consists only of individual aperçus that do not bring into play any theoretical, preconceived notions" (*GA* 20:348).

Schiller's own aperçus—no matter how idealistic—are informed by his probing analysis of modern civilization and its discontents as well as by his conviction that poetry has its role to play in restoring to modern man a capacity for wholeness through engaging him in an imaginative transaction with the fullest, the most perfect possible expression of mankind. And

Schiller's aperçus further show us that for him poetry is not a neutral semiotic system—though he was fully aware of the semiotic nature of language as the poetic medium—but a value-laden, meaning-oriented human activity. Consistent with his open-ended speculation, he prescribes no rules, offers no specifications for how the poet is to attain the fullest possible expression of the human ideal. He offers aperçus, insights, critiques, questions, procedural hints.

Nor does Schiller's typology of genres generate rules about which subject is appropriate for which genre or what actions may be included in a high genre such as tragedy without breach of decorum, without lowering the genre's dignity. We hear nothing about those endless neoclassic rules of decorum that governed most poetic choices, even to the point of specifying what characters in a drama may "kill one another with decency" (Bate, *From Classic*, 33). Bypassing the controversy over rules, just as he bypassed the other controversies that fueled the battle between ancients and moderns, Schiller dismisses all choice of subject matter as indifferent (*gleichgültig*)—one might even say immaterial. He insists that poetry's dignity and worth, whether tragic, comic, satiric, or pastoral, depend entirely on how the poet transforms his material into an aesthetic object. The most important key to such transformation is not social decorum but a manner of feeling, which imparts to the poem its dominant mood and its embodied *Empfindungsweise*. This nucleus of expressed feeling is similar to what Dilthey calls the aesthetic point of impression (*aesthetischen Eindruckspunkt*), which influences and structures our (and the poet's) perceptions (Makkreel 114). As Schiller conceives it, the poetic process begins in the subjective point of feeling and ends in a work that is both subjective and objective, concrete and general, individual and universal. For him, the highest poetic mode must achieve the most perfect balancing of these opposites, what he calls "generalized individuality" (*NA* 27:81). It must assimilate felt experience and universal ideas. Thus Schiller proves himself the consummate Romantic classicist as he combines a central emphasis on mode of feeling with the equally central challenge to embody this

Empfindungsweise in an aesthetic work that is not only "a true and beautiful unified whole but also the most multifarious possible whole" (21:288). The highest import—indeed, the unlimited import (*unendliche Gehalt*)—that Schiller demands of pastoral, as of all genuine poetry (20:469), involves the dynamic interplay of subjective and objective, sensibility and thought, feeling and form, particular and universal, praxis and theory. Schiller's *Naive and Sentimental Poetry* breaks new ground, as Wilhelm von Humboldt recognized when he wrote Schiller that henceforth nearly all aesthetic judgments needed to be rethought (36.1:48). It offers us an unsurpassed heuristic tool for looking at pastoral poetry from a perspective beyond generic rules and beyond the battle of ancients and moderns.

THE PASTORAL SPECTRUM:
FROM ARCADIAN RHETORIC
TO THE RHETORIC OF TRANSCENDENCE

Although the "rurall Muses"—
to borrow Spenser's term[1]—who preside over the pastoral microcosm are invariably less stern and solemn than their sisters who preside over heroic enterprises, they wear various masks. At one end of the spectrum we find the "mild pastoral Muse" whom Wordsworth invokes in his *Vernal Ode*:

> O, nursed at happy distance from the cares
> Of a too-anxious world, mild pastoral Muse!
> That, to the sparkling crown Urania wears,
> And to her sister Clio's laurel wreath,
> Prefer'st a garland culled from purple heath. . . .
> (75–79)

This pastoral muse demands of her votary—whether the central persona in the poem or the reader outside—nothing more than to shut out the world of business, the world of *negotium*, in order to relax in a "fit of pleasing indolence" (86), surrendering to the holiday mood of *otium*. Both speaker and reader are lulled into inactivity by the "soft murmur of the vagrant Bee" (90) until these hyblean murmurs benumb their senses and carry them into drowsy nirvana.

At the opposite end of the spectrum, the pastoral muse wears a sterner mask, usurping the role of Urania or Mnemosyne, whose prophetic visions encompass the past and future. Unlike the indolent muse who retires with her votary into half-oblivion, Mnemosyne enters the pastoral bower to prod, animate, even admonish her votary and make him conscious of his gifts and of his task. Thus she resembles the muses whom Hesiod describes as singling him out, while he was tending his sheep on Mount Helicon, to bestow on him the laurel and breathe into him "a divine voice to celebrate things that shall be and things that were aforetime" (*Theogony* 31–32). Pastoral inspiration at this end of the spectrum shades off into the heroic as the shepherd-poet is called upon to leave his pastoral abode and enter upon more rigorous enterprise.[2]

In Schiller's typology this pastoral spectrum ranges from poetic embodiment of nostalgic longing for lost innocence and simplicity to the inspirational vision of an exemplary future state. This spectrum is reflected in Romantic poetry not only in the role of the inspiring muse but also in the roles of the lyric speaker and of the implied reader. At one end of the spectrum—the poetic celebration of *otium*—the speaker establishes a sympathetic bond with the person addressed, sharing either nostalgia or an illusory moment of wish fulfillment. But at the opposite end the pastoral speaker dramatizes an exemplary ethos, straining for an authentic ideal that outdistances the ethos by which his auditor and reader lives. Between these extremes of relaxed and strenuous, norm-fulfilling and norm-breaking roles[3] there exist many mixed possibilities, often dialectically juxtaposed in the same poem.

Typically the "mild pastoral Muse" keys the reader to pastoral's sequestered pleasance and asks him to regard it as if its microcosm were the only existing world. And typically the persona placed in this pleasance weaves a communicative fabric that links him with the chosen few who share his pastoral ethos. Blake's *Introduction* to the *Songs of Innocence*, in both text and illustration, exemplifies this norm-sharing mode. The full-page illustration introduces the green miniature world shared by the poet-piper and child-muse in a tableau vivant of innocence. It immediately distances this green world from the ordinary world of daily life. The two figures are temporally as well as spatially enclosed in a moment of perfect communion: the child hovering above the shepherd-piper charismatically holds his gaze. Floating on a cloud, the cherubic child interestingly anticipates Blake's splendid illustration for Milton's *L'Allegro*, which shows the inspiring and inspired lark portrayed as an angelic cherub hovering in the sky. Both tableaux visualize the mysterious moment of inspiration that is also an annunciation. As Kathleen Raine observes, Blake's lark "sings for the Divine Humanity in all men" (2:160); he sings a truly pastoral song, the "song of Spring," as Blake reveals in using the motif again in *Milton*:

> Mounting upon the wings of light into the Great
>   Expanse:
> Reechoing against the lovely blue & shining heavenly
>   Shell:
> His little throat labours with inspiration; every feather
> On throat & breast & wings vibrates with the effluence
>   Divine
> All Nature listens silent to him. . . .
>   (31:32–36)

In the introductory tableau of the *Songs of Innocence*, the child does not himself sing a song of spring but inspires, ordains, and responds to the shepherd's pastoral song. In the illustration the shepherd-piper who looks raptly up at the child hovering on a cloud gives the impression of having been suddenly arrested in his wanderings and frozen in the very act of putting his reed pipe to his lips. The pose suggests a pattern that Wordsworth was to use to good effect in his lyrics and narrative poems—that of the halted traveler, usually an autobiographic persona, whose ordinary activity is interrupted and whose consciousness becomes detached from his familiar world as he encounters a figure seen in a supernal light.[4]

Blake's poem dissolves the static pose depicted in the illustration as the child directs the poet to "Pipe a song about a Lamb," and the poet responds in a perfect matching of inspiration and creation.

> Pipe a song about a Lamb;
> So I piped with merry chear,
> Piper pipe that song again—
> So I piped, he wept to hear.
>
> Drop thy pipe thy happy pipe
> Sing thy songs of happy chear,
> So I sung the same again
> While he wept with joy to hear.
>   (5–12)

Clearly the poet sings in "strains of unpremeditated art"[5]; the innocent child-muse strikes a responsive chord in the piper, resulting in spontaneous concord that is reflected in the rhetorical echoes: "Pipe a song . . . / So I piped," "Sing thy songs . . . / So I sung." Blake's rhetorical matching of direction and execution, injunction and action, echoes the syntactic economy of "God said, Let there be light: and there was light" (Genesis 1:3),[6] bringing his pastoral language close to the divine logos.

It is worth noting that Blake introduces this echo effect only into his piper's syntax as a mark of his innocent seeing and saying. By a brilliant strategy of omission he leaves it to the reader to supply, if he will, the pastoral commonplace of nature's woods and valleys reverberating with the shepherd's song, a *topos* prominent in pastoral poetry from Virgil to Yeats. For example, Virgil's *Sixth Eclogue* concludes with the image of the echoing valleys carrying Silenus's songs to the stars: "ille canit; pulsae referunt ad sidera valles" (84). Rather than invoking this echo *topos*, Blake leaves unsaid in his introductory lyric that nature is not a deaf or neutral but a sympathetic amplifier of human music. Blake leaves such echoes to the reader's surmise while he concentrates on the human interplay between the child-muse and adult poet-piper. For him the pastoral green is created by the human mind, not by nature's pleasance.

The shepherd is interrupted in his habitual activity of "Piping down the valleys wild / Piping songs of pleasant glee"; the text neither affirms nor denies whether nature sympathetically responds to his songs or silently absorbs them. The text simply offers a minimal expansion of the minimal emblem. As the voices of pastoral persona and child-muse harmonize, the child plays the role of responsive auditor in addition to that of patron-genius. He asks for the song, hears the song, and weeps or laughs in response to it. His tears and laughter round off the echoing circle of sympathetic responses that his visitation initiated. This truly is organized innocence! The poem comes as close as any modern poem can come to embodying the artless naive (in Schiller's sense) mode of pastoral, in which there is no discrepancy between real and ideal, in which the image of innocent and happy mankind epitomizes actual possibility. Naive language, Schiller said, springs spontaneously from naive thought and is so totally one with it that its spirit appears unconcealed within its corporeal husk (*NA* 20:426). Blake's *Introduction* to the *Songs of Innocence* exemplifies such naive language, which by spontaneously naming reality can grasp the "nature of things in figurative terms" (White 36–37). The lyric creates the illusion that word and act, appearance and reality, spirit and matter, meaning and sign are all firmly, inextricably fused in this pastoral syntax. The childlike simplicity of the monosyllabic words and short lines mirrors the naive thought that has not yet developed the art of involuted rhetoric. Its grammatical repertoire consists only of the imperative and indicative moods. It knows nothing of subordinate, coordinate, or interrogative construction, nothing of qualification, causation, or negation.

Both the visual and verbal representation of circular creativity invite the reader to enter the enchanting microcosm and share its communicative ideal. Both the water-color design and the childlike lyric entice the reader out of his familiar world into participating in the liberating illusion that the pastoral microcosm is all-sufficing. Nothing more is demanded of the reader than what Coleridge calls "that *negative* faith, which simply permits the images presented to work by their own force, without either denial or affirmation of their real existence by the judgment" (*BL* 2:134). The reader is not challenged to reflect about himself, to change his way of life, to forge new solutions to moral or social problems. The poem raises no provocative questions.

Yet we must not overlook the fact that, even in this self-sufficient microcosm of innocence, the notes of joy are not wholly unambiguous. Blake's language confirms Schiller's view that the modern poet's language will betray his divided sensibility even when he envisions harmonious wholeness. How are we, for example, to interpret the second half of Blake's *Introduction*? The child once more ordains a song (this time in written, not oral, form) to be recorded "in a book that all may read." Then he vanishes from sight. Clearly Blake seeks to enlarge the circle of happy communicativeness to include not only those who can hear the piper's songs but also those beyond the pastoral bower, the readers in their private rooms, separated from the poet-singer and from each other. Why then does the child-muse disappear just at the moment when his inspiration is needed for the most demanding task voiced so far? And how are we to interpret the piper's response that involves staining the clear stream?

> And I made a rural pen,
> And I stain'd the water clear,
> And I wrote my happy songs
> Every child may joy to hear.
> (17–20)

Gleckner interprets the progression dramatized in the poem as follows: "the glad animal sounds of the *Introduction* . . . give way to the voice of divine humanity through a recognition of experience and its concomitant woe." And he comments specifically on the implication of the final stanza: "Though the visionary inspiration (like the child on a cloud) be lovely, creation involves a knowledge of both ugliness and loveliness, joined with the imaginative ability to fuse both into a larger and higher loveliness. This cannot be done with aimless infantile piping; it must be done by means of mature conceptual creation in which both joy and sorrow are present, yet do not exist independently" (88). In Schiller's terms, Gleckner seems to suggest that the naive piper must become sentimental, that sense perception must give way to conceptual thought, the real yield to the ideal. Blake's lines certainly dwell on the loss of the kind of effortless creation that matches the original inspiration, an achievement that is surely not to be dismissed as "infantile piping." But does the song written by staining the "water clear" after the child has vanished necessarily represent "conceptual creation in which *both* joy and sorrow are present"? Conversant with visions as he was, Blake may more plausibly be dramatizing the gap between the original flash of revelation and the concomitant words on the page. As Shelley says, "When composition begins, inspiration is already on the decline, and the most glorious poetry that has ever been communicated to the world is probably a feeble shadow of the original conception of the Poet" (*Critical Prose* 30). Blake may, moreover, be contrasting the living voice and the dead letter of the written word. In distinguishing between "living speech" and "dead discourse," Plato interestingly used the image of staining clear water, which Blake fittingly applies to his pastoral piper. Plato's Socrates tells Phaedrus that it is not the lover of wisdom but a mere speechifier who writes his words "in water or that black fluid we call ink, using his pen to sow words that can't either speak in their own defense or present the truth adequately" (*Phaedrus* 276c). Blake seems similarly to contrast the written word's inadequacy to present the invisible inspiration with the living voice's greater expressiveness and immediacy.

The poem's ambiguous tonality elicits from the reader an ambiguous response. Initially the reader, like the child in the poem, is moved by the few sensuous details and simple acts that draw him into the poem's magic circle. The first half of the poem achieves the effect that Schiller ascribes to the naive poet who "moves us through nature, through sensuous verisimilitude, through living presence" ("durch sinnliche Wahrheit, durch lebendige Gegenwart"; *NA* 20:438). The positive effect on the reader is re-creative, freeing him for the moment from the anxieties and worries of his everyday life, allowing him to savor a liminal holiday in the happy counterfactual microcosm. Schiller, however, sees two moral dangers in this response. On one hand, the reader may simply seek to escape the pressures of his own world by regressing in imagination to a simple paradise. He may thus find relief in and through regressive quiescence instead of struggling for a progressive, higher harmony (451–52, 472). The other moral danger to which the pleasure of naive pastoral exposes the sentimental reader is having aesthetic pleasure turn into elegiac regret as the contrast intrudes itself on his consciousness between the poetic depiction of pure innocence and his actual experience of corruption. Schiller sees this intrusion as so inescapable that even the purest pleasure afforded by naive masterpieces will quickly become adulterated through the admixture of elegiac sensibility (20:449n). Living in an age of specialization and fragmentation, the modern reader finds the depiction of Edenic harmony and integrity both pleasurable and painful, both a reminder of what might be and of what can no longer be. The ambiguity invades all modern depictions of Edenic innocence. As Blake points out, many readers will respond to depictions of innocence by being offended because they reproach them with "the errors of acquired folly" (589).

As we have seen, Blake's *Introduction* to *Innocence* includes a hint of such tainted innocence, reinforcing the reader's mixed response. We need only to turn to other poems in the same volume to discover how uneasy Blake felt to speak consistently through the mask of the innocent piper, informing his miniature canvas with naive joy. Wagenknecht calls Blake's rhetorical posture the assumption of "pastoral ignorance" (15), the utterance of words that are "steadfastly innocent of their darker implications" (29). Blake's darker implications are masked by ignorance—ignorance of how readily innocence is undermined from within and without, both by natural instinct and by socially imposed norms. Where, for example, but in a postlapsarian world could a mother have learned the "wisdom" that the Little Black Boy's mother has passed on to her son? Her moral values belie the idyllic harmony of the pastoral community that the world of innocence predicates, and they taint the Arcadian images of the mother's lesson. "My mother taught me underneath a tree," the innocent boy fondly remembers,

> She took me on her lap and kissed me,
> And pointing to the east began to say.
>
> Look on the rising sun: there God does live
> And gives his light, and gives his heat away.
> And flowers and trees and beasts and men receive
> Comfort in morning joy in the noon day.
>
> And we are put on earth a little space,
> That we may learn to bear the beams of love,
> And these black bodies and this sun-burnt face
> Is but a cloud, and like a shady grove.
>
> For when our souls have learn'd the heat to bear
> The cloud will vanish we shall hear his voice.
> Saying: come out from the grove my love & care,
> And round my golden tent like lambs rejoice.
>   (7–20)

The mother's unquestioning acceptance of inequality in this world as a mere cloud obscuring the radiant equality and harmony in the next disturbs the reader's participation in this questionable concord. And so it is with some relief that we see the piper's pastoral mask slip and reveal the bard who erupts in antipastoral indictment:

Is this a holy thing to see,
In a rich and fruitful land,
Babes reduced to misery,
Fed with cold and usurous hand?
    (*Holy Thursday* 1–4, *Songs of Experience*)

Even though Blake could not long sustain the insulated vision of innocence, he came closer than any other Romantic poet to achieving a modern version of naive pastoral. Other poets only rarely followed his example of creating unself-conscious personas who evoke the concrete particulars of the pastoral bower without reflecting about themselves. Far more common among Romantic poets was the self-conscious struggle to achieve a timeless moment of pastoral harmony and community. Thus we find them assimilating pastoral moments into the introspective, dialectical poem that was one of their major achievements, the poem that M. H. Abrams has called the greater Romantic lyric. Abrams's paradigm of this Romantic lyric includes a meditative speaker in a particularized landscape carrying on a colloquy with himself, with an implied auditor, or with nature. In the course of the speaker's dramatic meditation, he "achieves an insight, faces up to a tragic loss, comes to a moral decision, or resolves an emotional problem. Often the poem rounds upon itself to end where it began, at the outer scene, but with an altered mood and deepened understanding which is the result of the intervening meditation" ("Structure" 528). Frequently these lyrics create pastoral spots of time that focus the speaker's change in mood from elegiac nostalgia to idyllic vision. Of the many examples that come to mind—*Frost at Midnight*, *Dejection*, *Intimations of Immortality*, *Ode to a Nightingale*, *Ode on a Grecian Urn*—Coleridge's *This Lime-Tree Bower My Prison* is one of the earliest, prototypical examples.

This Lime-Tree Bower opens with the speaker's self-pitying reflection on his state of imprisonment: he is physically immobilized and spiritually isolated. Coleridge's variation of the opening passage that he sent to Southey emphasizes the elegiac note even more strongly than does the published version:

> Well—they are gone: and here must I remain,
> Lam'd by the scathe of fire, lonely & faint,
> This lime-tree bower my prison.
>   (*CL* 1:334)

Lonely and faint, he feels doubly deprived. First he has been deprived of the beauties and feelings that, during his happy wandering through the countryside, might have nourished his mind not only for the present moment but also for future remembrance and restoration. Second, he has been deprived of the fellowship of his friends, deprived of a human community that would have blessed his communion with nature. Dispirited by the loss of such gifts, he undergoes what Coleridge on a different occasion calls "a process of intellectual *exsiccation*" (*CL* 2:713). His bower seems to him a prison, an empty space in an empty time.

Quietly and subtly this elegiac pastoral modulates to a more hopeful tone. As the speaker thinks of his absent friends, they no longer appear to him simply the measure of his misfortune. He gradually frees himself from being a spectator of his own misery as his imagination actively overcomes his passive self-pity. He dramatizes in the theater of his mind the progress of his friends downhill to a "roaring dell, o'erwooded, narrow, deep, / And only speckled by the mid-day sun" (10-11). This descent is not a further sinking into the recesses of his own mind; on the contrary, it marks his mind's movement from inward-focused regret to outward-focused intentionality, a movement which Coleridge explained in discussing the nature of meditative genius: "We imagine the presence of what we desire in the very act of regretting its absence, nay, *in order* to regret it the more livelily; but while, with a strange wilfulness, we are thus engendering grief on grief, nature makes use of the product to cheat us into comfort and exertion. The positive shapings, though but of the fancy, will sooner or later displace the mere knowledge of the negative" (Shedd 4:431).[7]

When Coleridge's speaker first imagines his absent friends' presence in his favorite landscape, he is making vivid to himself his solitary predicament. But then the activity of calling up the absent images indeed cheats him into comfort and exertion. The pleasurable energy of his imagination becomes increasingly powerful as he not only places before us images of a picturesque landscape but also animates the static scene by picturing his friends moving through the ever-changing scenery. Imagining his friends' descent into the sunless cavern followed by their ascent to panoramic views of hills and sea and sky, the poet gradually effaces himself from his own consciousness and allows the sensuous particulars of the imagined landscape—the world of sights and sounds—to occupy the center of his mental stage.

He thus makes present the rich cabinet of beauties whose absence had earlier sparked his discontent. And he also makes present the kind of happy pastoral community from which he had felt miserably excluded. I call this a pastoral community, although nowhere in this poem does Coleridge explicitly speak of himself and his friends as shepherds. But he imagines the happy wanderers as unencumbered by the burdens and restraints of the modern workplace while emphasizing their freedom and happiness: "Yes! they wander on / In gladness all" (26–27). Theirs is the happiness of a small circle of intimate friends (they were in fact Coleridge's most intimate friends— William and Dorothy Wordsworth and Charles Lamb)[8] rather than the shared interests of a larger society. They mutually intensify each other's pleasures without restricting each other's freedom. Theirs is the Epicurean ethos exemplified in Theocritus's *Idylls*, which, as Thomas Rosenmeyer argues, is most appropriate to pastoral. The proper freedom of pastoral accords with the Epicurean notion that "freedom is possible only if it is enjoyed in a circle of friends; true friendship, in turn, is enjoyable only if it is attended by liberty" (Rosenmeyer 105). Having attuned himself to such true companionship envisioned amidst nature's cornucopia, Coleridge's speaker might assert for him-

self what he asserts for his alter ego, "gentle-hearted Charles,"
that to him "no sound is dissonant which tells of Life" (75–
76). The speaker enchants himself with a visionary moment in
which pastoral community and communicativeness are trans-
formed into ecstatic vision. Having vividly painted a mental
canvas of the dramatic colors of the setting sun, dynamically
kindling clouds, groves, and oceans with brilliant light, he in-
vokes for his friend a transfiguring response:

> So my friend
> Struck with deep joy may stand, as I have stood,
> Silent with swimming sense; yea, gazing round
> On the wide landscape, gaze till all doth seem
> Less gross than bodily; and of such hues
> As veil the Almighty Spirit, when yet he makes
> Spirits perceive his presence.
> (37–43)

This moment marks the antipodal point from which the
speaker embarked on his mental journey. He began in a mood
that Coleridge described in a letter closely tied to *This Lime-Tree
Bower*: "I can *at times* feel strongly the beauties, you describe, in
themselves, & for themselves"—he told his friend, John Thel-
wall—"but more frequently *all things* appear little—. . . the uni-
verse itself—what but an immense heap of *little* things?" (*CL*
1:349). In such acedia, nature's language offers only the re-
sources of metonymy, the relation of part to part, like the
reduction of the lime-tree grove to a prison. Coleridge longs to
recover his capacity for seeing in nature the integrative thrust
of synecdoche: "My mind feels as if it ached to behold & know
something *great*—something *one* & *indivisible*—and it is only in
the faith of this that rocks or waterfalls, mountains or caverns
give me the sense of sublimity or majesty!—But in this faith *all
things* counterfeit infinity!—'Struck with the deepest calm of
Joy' I stand" (1:349). Having thus appropriated for himself the
joy he originally attributed to Charles Lamb, Coleridge quotes
further from *This Lime-Tree Bower* in a version that, more explic-

itly than the later revisions, emphasizes the dynamics of the reciprocal shaping power of mind and nature in the act of counterfeiting infinity:

> . . . and gazing round
> On the wide Landscape gaze till all doth seem
> Less gross than bodily, a living Thing
> Which acts upon the mind, & with such Hues
> As cloath th'Almighty Spirit, when he makes
> Spirits perceive his presence!
>   (*CL* 1:350)

And Coleridge remarks, "It is but seldom that I raise & spiritualize my intellect to this height" (1:350).

Two years earlier, in *Reflections on Having Left a Place of Retirement*, Coleridge summoned forth a similarly spiritualizing response to a panoramic view from a mountaintop—a view of clouds and fields, winding river, woods, hamlets, spires—leading the eye to its farthest reach:

> Dim coasts, and cloud-like hills, and shoreless Ocean—
> It seem'd like Omnipresence! God, methought,
> Had built him there a Temple: the whole World
> Seem'd *imag'd* in its vast circumference:
> No *wish* profan'd my overwhelméd heart.
> Blest hour! It was a luxury,—to be!
>   (37–42)

Recapitulating such a vision of divine omnipresence in *This Lime-Tree Bower*, Coleridge strikingly presents the kind of revelatory experience that Romantic poets frequently evoke as the highest reach of the human imagination. The experience is typically triggered by the poet's perception or sensation of an external object that will be suddenly, mysteriously transfigured. To capture in words such a revelatory moment challenges the poet to what Coleridge called the "grandest efforts of poetry . . . where the imagination is called forth, not to produce a distinct form, but a strong working of the mind, . . . the result being what the poet wishes to impress, namely, the substitution of a sublime feeling of the unimaginable for a mere image" (*Shakespearean Criticism* 2:103–4). The poet must so shape his verbal medium that it transports the reader's imagination from the visible, ordinary world into the realm of invisible, unimaginable sublimity. In *This Lime-Tree Bower* Coleridge articulates such an epiphany as illuminating his own existence only indirectly through imagining its efficacy for his friend.

Even though he has not affirmed such self-transmutation for himself, the speaker has freed himself from his spiritual prison and has lifted his spirit into a mystic, albeit vicarious, communion. From imaginary companionship in a ramble through the countryside, his imagination has launched an excursion into spaceless and timeless vision. Although he passes over his own capacity for epiphanal revelation in centering all his meditative energy on his friend, his own experience authenticates the experience projected for his alter ego: "So my friend / Struck with deep joy may stand, as I have stood, / Silent with swimming sense" (37–39). This is not egotistic self-aggrandizement, but a repetition of pastoral communicativeness and friendship in a finer tone.[9]

After this transfiguring moment, the speaker returns from his imaginary wanderings to view his lime-tree bower with new eyes. He discovers in his miniature world precisely the kind of renovating experience that he had hoped to store up for future years had he not been confined to his prison. Having distanced himself from his self-concern, having created an imaginary bond not only with his friends but with all creation, all life, he has received back from his creative effort a mirrored ray of inspiration. The process of renovation can best be explained by one of Coleridge's notebook memoranda in which he speaks of the mutual interpenetration of habits of feeling and moral action. Each is the cause of the other, he says, the "Light purifying, and the purified receiving and reflecting the Light, sending it off to others, not like the polish'd mirror by rejection from itself, but by transmission thro' itself" (*CN* 2:2435). This light metaphor aptly captures the complicated inner transformation that in *This Lime-Tree Bower* is both the cause and effect of the speaker's discovery that he is not banished to a world of shadows, but that even in his contracted horizon he can see leaves dappling in the sunshine, a "deep radiance" (52) overlaying the ivy on the walnut tree and dark branches of the elm gleaming "a lighter hue / Through the late twilight" (55–56). In short, the poem dramatizes the process by which the speaker's vision dissolves the apparent bower-prison and re-creates it as a bower paradise.

Solitary though he remains in his bower, he can easily fly on the wings of poetic imagination to his fellow imaginist, Charles Lamb. Coleridge fittingly closes his poem not with the melancholy mood in which he began his meditation but with the mellow mood of dusk, his speaker blessing the last rook as symbolic of the deep bond between himself, nature, and his friend. He captivates in and through the rook's flight the dynamic act of imagination that can, out of a fleeting observation of nature (the rook's black wing), create a symbol that embodies presence and absence, seeing and non-seeing, mind and object, self and other:

> when the last rook
> Beat its straight path along the dusky air
> Homewards, I blest it! deeming its black wing
> (Now a dim speck, now vanishing in light)
> Had cross'd the mighty Orb's dilated glory,
> While thou stood'st gazing; or, when all was still,
> Flew creeking o'er thy head, and had a charm
> For thee, my gentle-hearted Charles, to whom
> No sound is dissonant which tells of Life.
> (68–76)

The speaker blesses the bird because he imagines its having been visibly present to Charles at an earlier moment, etched against the sun's "dilated glory"; having become invisible to

Charles, the bird has become briefly present to the speaker, only to vanish into the evening sky as a "dim speck." This quick alteration of absence/presence/absence does not leave the solitary's bower empty and desolate. The sweep of his imagination extends the presence indefinitely and mirrors the orbit of the rook's flight even in the syntax of the meditation's final movement. Absorbed in the half-perceived, half-created symbol, the speaker's consciousness vaults across the confines of his prison to join his alter ego, Charles Lamb, who is also his silent auditor and inspiring muse. Clearly the speaker envisions for Charles the kind of paradisal blessings that a similar Coleridgean persona invokes for Sara Hutchinson:

> To her may all things live, from pole to pole,
> Their life the eddying of her living soul.
>   (*Dejection* 135–36)

In its dramatic turn from dispiriting to inspiring landscape, *This Lime-Tree Bower My Prison* assimilates pastoral modes and moods. In Schiller's terms, we can describe the speaker's mind as resisting the pull toward elegiac pastoral to which he seems to yield in the opening passage. By successfully capitalizing on the sentimental strength of transcending the limits of sense experience through the freedom of the imagination, he opens vistas on boundless space and time and achieves an idyllic moment in which the finite and the infinite coalesce.

Dramatic tension between elegiac and idyllic modes of pastoral is also central in the finest Romantic example of pastoral elegy, Shelley's *Adonais*. Painted on a much larger canvas than Coleridge's *Lime-Tree Bower*, it places in the foreground a more complicated pastoral persona to whom the speaker and the reader respond. The response ranges from empathy with Adonais's martyrdom to admiration, astonishment, and a desire to emulate his deification. The reader's response is complicated by the fact that Keats-Adonais occupies the central position on the poem's dramatic stage for only half the poem; he then moves into the background, where he continues to exert a magnetic power over the now foregrounded elegist. Not that the elegist is totally eclipsed in the first half. He assumes, however, more the role of chorus voicing ritualistic formulas of mourning even when he presents himself in the procession of mourners. Only later does he become both a private and public protagonist whose modes of feeling and perception have universal implications.

Having translated passages from Bion's *Lament for Adonis*, Moschus's *Lament for Bion*, Virgil's *Gallus Eclogue*, and having read and reread Theocritus's *Idylls* as well as the notable Renaissance elegies of Spenser and Milton, Shelley had a rich vocabulary and conceptual schema ready at hand for his pastoral elegy on the death of Keats.[10] Language, as Coleridge observed, "is the armoury of the human mind; and at once contains the trophies of its past, and the weapons of its future conquests" (*BL* 2:30–31). No Romantic poem more clearly bears out Coleridge's assertion about language as the armory of the mind than does Shelley's *Adonais*. Because he had such a large arsenal of pastoral *topoi* and elegiac conventions to draw on, Shelley could rapidly deploy his weapons for a new conquest when "sad occasion dear" (to borrow a pertinent phrase from *Lycidas*) compelled him. Assimilating Keats's fate to that of Adonis, he composed his elegy in less than three months.

The Adonis myth proved as heuristically rewarding a poetic paradigm for Shelley as the Oedipus myth was a psychological paradigm for Freud. Not only could Shelley readily allegorize such biographical details as the critics' attacks on Keats through the Adonis myth, but also, more significantly, he could dramatize a range of personal responses to life and death, universalizing them through the vegetation myth as well as through other conventions of the pastoral elegy. In fact the thematic conventions of pastoral elegy are so closely intertwined with the cyclical pattern of fertility cults that Earl Wasserman has argued that these myths and the poetic genre of pastoral elegy are nearly identical in structure: "Like the legend, the traditional artistic shape of the elegy expresses a way in which man has grasped and responded to the idea of life and death" (463).

Shelley opens his elegy with the formula borrowed from Bion: "I weep for Adonais—he is dead!" and immediately enlarges the personal lament to include all personae in the poem and readers of the poem in a universal injunction: "O, weep for Adonais! though our tears / Thaw not the frost which binds so dear a head!" (2–3). The speaker then further enlarges the scene as he calls upon the "sad Hour, selected from all years / To mourn our loss" (4–5), thus asking the reader to empathize not only with the elegist's personal loss but also with a whole life cycle coming to an end. Just as he asks the Hour to teach her own sorrow to her compeers, the speaker is teaching his readers to feel the universal loss in its full immediacy: "say: with me / Died Adonais" (6–7). Adonais has died at the appointed hour that marks nature's inexorably cyclical order:

> As long as skies are blue, and fields are green,
> Evening must usher night, night urge the morrow,
> Month follow month with woe, and year wake year to
> sorrow.
> (187–89)

If the Horae personify the mainspring of nature's cyclical life, they are but the handmaidens to Urania, the "mighty Mother" (10), the all-creative principle. Shelley conflates in her the goddess who loved Adonis, Plato's heavenly Aphrodite, Lucretius's Venus Genetrix, Milton's Urania (who, in turn, is a conflation of classical and Hebraic traditions), and Keats's Mnemosyne. Moreover, in her role of "most musical of mourners" (28), she is also Calliope, who mourns the loss of all her great epic poets—a *topos* borrowed from Moschus's *Lament for Bion*—as she bemoans the death of her "youngest, dearest one" (46). Her formulaic lament links Keats-Adonis to Bion and Lycidas, who also died before their prime; Keats is her

> extreme hope, the loveliest and the last,
> The bloom, whose petals nipt before they blew
> Died on the promise of the fruit. . . .
>   (51–53)

And just as Milton reminds us that Calliope could not save Orpheus from the bacchantes, Shelley shows Urania as helpless to save Adonis from fatal attack. Urania is left bereft both as epic muse who has lost all her "sons of light" (36) and as Aphrodite who has lost her lover because "Too soon, and with weak hands though mighty heart" he dared "the unpastured dragon in his den" (237–38). Even though the speaker does not recognize it, is she not, in addition to her other roles, a symbol for the power of poetry, which, though like Urania "chained to Time" (234), participates, like Adonis, in eternal life? In the *Defence of Poetry* Shelley speaks of the poet's words as being "instinct with spirit; each is as a spark, a burning atom of inextinguishable thought" (*Critical Prose* 26). Aphrodite resembles the poets who are "the hierophants of an unapprehended inspiration; the mirrors of the gigantic shadows which futurity casts upon the present; . . . the influence which is moved not, but moves" (35–36).

But such faith in poetry's power to produce the "interpenetration of a diviner nature through our own" (*Critical Prose* 31) is shaken to its roots by the silencing of the young Keats-Adonis's divine song: "Death feeds on his mute voice, and laughs at our despair" (27). The Shelleyan poet, like Urania, is forced out of his paradise of pure poetry, the *locus amoenus* of "ambrosial rest" (198). When he asks "where was lorn Urania / When Adonais died?" (12–13), the elegist's answer applies to himself as well:

>   With veiled eyes
> 'Mid listening Echoes, in her Paradise
> She sate, while one, with soft enamoured breath,
> Rekindled all the fading melodies,

> With which, like flowers that mock the corse beneath,
> He had adorned and hid the coming bulk of death.
>   (13–18)

Urania and the poet-eulogizer must leave such illusive paradises, such illusive defenses against total extinction, and face reality's dark truth by giving death its due. With empathy the speaker describes Urania fleeing her paradise, tormented by a "wound more fierce" than Adonais's:

>   Sorrow and fear
>   So struck, so roused, so rapt Urania;
>   So saddened round her like an atmosphere
>   Of stormy mist; so swept her on her way
> Even to the mournful place where Adonais lay.
>   (203–7)

Nowhere in this all-engulfing sorrowful tableau can the elegist find any consolation, not even in the survival of the dead poet's creations, which traditionally offers the consolation of poetry's immortality. The speaker can imagine all of Keats's creations, all the "glimmering Incarnations / Of hopes and fears, and twilight Phantasies" (111–12) only as desolate flocks now left unattended, mourning their shepherdless, homeless state. The only power these "passion-winged Ministers of thought" (74) retain is lovingly to administer last rites to the dead poet. Nor can the elegist find consolation in nature's rebirth. He can observe but not emulate spring, which had first been so tormented with grief that "she threw down / Her kindling buds, as if she Autumn were / Or they dead leaves" (136–38). But now spring discards such unseasonal despair and spreads a "joyous tone" (156). The speaker can observe that ants and bees, flowers and birds all participate in nature's rebirth, yet he does not feel this universal "quickening life" (164). Nature's cyclical renewal underscores the unchanging circularity of his own grief. For him must "Month follow month with

woe, and year wake year to sorrow" (189).[11] Chained and bowed
by the weight of sorrowful hours, he no longer finds efficacy in
the wish—sanctioned by nature's cycle of death and rebirth—
with which he had importuned the west wind: "Drive my dead
thoughts over the universe / Like withered leaves to quicken a
new birth!" (63-64). Neither Keats's poems nor his own seem in
this despairing mood to be an "unextinguished hearth" (66)
whose ashes and sparks can awaken mankind. He knows only
that a poet's creation like the "intense atom glows / A moment,
then is quenched in a most cold repose" (*Adonais* 179–80).

Does this elegiac meditation not only mourn a specific poet's
mortality but also declare the death of art? Does it not confirm
Hegel's conclusion, stated in his lectures on aesthetics (which
were delivered in 1820, the year before Shelley wrote *Adonais*),
that art as the highest embodiment of truth, as the highest
concrete aspiration of the human spirit, is a matter of the past
(*Sämtliche Werke* 12.1:16)? Heidegger reformulated Hegel's pro-
vocative utterance as a searching question that still needs to be
confronted in our own time: Does art continue to be, or has it
ceased to be, an essential and necessary event manifesting truth
that is decisive for our historical existence?[12] Before Shelley can
regain the resounding affirmative with which he answered this
question in the *Defence of Poetry*, he gives the negative alternative
its full expression in the first half of *Adonais*. Like Blake, he
feels impelled to embody error in order to vanquish it.

After sustaining his elegiac mood, his "melodious pain" (146),
for thirty-seven Spenserian stanzas—interspersed with brief but
violent attacks on the hostile critics, the "herded wolves" (244)
who presumably had hounded Keats to death—Shelley shifts to
a different key. In Schiller's terms, he has up to this point in
Adonais presented an elegiac speaker whose passion feeds only
on sorrowful reality. Suddenly his passion takes wings from an
idea, from a vision that compellingly reverses all earlier conclu-
sions, as he modulates from an elegiac to an idyllic perspective.
It now seems certain to the speaker that Keats's "pure" spirit is
not lost with his body's death, that it

> shall flow
> Back to the burning fountain whence it came,
> A portion of the Eternal, which must glow
> Through time and change, unquenchably the same. . . .
>   (338–41)

Sorrow and mourning acted out, fully expressed in a ritualis-
tic scenario, have served their purpose: they have purged the
speaker—and the reader—of narrow preoccupation with death,
with a ruined paradise of failed hopes, keeping with "phantoms
an unprofitable strife" (345). To see the dead poet only through
the metonymic trope of the dead vegetation god is to kill the
vivifying power of imagination. Shelley does not show or ex-
plain how he discovers his new perspective; like all sudden
conversions, the flash of illumination is inexplicable in itself but
knowable and expressible through its effect. From his new van-
tage point, the speaker glimpses previously invisible spiritual
horizons. His vision is no longer grounded in the experience of
his senses but orients itself by the world of invisible ideas. First
he sees that neither is the inspired young Keats-Adonais perma-
nently lost, nor has art lost its efficacy. It is not Adonais who is
dead, but those who see life only as material existence, those
who are imprisoned in the charnel house of narrow perceptions
and tormented by self-imposed delusions. The speaker invites
his audience to share his fresh apperception:

> He hath awakened from the dream of life—
> 'Tis we, who lost in stormy visions, keep
> With phantoms an unprofitable strife,
> And in mad trance, strike with our spirit's knife
> Invulnerable nothings.—*We* decay
> Like corpses in a charnel; fear and grief
> Convulse us and consume us day by day,
> And cold hopes swarm like worms within our living clay.
>   (344–51)

In thus transposing his song of lamentation into one of jubi-
lation, Shelley follows a pastoral tradition that was familiar to
him from Spenser's November Eclogue and Milton's *Lycidas*.
The tradition goes back to Virgil's Daphnis Eclogue, which, as
Renato Poggioli has argued, radically changed the structure and
ethos of pastoral elegy: "By setting a song of rejoicing beside a
song of grieving Vergil followed the pattern of the Adonis
festivals, or of the joint ritual celebration of death and resurrec-
tion of a vegetarian god. But Daphnis had been born and had
died a man: what we witness is his apotheosis, not his rebirth, a
novelty so unique within the pastoral canon as to induce many
interpreters to believe that it was determined by an exceptional
historical accident" (74). Both Milton and Shelley adopted and
modified this Virgilian novelty. Milton contributed fresh possi-
bilities to the paradigm by fusing Epicurean pastoral with a
Christian ethos, while Shelley exploited Orphic themes fused
with Platonic ideas.

Having gained his clear insight into the Keatsian realm of
pure eternal being, set over against the corrupt sphere of
earthly existence, Shelley's speaker stands at a crossroads, con-
fronted by the choice that Schiller regarded as inescapable for
the modern (sentimental) poet: whether he will orient him-
self by actual experience or by the world of ideas and ideals;
whether he will primarily view reality as an object of antipathy
(*Abneigung*) or the ideal as an object of sympathy (*Zuneigung*)
(*NA* 20:441). Swiftly the speaker frees himself from the world
of sense experience that has so far obsessed him and has driven
him to self-martyred suffering with and through the martyred
Adonais. He frees himself, too, from the bitter occasion that
moved him to savage satiric attack on Adonais's tormentors.
Schiller throws light on the discomforting, constricting effect
that such elegiac poetry as the first half of *Adonais* has on the
reader. Pathos that is not nourished by ideals will, according
to Schiller, manifest itself by shackling the reader's heart and
mind, whereas truly poetic pathos will leave the reader's psyche
in a state of free activity—a state of *Selbsttätigkeit* and *Gemütsfrei-*

heit (20:443). And he adds that only a poet who is animated by the ideal, not the real, world can free the reader from the confining emotions and limitations of experience.[13] Therefore the elegiac poet is well advised to draw his subjects from the realm of ideas, not from the external world. Even if he laments the loss of a real person, as Shelley does in lamenting Keats's death, Schiller insists that the modern poet must transform the real subject matter into an ideal one. Precisely such transformation of a finite into an infinite subject constitutes his poetic task (20:450).

Shelley meets the challenge of such a transformation in the second half of *Adonais*. It culminates in an ecstatic vision that, for a moment, holds in perfect equilibrium the finite and infinite, the human and divine, becoming and being. As the speaker gradually sees the mortal Adonais not as the antithesis of the ideal but as participating in it, he frees himself from his inadequate polar logic as well as from his equally inadequate cyclical organicism, both of which confirmed the antithesis between the linear time of human life and nature's cyclical renewal. Only by seeing beyond these finite contradictions can the speaker achieve the kind of union of contraries that Cusanus, for example, like other Renaissance Platonists, thought attainable. Cusanus explained that a circle and a straight line are incompatible only as long as they are conceived as finite but coincide when they are infinite (Wind 47).

In *Adonais* the elegist's horizon first expands by means of negative predications. Still trapped in antithetical thought, he sees Keats-Adonais as outsoaring "the shadow of our night" (352), becoming invulnerable to the "Envy and calumny and hate and pain" (353) of human existence:[14]

> From the contagion of the world's slow stain
> He is secure, and now can never mourn
> A heart grown cold, a head grown grey in vain.
>   (356–58)

Just like the lovers on Keats's marble urn, whose love will be forever warm, and like his nightingale singing in "full-throated ease" in a green bower, Keats will never again know

> The weariness, the fever, and the fret
>   Here, where men sit and hear each other groan;
> Where palsy shakes a few, sad, last gray hairs. . . .
>   (*Ode to a Nightingale* 23–25)

The congruence between Shelley's negative predications about the immortalized Keats and Keats's similar predications about the ethereal nightingale and the immortal urn, strongly suggests that what is at stake for Shelley is both the salvation of the individual soul and the theodicy of art. It is necessary to redeem art at a time when it is obscured by the "accumulation of facts and calculating processes" (*Critical Prose* 29). In both his *Defence of Poetry* and *Adonais* Shelley suddenly leaps beyond the opposition between material and spiritual, external and internal life. He transcends antithetical thought by way of visionary illumination. No longer does the speaker see the artist and his art as subject to mortality while nature is annually reborn; now he sees Keats-Adonais participating in a nature that is itself transfigured into a timeless paradise. By his enthusiastic affirmation of a universal redemption, the speaker has himself outsoared Urania, who is chained to the world of mutability. He sings, like the speaker of Keats's *Ode to Psyche*, by his own eyes inspired, enchanted by his unmediated vision of the transfigured Keats:

> He is made one with Nature: there is heard
> His voice in all her music, from the moan
> Of thunder, to the song of night's sweet bird. . . .
>   (370–72)

The echo of the speaker's earlier evocation of thunder and the nightingale's song as sounds of mourning underscores the new jubilant note in which he celebrates Adonais's immanent and transcendent cosmic presence by fusing the Adonis with the Orpheus myth.

Like Adonis, Orpheus is closely associated with the green world of pastoral. His association with different religious cults need not concern us here. What makes him a perfect symbol for Shelley's purpose, syncretizing him with Adonis and Keats, is his prowess in playing the lyre and his renown as a great singer who captivated all who heard him. The Duke's tribute in *The Two Gentlemen of Verona* is typical:

> Orpheus' lute was strung with poet's sinews,
> Whose golden touch could soften steel and stones,
> Make tigers tame, and huge leviathans
> Forsake unsounded deeps to dance on sands.
>   (3.2.77–80)

In Ovid's telling of the myth, Orpheus's power to enchant nature persists even after his death. Not only does all of nature mourn for him—the birds, beasts, rocks, and trees that in his life had been moved by his song—but as his dismembered head and his lyre float down the Hebrus River, their mournful prophecy is also echoed by nature (*Metamorphoses* 11:42–54). Thus Orpheus is truly one with nature. In his life, his music resonating with nature and love vivified the cosmos; in his death, his charismatic presence remains in nature's echoes of his surviving song. As Rilke says in his fifth sonnet to Orpheus, "Ein für alle Male / ists Orpheus wenn es singt" (once and for all it's Orpheus wherever there is a song). And for Neo-Platonists like Ficino, Orpheus symbolized the universal power of Eros that is consonant with the power of art. Both as lover and as theologian, he is credited with "finding a single voice for all the intimations of this world's beauty and the other world's that solicit a human mind" (Cody 29). In a fragmentary dialogue on Orpheus, Shelley praises the divine power of Orpheus's multiform melody that "clothed in sweetest sounds and varying words / Of poesy" both deepest joy and tumultuous grief:

Unlike all human works,
It never slackens, and through every change
Wisdom and beauty and the power divine
Of mighty poesy together dwell,
Mingling in sweet accord.
(83–87; *Oxford Shelley* 629)

Shelley would have found Orphic and neo-Platonic myster-
ies linked in the commentaries of his contemporary Platonist,
Thomas Taylor. He would have found attractive Taylor's argu-
ment that in Orphic theology "the deity is an immense and
perpetually exuberant fountain whose streams originally filled
and continually replenish the world with life" (171). Shelley
transferred this neo-Platonic Orphic image from the deity to
the poet in his *Defence of Poetry*: "All high poetry is infinite. . . . A
great poem is a fountain for ever overflowing with the waters of
wisdom and delight; and after one person and one age has
exhausted all its divine effluence which their peculiar relations
enable them to share, another and yet another succeeds, and
new relations are developed, the source of an unforeseen and
an unconceived delight" (*Critical Prose* 26). Such Orphic pleni-
tude in which the poet fills the universe with paradisal fresh-
ness and divinity is precisely the vision to which Shelley's elegist
rises in *Adonais* in his conversion from sorrow to joy, from
preoccupation with the world of appearances to openness to the
world of ideas. He breaks through to the insight that the deified
Keats is an Orphic power—

a presence to be felt and known
In darkness and in light, from herb and stone,
Spreading itself where'er that Power may move
Which has withdrawn his being to its own;
Which wields the world with never wearied love,
Sustains it from beneath, and kindles it above.
(373–78)

This insight is consolation of the highest order. It is a discovery that if man can degenerate to the level of wolves and vultures, he also has the power to ascend to higher being, to the informing motion and spirit that—to quote Wordsworth's *Tintern Abbey*—"impels / All thinking things, all objects of all thought, / And rolls through all things" (100–102). Shelley's elegist turned encomiast has himself been metamorphosed even as he envisions Keats's metamorphosis. His tribute echoes Pico della Mirandola's oration on the dignity of man, showing the heights to which man could rise by his own choice; "if, happy in the lot of no created thing, he withdraws into the center of his own unity, his spirit, made one with God, in the solitary darkness of God, who is set above all things, shall surpass them all. Who would not admire this our chameleon?" (Cassirer 225).

For Shelley this admirable chameleon who "withdraws into the center of his own unity" and is made one with God is, par excellence, the poet. Poetry is stamped with the image of divinity in man. It "makes immortal all that is best and most beautiful in the world" (*Critical Prose* 32). Thus Shelley can conclude that poetry "redeems from decay the visitations of the divinity in Man" (32). Given the poet's powerful "secret alchemy" that transmutes all that it touches, changing "every form moving within the radiance of its presence" (32), not only is Keats deified by being made one with the divine power of nature but nature is also vivified by the poet's interpenetrating radiance. Yet both in his *Defence of Poetry* and in *Adonais* Shelley admits that poetry's divine emanation is an ideal, a hypothetical state: "Could this influence be durable in its original purity and force, it is impossible to predict the greatness of the results" (*Critical Prose* 30).

Since experience confirms that pure inspiration occurs only as "evanescent visitation," Shelley ultimately proposes a metaphysical solution to the problem of redeeming the world. Unequivocally the speaker in *Adonais* arrives at a bold imperative, addressing himself, fellow poets, and sympathetic readers:

> Die,
> If thou wouldst be with that which thou dost seek!
> Follow where all is fled!
>   (464–66)

He does not gloss over his own reluctance to translate this imperative into action:

> Why linger, why turn back, why shrink, my Heart?
> Thy hopes are gone before; from all things here
> They have departed; thou shouldst now depart!
>   (469–71)

Again the speaker must struggle against the impulse to let his mind be absorbed by his bitter disappointments and disillusionments with this world, where even "what still is dear / Attracts to crush, repels to make thee wither" (473–74). Again he must teach himself, "dart thy spirit's light / Beyond all world's until its spacious might / Satiate the void circumference" (418–20). Only then can he perceive calmly that

> The soft sky smiles,—the low wind whispers near:
> 'Tis Adonais calls! oh, hasten thither,
> No more let Life divide what Death can join together.
>   (475–77)

Thus death becomes the gateway to true community, the community of the sacred few who are identified in *The Triumph of Life*: those like Socrates and Jesus who "as soon / As they had touched the world with living flame / Fled back like eagles to their native noon" (129–31). They are the "kings of thought / Who waged contention with their time's decay" (*Adonais* 430–31), constituting the Shelleyan pantheon who welcome Keats to the immortal community. Shelley explicitly rejects the Wordsworthian community to be attained by reforming this world, a faith that he himself had embraced in earlier days, believing that

Not in Utopia, subterraneous Fields,
Or some secreted Island, Heaven knows where,
But in the very world which is the world
Of all of us, the place in which, in the end,
We find our happiness, or not at all.
    (*Prelude* 10:724-28)

The idea of localizing what Wordsworth called the "One great
Society . . . / The noble Living and the noble Dead" (*Prelude* 10:
970-71) in "the world which is the world / Of all of us" was
anathema to Shelley. He called it "demoniacal."[15] To restrict all
hope for human perfectibility to what *this* world offers seemed
to Shelley a counsel of despair. To be discontent with the "nar-
row good we can attain in our present state" was to be on "the
right road to Paradise" (*Letters* 2:406). But discontent with cor-
rupt existence is, in *Adonais*, the negative impulse that the poet
must transmute into positive idealism if he is to embark on the
way to Elysium.

Shelley presents a complicated paradigm. Through identifi-
cation with the fate of Keats-Adonais, the speaker undergoes a
catharsis of his pity and anger that frees his imagination to
make the leap to a deified Keats-Vesper, an eternal among
eternals. And he struggles to free himself not only from his
elegiac feelings occasioned by Keats's death, but also from his
immersion in temporal process as such, a struggle for which he
has no guide. He must leave Urania behind since she is chained
to time; by his own light, by his own imaginative investment, he
must ascend to a perspective from which Keats-Adonais's death
can illuminate the overarching concord between beginnings
and endings, births and deaths. He comes to speak not only for
the poet's but for all human beings' need for an intelligible and
timeless order. As Frank Kermode puts it in *The Sense of an
Ending*, "we project ourselves—a small, humble elect, perhaps
—past the End, so as to see the structure whole, a thing we
cannot do from our spot of time in the middle" (8). Shelley's
persona struggles to reach a perspective from which death—
whether Keats's or his own—is not a moment of total disruption

and dissolution of all hope for the future, especially the hope for the vivifying power of the poet's word, but an apocalyptic paradigm that mysteriously informs the existence of the "sacred few." He moves toward a perspective that freshly illuminates the end. To borrow Kermode's words: "No longer imminent, the End is immanent" (25).

From his perspective, Adonais is not only beyond time, unified with the transcendent One, but also immanent in time, in the many that change and pass. The speaker hears Adonais's Orphic voice calling in the whispering wind and is enchanted, drawn to the prophetic fire that consumes "the last clouds of cold mortality" (486). In a magnificent concluding stanza Shelley offers an intimation of the speaker's apotheosis through the symbol of his soul's voyage. The final lines join mortal doubts and immortal longings in an open-ended, moving tableau:

> I am borne darkly, fearfully afar:
> Whilst burning through the inmost veil of Heaven,
> The soul of Adonais, like a star,
> Beacons from the abode where the Eternal are.
> (492–95)

As the reader follows the poet to this final perspective, the tension of earlier, contradictory perspectives through which he has been "borne darkly" is resolved as he yields to the lines' placidly moving current. The poet's final words elicit from the reader a passive response that contains within it, however, the latent energy for further active movement. The reader here experiences the kind of alternate rhythm that Coleridge thought characteristic of the mind's activity. He illustrates this activity by that of a water insect which "*wins* its way up against the stream, by alternate pulses of active and passive motion, now resisting the current, and now yielding to it in order to gather strength and a momentary *fulcrum* for a further propulsion. This is no unapt emblem of the mind's self-experience in the act of thinking" (*BL* 1:124).

All through *Adonais* Shelley creates a series of resting places in the form of earthly paradises, a series that culminates in the promise of eternal paradise. Through varying evocations of the *locus amoenus*, Shelley's persona in the poem and the reader outside it enjoy brief recreative tableaux, each of which serves as a "momentary fulcrum for a further propulsion." Thus, for example, we are allowed an early resting place in the image of Rome, the eternal city, which seems to attenuate the awesome power of death. The speaker enjoins the reader through his address to Urania—

> Come away!
> Haste, while the vault of blue Italian day
> Is yet his fitting charnel-roof! while still
> He lies, as if in dewy sleep he lay;
> Awake him not! surely he takes his fill
> Of deep and liquid rest, forgetful of all ill.
> (58–63)

This azure vault grants the illusory consolation of Keats's imminent awakening yet leads quickly to disillusionment. Shelley's dialectical thought winds its way through similar putative, paradisal encounters—whether in the form of Keats's "passion-winged Ministers of thought / Who were his flocks" (74–75) or in the extended tableau of nature's rebirth (155–77)—to another image of Rome as *concordia discors*:

> Go thou to Rome,—at once the Paradise,
> The grave, the city, and the wilderness;
> And where its wrecks like shattered mountains rise,
> And flowering weeds, and fragrant copses dress
> The bones of Desolation's nakedness
> Pass, till the Spirit of the spot shall lead
> Thy footsteps to a slope of green access
> Where, like an infant's smile, over the dead,
> A light of laughing flowers along the grass is spread.
> (433–41)

This paradoxical *locus amoenus* is the last terrestrial resting place in the speaker's progress of mourning and propels him toward his ultimate resolution:

>   Die,
> If thou wouldst be with that which thou dost seek!
> Follow where all is fled!—Rome's azure sky,
> Flowers, ruins, statues, music, words, are weak
> The glory they transfuse with fitting truth to speak.
> (464–68)

Through his dialectics, Shelley has found the language that can speak "with fitting truth" of mysteries that are unpresentable, inexpressible. He finds himself, as he said in his *Essay on Life*, "on that verge where words abandon us, and what wonder if we grow dizzy to look down the dark abyss of—how little we know" (Reiman 478). Yet he knew that he must find words, that he must speak by indirection, as he explained in his dialogue on Orpheus:

> I talk of the moon, and wind, and stars, and not
> Of song; but, would I echo his high song,
> Nature must lend me words ne'er used before,
> Or I must borrow from her perfect works,
> To picture forth his perfect attributes.
> (98–102; *Oxford Shelley* 630)

In *Adonais* Shelley similarly borrows his language from nature, straining the familiar world into unfamiliar synecdochic tropes while keeping it undefiled by mundane pursuits. In anthropomorphic images such as "That Light whose smile kindles the Universe" (478), he offers glimpses into the infinite without abandoning finite existence. He achieves precisely what Schiller had hoped for in his projected idyll about Hercules's union with Hebe, an idyll that was to make manifest Hercules's apotheosis and yet not abandon human concerns. Shelley's concluding vision comes close to embodying the ecstatic effect Schiller projected—a vision of pure light, pure freedom, pure potentiality, in which all mortal shadows and barriers have vanished (NA 28:120). Shelley does not press his ecstatic conclusion to the point of extinguishing all sense of mortality, but his own vision of the autobiographic persona's soul sailing toward the realm of pure light solves the problem of how to embody poetically both movement and stasis in an idyllic moment. Schiller's theory of the idyll illuminates Shelley's poetic achievement of creating an impression of tranquility that does not eliminate the tension of opposing forces but holds them in perfect equilibrium.[16] Precisely because the poet removes all obstacles standing in the way of the speaker's reaching his ideal, he runs the risk of dissolving all tension and ending in quiescence. Shelley avoids this pitfall by delicately touching the dissonant chords of the speaker's remaining unresolved fears, even as he clairvoyantly moves toward eternal concord.

There is no evidence that Shelley knew Schiller's poetics. But he shared more strongly than any other poet of the time Schiller's hopes for reforming the world by first reforming the individual, and to reform the individual through the influence of ideas, through the interpenetration of man as bound to the senses and man as ascending to the ideal. Schiller's theory of the idyll fascinatingly highlights the spectrum of pastoral responses that Shelley's *Adonais* embodies in the two central personas and evokes in the reader, ranging from the pathos of sorrow and pity that inhibit the freedom of the imagination to the theopathy that liberates the imagination to encompass infinite potentiality. *Adonais* shows the way from a lost Arcadia to an attainable Elysium. And yet, for all its incomparable achievement—and the poem indeed loads every rift of its subject with precious ore, as Keats once advised Shelley to do[17]—it leaves one Schillerian task unattempted: to create an image of paradisal happiness and innocence, an image of human perfectibility, as a goal achievable in the modern world of technological progress and social complexity. Shelley's poem succeeds in embodying vastly complex responses to universal questions about life and death, change and permanence, language and art. Yet, while his visionary pastoral, like all major pastoral poetry, implies a social model of community, it suggests no model for reforming this world into a better community; it offers only the alternative of leaving the world behind for an eternal ideal. In his *Defence of Poetry* Shelley had credited the poets of the age of Petrarch and Dante with creating just such a model of this-worldly renovation: "the familiar appearance and proceedings of life became wonderful and heavenly; and a paradise was created as out of the wrecks of Eden. And as this creation itself is poetry, so its creators were poets; and language was the instrument of their art" (*Critical Prose* 22–23). Like Schiller, who never matched in poetry the idyllic possibilities that his poetics projected, Shelley never embodied in his mature poetry a physical rather than a metaphysical model for creating a modern paradise out of the "wrecks" of Eden.

"MY VALLEY BE MY WORLD":
HOME AT GRASMERE AS A FAILED IDYLL

No didactic poem has yet appeared, Schiller wrote in 1795, in which the informing idea is itself poetical. Most *Lehrgedichte* alternate between abstract ideas and imaginative concreteness or else fetter the imagination altogether, instead of achieving an interpenetration of universality and particularity, reasoned thought and free play of the imagination (*NA* 20:453). Schiller's criteria for legitimate didactic poetry resonate in Coleridge's expectations and plans for Wordsworth's *Recluse* as the "first & finest philosophical Poem" to be created by "the only man who has effected a compleat and constant synthesis of Thought and Feeling and combined them with Poetic Forms, with the music of pleasurable passion and with Imagination or the *modifying* Power in that highest sense of the word . . . in which it is a dim Analogue of Creation, not all that we can *believe* but all that we can *conceive* of creation" (*CL* 2:1034). Such a synthesis of thought and feeling placed in the service of an ideal creation presents a Coleridgean version of Schiller's concept of the idyllic mode as a poetic ideal.

Unfortunately Coleridge's earliest contributions to laying out the blueprint for Wordsworth's great philosophical poem have not survived. Conceived during the winter of 1797–98 at Alfoxden, when Coleridge and Wordsworth almost daily talked at length about present and future poetic projects, the *Recluse* grew into a poetic scheme of awesome proportions. Although Wordsworth completed the prospectus rapidly, the poem itself grew only in intermittent spurts. In Coleridge's presence, as Darlington remarks in her introduction to *Home at Grasmere*, "there were long, thought-provoking conversations; in his absence, Wordsworth begged for instruction to help him find his way" (5–6), while the poem itself languished. Wordsworth's dependence on Coleridge for inspiration and instigation is shown in two letters to Coleridge in March 1804, after he left for Malta. With supreme egotism, Wordsworth speaks of his fears that Coleridge might die before he gathered and sent for safekeeping his scattered notes on the *Recluse*: "I am very anxious to have your notes for the Recluse. I cannot say how much importance I attach to this, if it should please God that I survive you" (*EY* 452). Still more urgently he writes, "I cannot help saying that I would gladly have given 3 fourths of my possessions for your letter on The Recluse at that time. I cannot say what a load it would be to me, should I survive you and you die without this memorial left behind. Do for heaven's sake, put this out of the reach of accident immediately" (464).[1]

For specific details on the collaborative plans for Wordsworth's philosophical *magnum opus*, we must turn to comments involving the publication of the *Excursion* as the "intermediate part" of the projected tripartite *Recluse*. In his Preface to the *Excursion* (1814) Wordsworth speaks of his "determination to compose a philosophical poem, containing views of Man, Nature, and Society; and to be entitled, The Recluse; as having for its principal subject the sensations and opinions of a Poet living in retirement" (*Prose* 3:5). The prose Preface ends with the famous verse Prospectus expressing the "design and scope of the whole Poem," a Prospectus which, besides having Miltonic echoes, also reverberates with Schiller's plea that the poet lead us forward toward a realizable goal of civilization rather than backward toward an Arcadian dream:

> Paradise, and groves
> Elysian, Fortunate Fields—like those of old

Sought in the Atlantic Main—why should they be
A history only of departed things,
Or a mere fiction of what never was?
(105–9)

Wordsworth, however, parts company with Schiller and Cole-
ridge when he insists that such a model of attainable bliss is to
be found as "A simple produce of the common day" (113) that
can be expressed by words "Which speak of nothing more than
what we are" (117).[2] Such matter-of-factness contradicts Schil-
ler's conviction that the modern poet's richest province is the
realm of ideas, the conception of the possible, of the counter-
factual or metaphysical (in its literal sense). Schiller believed
that it was indeed imperative to speak of something more than
"what we are." Only by transfiguring the manners and morals,
the character and wisdom of his own time could the modern
poet, through the art of idealization, create a model of human-
ity's wholeness for his age (*NA* 20:437). Surprisingly enough, on
close examination Wordsworth's "simple produce of the com-
mon day" turns out not to exclude such an art of idealization.
Paradoxically, Wordsworth insists on simple reality as "Surpass-
ing the most fair ideal Forms" (Prospectus 101) and invokes the
Miltonic Urania, the "dread Power" (158), to inspire him so that
his life might "Express the image of a better time, / More wise
desires, and simpler manners" (161–62).

But we must turn to Coleridge for the strongest assimilation
of Schiller's humanistic aesthetics into his conception of what
was to be the finest and only true philosophical poem. The
synopsis of the *Recluse* that he sent to Wordsworth in 1815
sounds as if Coleridge expected a Wordsworthian version of the
ideas in both the *Letters on the Aesthetic Education of Man* and
Naive and Sentimental Poetry. Put briefly, Coleridge's expectations
included philosophical commentary (1) on the human faculties
from a physical, psychological, and moral perspective; (2) on
the evolution of human society from "savage" to "civilized,"
including "a manifest Scheme of Redemption," as the means of
reconciling man with nature; (3) on "the necessary identity of a

true Philosophy with true Religion." And the whole poem was to reveal the "necessity of a general revolution in the modes of developing & disciplining the human mind by the substitution of Life, and Intelligence . . . for the philosophy of mechanism . . . which idly demands Conceptions where Intuitions alone are possible or adequate to the majesty of the Truth." Finally, Coleridge epitomizes his own scheme in a terminology that brings him closest to Schiller's "coalition" of naive and sentimental modes of feeling: "In short, Facts, elevated into Theory— Theory into Laws—& Laws into living & intelligent Powers— true Idealism necessarily perfecting itself in Realism, & Realism refining itself into Idealism" (*CL* 4:574–75).[3]

Idealism perfecting itself in realism and realism refining itself into idealism: here is a capsule definition of the informing principle of Schiller's idyllic mode, even to the point of assimilating in the terms "perfecting" and "refining" Schiller's recurring alchemical metaphor for a baser substance being transmuted into a higher value. Schiller's idyllic mode transmutes reality into a poetic revelation of the ideal of humanity, which, as Coleridge says of the Scriptural symbol, is "characterized by a translucence of the Special in the Individual or of the General in the Especial or of the Universal in the General. Above all by the translucence of the Eternal through and in the Temporal. It always partakes of the Reality which it renders intelligible; and while it enunciates the whole, abides itself as a living part in that Unity, of which it is the representative" (*Lay Sermons* 30).

Both Coleridge and Schiller transferred their hope for the complete revelation of truth for their own time from sacred to profane texts. Both expected that the highest poetic mode contain, like the Bible, "a Science of *Realities*: and therefore each of its elements is at the same time a living *Germ*, in which the Present involves the Future, and in the Finite the Infinite exists potentially" (*Lay Sermons* 49). To use Schiller's terminology, we might say that in this poetic science of realities, the sentimental *Empfindungsweise* restores the finite realities of the naive without sacrificing the sentimental revelation of the infinite. Precisely such an ideal form of poetry or human ideal realized in poetry is Coleridge's expectation that the *Recluse* create "the Colors, Music, imaginative Life, and Passion of *Poetry*; but the matter and arrangement of *Philosophy*—not doubting . . . that the Totality of a System was not only capable of being harmonized with, but even calculated to aid, the unity . . . of a *Poem*" (*CL* 4:574). This unity was clearly to be an "omniformity"[4] that could accommodate a "manifest Scheme of Redemption," uniting the individual and the universal, the psychological with the philosophical, in its translucent symbolism.

We know that Wordsworth found Coleridge's profound expectations both persuasive and overwhelming, both inspiring and inhibiting. He accepted his assigned mission but felt powerless to proceed with it. Yet he made an exuberant start about 1800, just after he finished his earliest version of the *Prelude*, a poem he was later to describe as "preparatory" to the *Recluse* (*Prose* 3:5), the "moral and Philosophical Poem" to which he resolved to devote the prime of his life and the "chief force" of his mind (*EY* 454). As he tackled the first book of the *Recluse*, his imagination flowed freely as long as he dwelled on details of his reclusive world, but it became stymied when he tried to pass on to reclusive meditations on human nature and on man's relation to society, not to mention schemes of redemption. The fact that the expected setting—Wordsworth "settled in an abiding Home" (*CL* 4:574)—became the whole of *Home at Grasmere* (*The Recluse*, Book One, Part One), leaves the reader to fill in the large gap of the rest of Book One. One way of solving this puzzle is to see the relation of the part to the whole through Kenneth Johnston's playful analogy that asks us to picture an archaeologist coming into a "metaphorical Westmorland valley" where he discovers what appears to be the facade of a ruined Gothic cathedral. He remarks that on this facade "ordinary scenes from rural life are carved and arranged in bizarre patterns. What can the whole have been like? the explorer wonders excitedly, not knowing the wall was never more than a freestanding prototype. And he goes on in the bliss of ignorant expertise to reconstruct in theory what the original architect could not complete in stone" ("Home" 1).

It is not entirely fair to attribute this edifice complex to the holistic preconceptions of Wordsworth's critics, since Wordsworth himself clearly suffered from it as well. After he finished the *Prelude* in 1805, he felt dejected rather than exhilarated: "when I looked back upon the performance it seemed to have a dead weight about it, the reality so far short of the expectation; it was the first long labour that I had finished, and the doubt whether I should ever live to write the Recluse and the sense which I had of this Poem being so far below what I seem'd capable of executing, depressed me much." And he goes on to speak of the *Prelude* as "a sort of portico to the Recluse, part of the same building, which I hope to be able erelong to begin with, in earnest" (*EY* 594). Clearly Wordsworth felt the burden of his calling, much as did Wallace Stevens when he received the National Book Award in 1955 and said, "It is not what I have written but what I should like to have written that constitutes my true poems, the uncollected poems which I have not had the strength to realize" (246).

Even if we ignore Wordsworth's intentions and aspirations and accept Johnston's contention that *Home* was all that Wordsworth could possibly complete—"a freestanding prototype"—we cannot ignore the artistic difficulties that it fails to solve as a prototype of pastoral landscape and inscape, of realistic-idealistic *locus amoenus* and social community. The poem compounds the difficulties inherent in the pastoral mode by making a static Grasmere rather than a dynamic persona the center of a long poem. It foregrounds what had been the background setting for philosophical meditation in the retirement tradition that goes back to Plato's *Phaedrus* and culminates in Pope's epistles, in which, as Maynard Mack shows, "seventeenth-century Christian humanism, and Horatian and other Roman precedents speak with a single voice" (113). Wordsworth was to experiment with such varied retirement patterns in a manuscript fragment of 1808, *The Tuft of Primroses*, parts of which he assimilated into the *Excursion*, using the *topos* of the happy man in his "abiding Home," far from the madding crowd. It generates his persona of St. Basil, his *beatus vir*, who retires to his hermitage neither to insulate himself against the world's evils in "a refuge from distress or pain" nor to enjoy *otium*, pure furlough from duty, a "breathing time, vacation, or a truce" (*PW* 5: Appendix C, p. 354).[5] He sought the cloistered life as an end in itself in which to realize his ideal of community, seeking not freedom from the world's restraints but principles of self-rule and self-restraint. In a daring experiment, Wordsworth tries to place this explicitly Stoic pastoral ideal of rational preference for repose into a setting that threatens the cloistered harmony. Like the speaker of *Home*, the poet in *The Tuft of Primroses* longs to confirm Grasmere as a sacred precinct for a "wardenship of spirits pure" (249), a place "inviolate for nobler purposes" (251). But Wordsworth here does not try to sustain the idyllic mode at all cost, and he allows satiric and elegiac feelings to surface. Despite his compelling hopes to discover his ideal in the real Grasmere, the speaker does not avert his eyes from the visible signs of human mortality and human devastation. He faces the vanity of founding the future in the present:

> In vain: the deafness of the world is here
> Even here, and all too many haunts
> Which Fancy most delights in, and the best
> And dearest resting-places of the heart
> Vanish beneath an unrelenting doom.
>   (259–63)

Such "bitter language of the heart" (*Excursion* 3:462) Wordsworth suppressed in *Home at Grasmere*, suppressing with it the tensions, complexities, discords, and countercurrents that might have made his static ideal into a dynamic equilibrium of opposing forces. In *Home* he defuses the destructive potential the speaker glimpses once or twice, either by allegorizing it or by containing it in homiletic recitals. Thus, for example, he distances a possible threat to his idyllic relationship with Dorothy by hinting at the fate that may have befallen a pair of swans who, like themselves, had chosen Grasmere as "their safe retreat" (332). But the swans' absence is offset by the human pair's unbroken presence; the passing speculation that the swans may have fallen prey to a shepherd's "deadly tube" (352) is immediately reproved as "unworthy recompense" (360) for the valley's hospitality and is displaced by the poem's dominant allegory of the "happy Valley" (378):

> Ah! if I wished to follow where the sight
> Of all that is before my eyes, the voice
> Which is as a presiding Spirit here
> Would lead me, I should say unto myself,
> They who are dwellers in this holy place
> Must needs themselves be hallowed.
>   (362–67)

This passage, following upon the overt threat to the swans and the covert threat to the human protagonists, illustrates Empson's point that "the feeling that life is essentially inadequate to the human spirit, and yet that a good life must avoid saying so, is naturally at home with most versions of pastoral" (110).

A second way in which Wordsworth neutralizes threats to his Edenic harmony is by containing evidence of socioeconomic change and personal suffering in a series of homilies. Evidently wishing to introduce some social realism into his retirement poem, Wordsworth in 1806 added a section that shifts from self-exploration to impersonal narratives connected with the inhabitants of three cottages located in his chosen valley.[6] He adopts the role that Coleridge thought peculiarly suited to him, that of *"Spectator ab extra" (Table Talk* 175). He tells the moralizing tale of an adulterous sheepfarmer who becomes a self-exiled outcast of society and dies of grief: "He could not bear the weight of his own shame" (532). The second tale extols the virtues of six daughters who spin and garden and by their busy cheerfulness console their widowed father. A story of sorrow assuaged, despondency corrected. Both tales are unambiguous in their simplistic moral import. More interesting is the third story, of a widow whose past joys are enshrined in the emblematic grove of firs that she and her husband had planted "with joint hands" (639) to provide shelter for their sheep, a grove "now flourishing while they / No longer flourish; he entirely gone, / She withering in her loneliness" (640–42). This tale is the most interesting because it remains untold—Wordsworth leaves it a treasure of the "silent mind" (643). It is displaced by self-reflection, by questions about the poet's craft and the nature of the poetic medium. The poet's doubts surface, doubts about his vocation as translator of the private language of suffering, about the gap between the poet's words and words uttered under the actual pressure of feelings.[7] The poet wonders whether there is a language that could capture the immediate feelings:

> Is there not
> An art, a music and a stream of words
> That shall be life, the acknowledged voice of life?
> (620–22)

His image of a stream of words expands into another question:

> Is there such a stream,
> Pure and unsullied, flowing from the heart
> With motions of true dignity and grace,
> Or must we seek these things where man is not?
> (628–31)

Here Wordsworth first envisions the "acknowledged voice of life" in a metaphor borrowed from nature (a pure and unsullied stream) only to discover a new perplexity: whether in fact the voice of life can be forged in a human context or must be sought "where man is not." Having heard the tale of human suffering from the sufferer's own lips, the poet now becomes skeptical about whether he dares to retell it in human language. He reflects here an anxiety about language that he would probe more deeply a few years later, in his third *Essay upon Epitaphs*: "Language, if it do not uphold, and feed, and leave in quiet, like the power of gravitation or the air we breathe, is a counterspirit, unremittingly and noiselessly at work, to derange, to subvert, to lay waste, to vitiate, and to dissolve" (*Prose* 2:85). To neutralize this counterspirit, Wordsworth turns to the non-human realm in his search for the unadulterated word, the word that is coessential with feeling. He resorts to the simile of the breeze, one of his favorite inspirational tropes:

> Methinks I could repeat that tuneful verse
> Delicious as the gentlest breeze that sounds
> Through that aerial fir-grove, could preserve
> Some portion of its human history. . . .
> (632–35)

Even though he chooses to remain silent, Wordsworth thus assures himself and his auditor that he could overcome the difficulty of producing an authentic language. He could just possibly recuperate in poetry the immediacy of human life that can be expressed only in a medium that is as diaphanous as the breeze blowing through the widow's symbolic fir-grove.

More frequently than using the strategy of preserving tales in the silent mind—a strategy that could hardly yield a long poem—Wordsworth escapes the disruptive forces both within the fabric of language and within the larger fabric of society by subordinating his speaker to nature, acting as a ventriloquist speaking for and through Grasmere's serene and unchanging mask. The speaker submerges himself, for example, as he calls on the hills to embrace him and enclose him (129):

> I would call thee beautiful, for mild
> And soft and gay and beautiful thou art,
> Dear Valley, having in thy face a smile
> Though peaceful, full of gladness.
> (133–36)

Through such an inane mask the speaker avoids all vigorous argument, all passionate debate of the kind Wordsworth engages in under the mask of St. Basil with his friendly adversary Gregory Nazianzen, who, resisting conversion, derides the Pontic retreat as the "Arcadia of a golden dream" (*Tuft of Primroses* 429; *PW* 5: Appendix C, p. 358).

No discordant voices are heard in the uniformly static Grasmere paradise. Not even the concordant voice of Dorothy—the Emma of the poem—is allowed a separate theme. She exists only as a shadowy double, a muffled echo of the speaker, an invisible genius loci of Grasmere:

> Where'er my footsteps turned,
> Her Voice was like a hidden Bird that sang;
> The thought of her was like a flash of light
> Or an unseen companionship, a breath
> Or fragrance independent of the wind. . . .
>   (109–13)

She is something between a Blakean emanation and a Jungian anima. But Wordsworth offers no Blakean drama of a fragmented self struggling toward wholeness. The speaker's wholeness is a given; his reunion with his Emma "to part no more" is the visible sign of the "surpassing grace" (122) that nature has bestowed on her chosen son. Emma is a far cry from the "dearest Friend" who in *Tintern Abbey* serves so brilliantly as a complementary alter ego, doubling the speaker's consciousness through the younger, more spontaneous, joyful self, embodied in Dorothy—"in thy voice I catch / The language of my former heart" (116–17). Moreover, she not only symbolizes the speaker's past but also is his link to the future, a future in which he may be physically absent but nevertheless will be present, like the landscape, inscribed in her memory, shaping her philosophic mind.

Such complex interweaving of past, present, and future, of self, alter ego, and landscape, is the hallmark of Wordsworth's best autobiographical meditations. To eliminate complexity and ambiguity of perspective is to reduce chiaroscuro painting to a monochromatic surface, to reduce dialogue to monologue, polyphony to homophony. Why then did Wordsworth suppress such multivalent vision in *Home* in favor of a simple doubling of the "I" into "we," a placid life mirroring his own in its mirroring his faithful abode's? Was he afraid that any discordant, dissenting, or even modulating point of view might release his latent skepticism about this all-sufficing retreat? Was he afraid of being overpowered by language's vitiating counterspirit if he dared forge a polyphonic voice of life?

Wordsworth's chief defense against the intrusion of the imagination of disaster is his metaphoric armature of "sublime retirement" (732), his archetype of an autonomous microcosm. The speaker sets up an unrelenting barrage of encomia celebrating his "self-sufficing world" (204)—

> This small abiding-place of many men,
> A termination and a last retreat,
> A Centre, come from whereso'er you will,
> A Whole without dependence or defect,
> Made for itself and happy in itself,
> Perfect Contentment, Unity entire.
>   (165–70)

Although these utterances leave no doubt about the speaker's vision of his sanctified abode as paradisal perfection, they reveal nothing about the process by which an individual living in an age of dislocating political, social, and economic changes could gain such undefiled wholeness, such undiminished self-realization. What way of life leads to this "hallowed spot" (250) where the poet and his sister found the promise to secure for themselves "in the midst of these unhappy times" (253),

> A portion of the blessedness which love
> And knowledge will, we trust, hereafter give
> To all the Vales of earth and all mankind?
>   (254–56)

Was such "unappropriated bliss" (85) to be the unearned inheritance, the free gift of beatitude, bestowed by bountiful nature on her favored beings?

It is difficult to speak of Wordsworth's encomia without resorting to the language of fairytale romance. Wordsworth was, after all, writing at a time when the public policy of enclosure led to the expropriation of the land on which independent farmers and laborers had built their cottages. Exploited by the landowners, these formerly self-sustaining workers became part of a surplus population that provided cheap labor (Thompson 220). Wordsworth blithely displaces such exploitative expropriation by blissful appropriation. In terms of his own vocation, the poet's homecoming to Grasmere does not so much suggest the Virgilian task of pastoral progression as sound the note of regression into infantile wish-fulfilling dreams of a return to the all-giving Mother, displaced by the image of "This all in all of Nature" (205).

Wordsworth claims to dismiss

> . . . all Arcadian dreams,
> All golden fancies of the golden age,
> That bright array of shadowy thoughts from times
> That were bright before all time, or are to be
> When time is not. . . .
> (829–33)

Yet he reaches into the shadowy depths of his own self to create his private Arcadian dream, his golden age, his family romance with Grasmere. Disappointingly enough, he does not reflect on this myth-making impulse, although he had already proved himself masterful at self-analysis in the *1799 Prelude*. There he raised incisive questions about the perspective from which he viewed his moments of visionary joy in another Cumberland valley:

How shall I trace the history, where seek
The origin of what I then have felt?
Oft in those moments such a holy calm
Did overspread my soul that I forgot
The agency of sight, and what I saw
Appeared like something in myself—a dream,
A prospect in my mind.
  (2:395–401)

He thus leaves open the question of where the experience
of "holy calm" originates: "Who knows the individual hour in
which / His habits were first sown, even as a seed" (2:245–46)?
He can only resort to metaphoric language to approximate the
tenor of the experience; words are, as Coleridge said, "the only
signs that a finite being can have of its own thoughts" (*Philo-
sophical Lectures* 173). The poet can use these signs to under-
stand his mood in terms of a veil spread over his spirit, inter-
posing itself between his mind and nature, making his eyes look
inward into the prospect of his mind.

 In *Home at Grasmere*, by contrast, Wordsworth eschews such
probing of the psychological processes that lie behind his pro-
claimed feeling of blessedness. He submerges the poet's indi-
vidual sensibility in the universal image of paradise as mystical
center, a center where, according to many archaic traditions,
heaven is near earth, the divine commingling with the human.[8]
As Wordsworth elaborates his paradise into a cosmic center, he
recapitulates a primeval myth while simultaneously claiming
Grasmere's uniqueness. Its perfection resides not only in the
perceptible landscape—perpetual streams, sunny hills, green
fields and mountains—but in the imperceptible sublimity it im-
prints on the beholder through the "one sensation that is here"
(156)—

Here as it found its way into my heart
In childhood, here as it abides by day,
By night, here only; or in chosen minds
That take it with them hence, where'er they go.

'Tis (but I cannot name it), 'tis the sense
Of majesty and beauty and repose,
A blended holiness of earth and sky,
Something that makes this individual Spot,
This small abiding-place of many men,
A termination and a last retreat,
A Centre, come from whereso'er you will,
A Whole without dependence or defect,
Made for itself and happy in itself,
Perfect Contentment, Unity entire.
    (157–70)

This unique, inexpressible encounter, first imprinted on the speaker's consciousness in childhood, resonates with the archetypal symbolism of the center described by Eliade as an axis mundi, a place consecrated by a hierophany, a "blended holiness of earth and sky" (*Cosmos* 12–16). Typically such hierophany, according to Eliade's ethnological studies, does not merely sanctify a given profane spot but goes so far as to "ensure that sacredness will continue there. *There*, in *that* place, the hierophany repeats itself. In this way the place becomes an inexhaustible source of power and sacredness and enables man, simply by entering it, to have a share in the power, to hold communion with the sacredness" (*Patterns* 368).

Wordsworth signals such communion with sacredness by the rhetorical *topos* of inexpressibility: the consciousness that this particular moment is numinous yet unnameable, unforgettable yet unsayable. It is charged with an inexpressible "overplus of meaning."[9] Rather than foregrounding the paradox of saying what is unsayable, however, Wordsworth evades any integrative strategy by alternating between wholes and parts, between archetypal symbols ("blended holiness of earth and sky," "a last retreat," a "Centre," "Unity entire") and verisimilar particulars (the lake with its one green island, surrounding crags, tree-lined shores, church and stone cottage) (137–40). Thus he establishes his "loved abode" (108) as both real and ideal, visible and invisible, personal and archetypal, historical and mythical.

In Kantian terminology, we might say that Wordsworth places Grasmere at the juncture of the world of sense and the world of ideas. It points to the goal marked by Coleridge as "Idealism perfecting itself in Realism, & Realism refining itself into Idealism" (*CL* 4:575). When, early in the poem, Wordsworth depicts himself in his "home / Within a home" (261–62), he seems to aim at such realistic idealism, claiming an all-surpassing congruity between desire and fulfillment, imagined ideal and experienced reality:

> The boon is absolute; surpassing grace
> To me hath been vouchsafed; among the bowers
> Of blissful Eden this was neither given
> Nor could be given—possession of the good
> Which had been sighed for, ancient thought fulfilled,
> And dear Imaginations realized
> Up to their highest measure, yea, and more.
> (122–28)

That in such passages Wordsworth could free the mind from the confines of reality without losing himself in metaphysical vapors is a measure of his greatness. On the one hand, he concretely pictures his journey toward Grasmere, his "individual nook" (251), as a recognizable experience in a recognizable landscape. On the other hand, he eulogizes this valley as "an image for the soul, / A habit of Eternity and God" (214–15), thus dematerializing it, deconstructing this "Home of untutored Shepherds" (665) in order to re-create it as a counterfactual, eschatological home. Grasmere as a "habit of Eternity and God" is consistent with Wordsworth's proclamation in *The Prelude* that

> Our destiny, our nature, and our home
> Is with infinitude, and only there;
> With hope it is, hope that can never die,

Effort, and expectation, and desire.
And something evermore about to be.
    (6:538–42)

This "hope that can never die," this trust in limitless futurity,
is Wordsworth's declaration of independence from hope at-
tached to the disappointing world of reality. As Schiller pointed
out, "all reality, as we know, lags behind the ideal; all that exists
has its limits; only thought is limitless" (*NA* 20:474). Words-
worth seems to confirm Schiller's view when he says of his
homecoming to Grasmere that

            the distant thought
Is fetched out of the heaven in which it was.
The unappropriated bliss hath found
An owner, and that owner I am he.
    (*Home* 83–86)

But at the same time Wordsworth betrays anxiety at thus leaving
behind the commonplace truths, which he defended as the
informing values of his art. He brings them into his grammar of
hope, asserting extravagantly that the "Realities of life" (54)
have been to him "more bountiful than hope, / Less timid than
desire" (58–59).

Wordsworth never quite resolves this question of primacy: Is
the numinous import of *Home* to serve as a utopian goal to
which the reader should aspire? Or is the "calmest, fairest spot
of earth" (MS D 73) intended as a realistic alternative to the
dissonant world of industrial England? Is Wordsworth trying to
break ground for a radically new ethos, or is he merely conserv-
ing an old and threatened ideal of life? Although he appears to
believe in an inscrutable workmanship by which the real can be
transmuted into the ideal without losing its earthliness, his po-
etic alchemy proves an inconclusive and evasive experiment.

Above all, Wordsworth's experiment is compromised by his
rhetorical insulation of his ideal abode from the larger world.

His recurrent image of peacefully embowered existence disturbs the reader with the sense of the darker realities so firmly shut out. The reader is all too aware of the "common world" (249), "the living and dead wilderness / Of the thronged World" (MS D 613–14) from which the speaker and his favorite companion have seceded. They dwell at "happy distance from earth's groaning field, / Where ruthless mortals wage incessant wars"—to borrow Wordsworth's apt phrases from *Composed by the Side of Grasmere Lake* (7–8). Does Wordsworth not protest too much when he details motives for retirement, or rather, enumerates the motives that did *not* lead him to this "abiding-place?"

> I came not dreaming of unruffled life,
> Untainted manners; born among the hills,
> Bred also there, I wanted not a scale
> To regulate my hopes; pleased with the good,
> I shrink not from the evil in disgust
> Or with immoderate pain.
> (428–33)

The double negatives of the litotes of "not dreaming" of "unruffled life" and "untainted manners" opens up a chink in the enclosed pleasance to admit the ruffled and tainted reality beyond the pale. Yet the negatives immediately cancel out the corrupt world, while the speaker insists paradoxically that he did not dream of doing so.[10] The litotes function to contain and conceal the antipastoral forces that might threaten the bower's "protection for the mind" (458). Continual use of negative prefixes reinforces the rhetorical work of the litotes to admit and yet render impotent such images as "hunger's abject wretchedness" (445), which is here unknown—here where the worker in the field is "unenslaved" (443). Yet in coupling such language of negation with a lexicon of protective custody—"safe retreat" (332), "enclosure" (466), "shelter" (132), "these narrow bounds" (878), "Mountain sanctuary" (685), "lofty barriers" (455)—Wordsworth's rhetoric does not so much repel as invite an invasion of hateful contraries. His rhetoric can ultimately neither dissolve nor resolve the antithesis between sacred Grasmere and the profane world.

Wordsworth's dilemma illustrates the difficulty that Schiller saw confronting the modern (sentimental) poet who attempts to write in the idyllic mode: even if such a poet does not explicitly present the antithesis between real and ideal, even if he presents an inviolate perfection, the antithesis unconsciously betrays itself with every stroke of the pen (*NA* 20:449n). It betrays itself in the homogenized harmony that dominates Wordsworth's pleasance, in its solipsistic self-sufficiency, in its absence of dynamic intensity and of economic factuality.

It seems fair to conclude that Wordsworth succeeds only too well in implementing the strategy urged on him by Coleridge, the strategy of "devoting himself to his great work—grandly imprisoning while it deifies his Attention & Feelings within the sacred Circle & Temple Walls of great Objects & elevated Conceptions" (*CN* 1:1546).[11] He does indeed imprison his feelings within the walls of his "noblest Temple" (*Home* 194) to enshrine the life of divinity and truth, of "singleness and unity and peace" (203). The hope for such a homecoming to unity and peace may offer the modern reader a Lethean draft that obliterates all painful reality, but it does not offer a source for the inspiriting draft that Dante calls Eunoë, which revives, rejuvenates, reanimates. Clearly the moral energy of Dante's earthly paradise is missing as is the dynamic paideia of Milton's Eden. As Barbara Lewalski has shown, Milton departed from the hexameral tradition by uniquely dramatizing Adam and Eve's emotional and intellectual growth. Although Milton's "sovran Planter" originates all action by implanting Adam and Eve in the Garden, he there expected them to "grow and perfect themselves through cultivation, and to bear appropriate fruits" (93). Whereas Milton thus emphasizes an Edenic process of growth, Wordsworth surprisingly depicts a paradisal stasis of passive contentment, of "full complacency," as the following tribute to Grasmere illustrates:

> Hail to thee,
> Delightful Valley, habitation fair!
> And to whatever else of outward form
> Can give us inward help, can purify
> And elevate and harmonize and soothe,
> And steal away and for a while deceive
> And lap in pleasing rest, and bear us on
> Without desire in full complacency,
> Contemplating perfection absolute
> And entertained as in a placid sleep.
>   (388–97)

Such an ideal of contemplative quiescence, imperturbable imaginings, and soothing nirvana is a far cry from the energetic repose (*energische Ruhe*) that Schiller stipulated as a sine qua non of the idyll (*NA* 20:466n) and that Milton specified through his images of gardening and harvesting. In Wordsworth's soothing, harmonizing valley we miss, as Herbert Lindenberger has rightly said, the "forward movement, the struggle toward definition, the whole larger drama of interaction" (*On Prelude* 165) that Wordsworth achieved in *The Prelude*. *Home*'s central defect lends weight to Schiller's contention that the greatest difficulty confronting the modern poet who attempts the idyllic mode lies in achieving movement within rest, tension within equipoise (*NA* 20:473). The difficulty lies in creating an equilibrium of opposing impulses, a *concordia discors* or unified manifoldness—what Coleridge calls "Multëity in Unity" (*BL* [1907] 2:232)—rather than a simple structure and uniform import.[12]

Although Wordsworth's *Home at Grasmere* fails, on the whole, to infuse intensity and vitality into his idyllic vision, one passage comes close to embodying formative energy and dynamic tranquility in an ideal moment. I am speaking of the opening passage, in which the poet-narrator recaptures the moment in his boyhood when the paradisal valley first claimed him. He vividly reenacts this covenantal moment:

> Once on the brow of yonder Hill I stopped,
> While I was yet a School-boy . . .
> And with a sudden influx overcome
> At sight of this seclusion, I forgot
> My haste—for hasty had my footsteps been,
> As boyish my pursuits—[and sighing said],
> "What happy fortune were it here to live!
> And if I thought of dying, if a thought
> Of mortal separation could come in
> With paradise before me, here to die."
> 　　(1–2, 5–12)

The speaker thus recovers in all its particulars not only the "sudden influx" that transfixed and enraptured him, but even the exact words that rose spontaneously to his lips. The verbal expression displaces the physical motion of his boyish pursuits.[13] Significantly, the recuperated utterance focuses on a thought of contingent happiness that dwells both on life and on death, both on timeless bliss and on "mortal separation." The subjunctive of happiness immediately generates the conditional of death.

This boyhood idyll exemplifies the distinctive Wordsworthian mode of the halted traveler: an imaginative encounter arrests the ordinary continuum of the narrative, separates the protagonist from familiar nature, and evokes a feeling of solitude and isolation or a thought of death (Hartman, *Wordsworth's Poetry*, 17–18). The idyllic encounter displays all these paradigmatic effects: it creates intensity within repose, dissonance within harmony, and compels them into a powerful *concordia discors*. The thought of death produces a counterweight to the promise of infinite joy, adding a penseroso voice to the dominant allegro. The speaker touches the *Et in Arcadia Ego topos* lightly, unelegiacally, almost with a Keatsian note of "easeful Death" in a moment when "more than ever seems it rich to die" (*Ode to a Nightingale* 52, 55).[14] An interesting passage in the *1799 Prelude* catches this same mood in a similar boyhood visionary experience. Here, too, Wordsworth includes the boy's exact recollected thoughts, as the radiance of the setting sun over the hills of Lake Coniston generates a thought of death in the midst of joyful rapture:

> And there I said,
> That beauteous sight before me, there I said
> (Then first beginning in my thoughts to mark
> That sense of dim similitude which links
> Our moral feelings with external forms)
> That in whatever region I should close
> My mortal life I would remember you,
> Fair scenes! that dying I would think on you:
> My soul would send a longing look to you. . . .
>   (2:161–69)[15]

The intrusion of death into Arcadia is not the only dissimilitude in the joyful similitude between internal and external landscape in the opening episode of *Home at Grasmere*. The brief narrative also embodies the tension between physical stasis and imaginative motion, suggesting the sense of power in repose. The boy's arrested pursuit—"Long did I halt; I could have made it even / My business and my errand so to halt" (20–21)— releases his mind to pursue clouds and breezes in a playful chase: "Who could look / And not feel motion there?" (24–25). With increasing rapidity and intensity, his imagination follows the fleeting forms from earth to sky, naming them as if he were Adam seeing and naming God's creation for the first time:

> Sunbeams, Shadows, Butterflies, and Birds,
> Angels, and winged Creatures that are Lords
> Without restraint of all which they behold.
> I sate, and stirred in Spirit as I looked,
> I seemed to feel such liberty was mine,
> Such power and joy. . . .
>   (31–36)

The imagination's free play in this passage recalls Coleridge's "idle flitting phantasies" in the *Eolian Harp* (40), dancing sunbeams and "twilight Elfins" (21) that lead to the speaker's recognition of "Rhythm in all thought, and joyance every where" (29). As if to restrain his Coleridgean "shapings of the unregenerate mind" (55), Wordsworth will not let his spirit rove unchecked beyond the visible world into metaphysical speculation. Even though his spirit rejoices in its freedom, it also sets boundaries to its exuberant excursions. The speaker resolves that his imagination's power will serve only this end:

> To flit from field to rock, from rock to field,
> From shore to island, and from isle to shore,
> From open place to covert, from a bed
> Of meadow-flowers into a tuft of wood,
> From high to low, from low to high, yet still
> Within the bounds of this huge Concave; here
> Should be my home, this Valley be my World.
> (37–43)

Thus Wordsworth brings this idyll within an idyll to a close with an epideictic flourish. Only in this passage—and never again in *Home at Grasmere*—does Wordsworth generate a lexicon of an autonomous world out of an organized plenitude, a *concordia discors* of visual particulars and spatial relations. The particulars are not deliberately composed into a controlled landscape in the style of Constable; rather, they cohere in the imagination's free play, capturing a complex mood in the style of Turner's seascapes.[16] Schiller's formulation of this kind of aesthetic activity is to the point. Objecting to the premature constraining of the imagination by the understanding, he writes to Körner in 1788:

> It seems not to be a good thing, and prejudicial to the creative work of the psyche, if the understanding submits to the

onrush of ideas to over-sharp scrutiny at the very gates, as it were. An idea considered in isolation may seem very unimportant or very extravagant; but it will perhaps gain weight from another which follows hard upon it; . . . the understanding cannot judge of any of this unless it holds fast long enough to view it in conjunction with these other ideas. In the creative mind, by contrast, so it seems to me, the understanding has withdrawn its sentinels from the gates, the ideas rush in *pêle-mêle*, and only then does it scrutinize and review the whole company of them.—You critics, or whatever you may like to call yourselves, are ashamed of, or fear, those fleeting moments of inspired frenzy which are characteristic of truly creative minds, and the longer or shorter duration of which distinguishes the thinking artist from the mere dreamer. Hence your complaints of barrenness; it is because you reject too soon and discriminate too severely.[17]

Only in his brief boyhood idyll does Wordsworth withdraw the sentinels of the understanding in *Home*, allowing the onrushing images to create a rich canvas of impressionistic brushstrokes without imposing discrete, unambiguous forms—that is, images translatable into unambiguous meaning. Keeping the "false secondary power"[18] from repressing or overscrutinizing the free flowing ideas has the effect on the reader that Hillis Miller has ascribed to Wordsworth's best poems. He bases his conclusion on *Composed upon Westminster Bridge*, but what he says of the implications of the figurative language in this sonnet holds with equal validity for the opening passage of *Home*; here, too, Wordsworth's figurative language "leads the interpreter away from an unambiguous mimetic reading toward the recognition that the poem expresses an oscillation between consciousness and nature, life and death, presence and absence, motion and stillness" ("Still Heart" 307).

Wordsworth's achievement of such multeity in unity, dynamic movement within ordered form, remains an anomaly in *Home at Grasmere*. He did not solve the problem of how to use his seminal boyhood encounter with the ideal valley as a paradigm for a sustained, future-oriented, creative meditation on "Man, on Nature and on human Life" (*Home* 959). The seminal episode remains a single dynamic spot of time in a static panegyric, a failed idyll.

4

THE RHETORIC OF PASTORAL INSPIRATION

In *Home at Grasmere* Words-
worth attempted a mythopoeic narrative that did not progress
beyond the mythic setting of a sanctuary (Grasmere) and a
guardian of authentic existence (the poet). Rilke's words from
Duino Elegy 9, "*Hier* ist des *Säglichen* Zeit, *hier* seine Heimat"
(43)—"here is the time of the expressible, here is its home"—
capture this Wordsworthian sense of sanctified time and place,
the sanctified "here" that is the "last retreat" (*Home* 166) for the
sayable, the expressible. By contrast, we might call *The Prelude* a
journey into and encounter with the unsayable, the unfathom-
able, the inexpressible. It is telling that even when Wordsworth
completed his manuscript in 1839 for posthumous publication,
he left it unnamed, "title not yet fixed upon."[1]

To investigate Wordsworth's rhetoric of inspiration in *The
Prelude* is an attempt to identify Wordsworth's distinctive way of
deploying pastoral metaphors to say that which "lies far hidden
from the reach of words" (*Prelude* 3:185). Wordsworth brings
this central difficulty of speaking of hidden depths into the
foreground of his poem as he pauses in his narrative, having
retraced his life up to an "eminence"; retrospectively he can see
his theme:

> Of Genius, Power,
> Creation and Divinity itself
> I have been speaking, for my theme has been
> What pass'd within me. Not of outward things
> Done visibly for other minds, words, signs,
> Symbols or actions; but of my own heart
> Have I been speaking, and my youthful mind.
>   (3:171–77)

Thus Wordsworth simultaneously claims that he has been speaking of invisible creative powers and that these powers cannot be spoken of, cannot be communicated to other minds through the public language of words, signs, symbols, or actions. Clearly he will, like Milton, attempt "Things unattempted yet in Prose or Rhyme" (*Paradise Lost* 1:16). He will penetrate the mazes of his inner world, whose contours lie hidden from the reach of words. He once pinpointed the difficulty of such a venture: "Archimedes said that he could move the world if he had a point whereon to rest his machine. Who has not felt the same aspirations as regards the world of his own mind?"[2] Where was the fixed point from which he could launch his voyage into this invisible world of his own mind? How could he find his bearings in its ever shifting topography and uncover its dynamic formative processes? To explore the complexities and paradoxes in which Wordsworth involves himself in *The Prelude* as he traces the "broken windings" (2:289) of his labyrinthine path is a task for which the critic as well as the poet needs the "chamois' sinews, and the eagle's wing" (2:290).

M. H. Abrams has made an important contribution to such an investigation by identifying the distinctive lexicon Wordsworth developed for speaking of transactions between mind and nature. It is the language that we most readily recognize as bearing Wordsworth's personal signature: "Natural objects enter, flow, are received, and sink down into the mind, while the mind dwells in, feeds on, drinks, holds intercourse with, and weaves, intertwines, fastens, and binds itself to external objects, until the two integrate as one." Abrams persuasively claims that these recurrent metaphors enabled Wordsworth to say "about the development of man's cognitive and emotional development with the milieu into which he is born, what had never been explicitly said before, and with a subtlety that has not been exceeded since" (*Natural Supernaturalism* 281). That is to say: this lexicon of primal, vital interaction, based on such elementary human functions as eating and drinking, effectively evokes a complex network of subject-object, mind-nature relationships. In short, Abrams illuminates that aspect of the interrelation of internal and external realms for which Wordsworth has solved the problem of language.

But there is another permutation of this mind-nature relationship for which Wordsworth had no such functional lexicon. This is the relationship of the poetic mind with nature as a language, both in the traditional sense of the Book of Nature—one of the two sacred books through which God reveals himself—and in the Wordsworthian sense of nature as language, nature as both the means to and end of discovering and disclosing the deep truth that is imageless. To read the traditional Book of Nature is to decipher and interpret the visible creation in order to approach the invisible spirit it embodies. But Wordsworth's reading of nature goes beyond such disclosing of the divine presence, although it includes it. His relation to the text of nature constitutes what Heidegger calls an experience *with* language: "In experiences *with* language, language itself utters itself."[3] But when and how does language speak itself, voice itself? Strangely enough, says Heidegger, when we cannot find words for something that seizes us, rushes in upon us. In such moments "we feel from afar the soul of language itself touching us fleetingly" (161). Paradoxically, in moments when words fail us, when we have become conscious of the limits of language, we come closer to the essence of language than when we readily use words to speak our thoughts. When language suffices, we use it to speak of events, to explain our actions, to state our wishes. But when we are thrown back on silence, we perceive the rhythms—one might say the syntax—of inner experience. "Silence," says Carlyle's Professor Teufelsdröckh, "is the element in which great things fashion themselves together; that at length they emerge, full-formed and majestic, into the daylight of life. . . . Speech is of Time, Silence is of Eternity" (*Sartor* 174). This timeless yet meaningful silence reveals the true power of language, which is concealed in the articulated, time-bound utterance. Only poets, according to Heidegger, can reveal this timeless existence in language; only they can find words for our experience *with* language that touches on the inmost fabric of our being (*Unterwegs* 159, 169). Such poetic language makes special demands on both poet and reader. In Jean-Paul Sartre's words, "the reader is conscious of disclosing in creating, of creating by disclosing." The literary work of art, he goes on to say, "though realized *through* language, is never given *in* language. On the contrary, it is by nature a silence and an opponent of the word" (44). Wordsworth seeks to make nature reveal this power of language that is concealed in the articulated form. He speaks of certain encounters with nature in terms of encounters with language. He reaches for experiences that lie "far hidden from the reach of words," silent moments in which he feels the breath of the language of nature, the breath of nature as language.

Early in the first book of the *Prelude* Wordsworth recalls such an experience in his boyhood, a moment of suspense as he was plundering a raven's nest:

> Oh! at that time,
> While on the perilous ridge I hung alone,
> With what strange utterance did the loud dry wind
> Blow through my ears! the sky seem'd not a sky
> Of earth, and with what motion mov'd the clouds!
> (1:346–50)

In this moment the speaker is overwhelmed by nature's address as he sees the earthly sky transformed into something unearthly and as he hears the wind's "strange utterance" in his ears. "As a man is So he Sees," Blake told Dr. Trusler in 1799 (677). And we can deduce what a man is or has become from what he sees.

The transformed earth that Wordsworth's persona sees as a boy points to the unutterable experience that transforms him as he responds to nature's strange utterance. Nature's mysterious language captivates the responsive listener and speaks to him "Rememberable things" (1:616). Wordsworth seeks through this boyhood incident to lead the reader into (in Coleridge's words) the "twilight realms of consciousness," " modes of inmost being" to which "the attributes of time and space are inapplicable and alien, but which yet can not be conveyed, save in symbols of time and space" (*BL* 2:147). Nature as language provides such symbols of time and space to articulate the otherwise inchoate realms of inmost being. The "universal language" that nature speaks is, as an early manuscript fragment of the *Prelude* makes clear, a holistic language that simultaneously impresses on the mind the visible forms of "beauteous objects" and moves the mind with the invisible "soul of things":

> How oft the eternal spirit, he that has
> His life in unimaginable things
> And he who painting what he is in all
> The visible imagery of all the worlds
> Is yet apparent chiefly as the soul
> Of our first sympathies. . . .
>   (MS JJ, *1799 Prelude*, p. 126)

Wordsworth traces back to the very "twilight of rememberable life" (*1799 Prelude* 1:298) nature's wordless, primal communion, received subliminally by the child.[4] He enters even more deeply into the "broken windings" (2:289) of his labyrinthine task by tracing inexpressible yet indelible impressions back to their source in the child's preverbal sensibility. Daringly Wordsworth enters the labyrinth of human consciousness, penetrating to "our dawn of being" (1:584) when our "mute dialogues" (2:283) with our mother's heart first become imprinted. He discovers in these mute dialogues between infant and mother a powerful model for the child's (and adult's) "unconscious intercourse" with nature (1:589). Just as the infant gathers from his mother's eye unspoken feelings that "pass into his torpid life / Like an awakening breeze" (2:244–45), so he is also quickened by nature's radiant presence. The infant-mother intercurrent flows over into and is contained in the infant-nature relationship. Therefore the infant leads a blessed life:

> Nurs'd in his Mother's arms, the Babe who sleeps
> Upon his Mother's breast, who, when his soul
> Claims manifest kindred with an earthly soul
> Doth gather passion from his Mother's eye!
> Such feelings pass into his torpid life
> Like an awakening breeze. . . .
>   (2:240–45)

It is worth noting that the "infant Babe," who literally is *infans* (one who does not speak), here communes silently with a kindred "earthly soul." In a manuscript fragment that also articulates the infant's "first born affinities," Wordsworth uses the same breeze image to praise the cosmic spirit that runs through nature and through the human soul:

> Oh bounteous power
> In childhood, in rememberable days
> How often did thy love renew for me
> Those naked feelings which when thou wouldst form
> A living thing thou sendest like a breeze
> Into its infant being.
>   (MS JJ, *1799 Prelude*, p. 126)

Thus Wordsworth uses the breeze as an integrative synecdoche for those first awakenings of the infant sensibility, effected by dynamic but silent interchange with a motion and a spirit that is his mother's and nature's, an emanation (in Coleridge's words) of "the one Life within us and abroad, / Which meets all motion and becomes its soul" (*Eolian Harp* 26—27), "one intellectual breeze, / At once the soul of each, and God of all" (49–50). Wordsworth was much closer to Coleridge's near-pantheism in his *1799 Prelude* than in his later versions. In one manuscript fragment he condemns the false distinctions made by our analytic reason—that "false secondary power"—through which we lapse from the "one interior life" "In which all beings live with god themselves / Are god existing in one mighty whole" (MS 33, p. 165). And the same "intellectual breeze" guarantees the renewal of those "naked feelings," those unrememberable experiences in later "rememberable days."

The silent language through which the infant carries on his "mute dialogue" organizes and interprets for him the detached fragments of his experience:

> his mind
> Even [in the first trial of its powers]
> Is prompt and watchful, eager to combine
> In one appearance, all the elements
> And parts of the same object, else detach'd
> And loth to coalesce.
>   (2:245–50)

Thus the infant's response is not only reflexive but also outwardly active; it fulfills instinctive needs even as it satisfies a need for synthetic shaping. His awakened powers focus not only on material things but also on appearances, forms, shapes, in the kind of surplus of aesthetic pleasure that Schiller sees as the means by which the human being transcends the confines of his animal nature (*AL* 27.1–2). Even at the threshold of consciousness, the child's mind

> Even as an agent of the one great mind,
> Creates, creator and receiver both,
> Working but in alliance with the works
> Which it beholds.—
>   (2:272–75)

When Wordsworth adds, "Such, verily, is the first / Poetic spirit of our human life" (2:275–76), he identifies the child's subliminal communings as a kind of poetic *Ursprache* (primal language). Wordsworth seeks to recapture this first poetic spirit of our life; he interrogates those twilight memories of nature's influx into his wordless thoughts. He inspires himself as he recollects himself as being inspired by the awakening breeze. He recollects knowledge gained as an infant from nature's mysterious voice, which he heard in the murmurs of "the fairest of all Rivers" that "sent a voice" which flowed along his dreams (1:273, 275–76). Listening to nature's language, he discovers in it a token that, even "Among the fretful dwellings of mankind," he will be assured of the calm which "nature breathes among the fields and groves" (1:283–85).

Even though nature's rhythmic cadences thus speak a language of pure inspiration, animating and quickening the burgeoning poetic spirit, only the receptive spirit can be thus inspired. Wordsworth makes the point explicitly in his second essay *Upon Epitaphs* when he speaks of the language that preserves the "primary sensations of the human heart, which are the vital springs of sublime and pathetic composition" yet cannot be heard except by those who listen with correspondent "primary sensations" (*Prose* 2:70). Because for Wordsworth these primary wordless sensations speak through the poet's words, only those who live such silent language and listen "promptly and submissively in the inner cell of the mind" (2:70) can hear the poet's utterance together with its wordless undercurrent. In a deceptively simple quatrain Goethe suggests the close reciprocity between passive and active sensation, speaking, however, of the eye rather than the ear:

> Wär nicht das Auge sonnenhaft,
> Die Sonne könnt es nie erblicken;
> Läg nicht in uns des Gottes eigne Kraft,
> Wie könnt uns Göttliches entzücken.[5]
> (*GA* 1:629)

In Wordsworthian terms, only those who have preserved the power of "godlike hours" in themselves and know "what majestic sway we have, / As natural beings in the strength of nature" (*Prelude* 3:192–94) can feel the "Visionary Power" that "Attends upon the motions of the winds / Embodied in the mystery of words" (5:619–21). For Wordsworth, as for Coleridge, nature is "that eternal language" which God utters "who from eternity doth teach / Himself in all, all things in himself" (*Frost at Midnight* 60–62). Or, as Coleridge says elsewhere, the "language of nature is a subordinate *Logos*, that was in the beginning, and was with the thing it represented, and it was the thing represented" (*Shakespearean Criticism* 1:185).

Wordsworth displays this "subordinate Logos" in and through the metaphor of the "awakening breeze" (2:245) that dominates the opening passage of the *Prelude*. It constitutes the originating word awakening the human spirit to "bliss ineffable" in the awareness that the "sentiment of Being" reaches over everything, even "beyond the reach of thought" (2:420–22). The breeze evolves quickly into one of those symbols of time and space to which the poet must resort in order to speak of the "twilight realms of consciousness" that Coleridge insisted transcend the categories of time and space (*BL* 2:147). Yet, not until 1805, in the process of completing his thirteen-book *Prelude*, did Wordsworth discover in the breeze the central symbol for his opening invocation. What he then wrote as an induction, as what he later called a "glad preamble" (7:4), turned, in fact, into a complex opening movement whose leitmotif is the synecdochic breeze.

I want to explore the hermeneutic and rhetorical implications of this opening passage, which elaborates the central analogy between nature's breeze and poetic inspiration into a fertile repertory of analogical relationships. Wordsworth here invests a familiar trope with fresh evocative power. The passage well exemplifies what Fritz Strich calls the magic conjuring power of language (*Sprachbeschwörung*). He suggests that it is typical of Romantic poetry that its language calls into being, whereas the language of classical poetry gives shape to being (172).

The opening movement of the *Prelude* falls into two parts: the preamble proper (1:1–54) and Wordsworth's re-view of the preamble (1:55–67). The preamble presents a spontaneous, hymnal apostrophe to the inspirational "gentle breeze" (1:1); the review glosses this spontaneous utterance, the poet turning exegete to his own text.

The poet opens with an enthusiastic tribute to the animating breeze. He first inobtrusively anthropomorphizes it as "half conscious" of its effect before he ushers in a fully personified breeze greeted as "welcome Messenger," "welcome Friend!" (1:5):

> Oh there is blessing in this gentle breeze
> That blows from the green fields and from the clouds
> And from the sky: it beats against my cheek,
> And seems half conscious of the joy it gives.
> (1:1–4)

This breeze is emphatically naturalistic and animistic: it blows from the fields and from the sky. It palpably beats against the speaker's cheek. Yet it is both a physically perceptible breath of fresh air and an invisibly animating spirit. Even when the speaker calls it the "sweet breath of Heaven" (1:41), he still insists on its tangible presence: he feels it blowing on his body before he recognizes its intangible, inspiring power. This eolian presence closely resembles those pagan genii whom Wordsworth frequently apostrophized in the *1799 Prelude* as "Beings of the hills," "Powers of earth," "Genii of the springs," whose ministry made "the surface of the universal earth / With meanings of delight, of hope and fear, / Work like a sea" (1:130, 186, 196–98).

The syntax of the vocative opening apostrophe ("Oh there is blessing in this gentle breeze") throws the central emphasis on the breeze's visitation; only in line 9 does the poet take the center of the stage. Even then he first speaks as a fictive persona (a "captive") before speaking in his own persona, the autobiographical "I" who is both the narrator and the subject of this narrative:

A captive greets thee, coming from a house
Of bondage, from yon City's walls set free,
A prison where he hath been long immured.
Now I am free, enfranchis'd and at large,
May fix my habitation where I will.
    (1:6–10)

Wordsworth builds up his repertoire of the creative breeze by playing it off against an apparent antithesis. The breeze that blows across the fields symbolizes freedom, while the speaker characterizes himself as a prisoner; the breeze emanates from nature, while the speaker abides in the city. But the poet resolves these apparent opposites into a *discordia concors* in this sacramental moment when the breeze's blessings are received by the newly enfranchised sojourner.

The biblical echoes of the release from captivity enlarge the range of Wordsworth's root metaphor of the vital breeze.[6] He makes the joy brought by the breeze resonate with echoes of Israel's release from Egypt's bondage and God's promise that he would bring the children of Israel into the land of their fathers, "a land flowing with milk and honey" (Exodus 13:5). It is worth remembering that Dante used the exodus from Egypt as an illustration of his "polysemous" meaning of the *Divine Comedy*. He comments in his letter to Grande della Scala: "if we look to the letter alone, the departure of the children of Israel from Egypt in the time of Moses is indicated to us; if to the allegory, our redemption accomplished by Christ is indicated to us; if to the moral sense, the conversion of the soul from the woe and misery of sin to a state of grace is indicated to us; if to the anagogical sense, the departure of the consecrated soul from the slavery of this corruption to the liberty of eternal glory is indicated" (Gilbert 202). Wordsworth secularizes and synopsizes such polysemous biblical parallels, collapsing the moral and anagogical levels into a single, this-worldly symbolism. Thus in the context of his preamble, the poet's departure from a house of bondage suggests the conversion of the soul from acedia and lethargy to renewed creativity. It suggests further, as in Dante's interpretation, the release of the consecrated soul from the enslavement by false ideals, by mind-forged manacles, though without leading (as in Dante's version) to the "liberty of eternal glory." Instead, Wordsworth arrests this spiritual conversion at the point of his spirit's reveling in liberty as such, not liberty for a transcendent goal. He knows that he must now choose his way but delays committing himself to a specific choice. He contemplates first the choice of a home, an authentic dwelling to harbor his newborn creativity. Unlike Milton's Adam, he finds that the world is all before him not after being expelled from paradise, but after his release from bondage propels him into a paradisal plenitude:

> What dwelling shall receive me? In what Vale
> Shall be my harbour? Underneath what grove
> Shall I take up my home, and what sweet stream
> Shall with its murmurs lull me to my rest?
> The earth is all before me. . . .
>   (1:11–15)

Biblical and Miltonic associations reverberate in the "miraculous gift" by which Wordsworth's autobiographic persona feels released from the physical confines of the city walls and from the inner yoke of his "own unnatural self" (1:24). "I breathe again" (19), he exclaims at this moment of springlike revival of the spirit after a wintry season of desolation, the revival bringing with it the hope of future joy to be savored in a promised land, a restored Eden. Even without providential guidance, his feeling of total harmony within himself as well as between himself and the natural world inspires joyful confidence. Nature is providential. Its spirit is identical with the prophetic spirit Wordsworth evokes in the concluding passage of *Home at Grasmere* (later revised as the Prospectus to *The Recluse*)—"Thou who art breath and being, way and guide" (*Home* 1043). Thus renewed and inspired, he celebrates this moment when

with a heart
Joyous, nor scar'd at its own liberty,
I look about, and should the guide I chuse
Be nothing better than a wandering cloud,
I cannot miss my way.
    (*Prelude* 1:15–19)

The speaker delights in a present moment of drifting, of hover-
ing between past and future, of feeling totally uncommitted. He
has freed himself not only from some false personal commit-
ments but also, temporarily, from all social and political order
and structure. He relishes the life of a happy nomad—a nomad
of the mind as well as of the world—who allows his imagination
free play with unlimited possibilities rather than focusing it on
drawing a blueprint for his future life. Neither moral nor aes-
thetic principles are his guide but the drifting clouds or even "a
twig or any floating thing upon the river" (1:21–22). He finds
himself in transit, as he says of another holiday experience,
from the "smooth delights" of simple youth to something that
resembles an "approach / Towards mortal business" (3:550–53).
With subtle self-knowledge, Wordsworth reveals that such "mid-
way residence" in a "privileg'd world / Within a world" (3:553–
54) suited the gradual maturing of his visionary mind far better
than being suddenly "bolted forth, / Thrust out abruptly into
Fortune's way / Among the conflicts of substantial life" (3:557–
59).

Wordsworth's "midway residence" interestingly resembles the
middle phase of typical rites of passage. As Van Gennep has
shown, in all "ritualized movement there was at least a moment
when those being moved in accordance with a cultural script
were liberated from normative demands, when they were in-
deed, betwixt and between successive lodgments in jural politi-
cal systems. In this gap between ordered worlds almost any-
thing may happen."[7] In such a gap between ordered worlds,
such a free-floating interval, Wordsworth's lyric speaker feels
the intense revival of poetic inspiration. Once more opposites

meet in this extraordinary spot of time. Upon his holiday mood
of ease and relaxation intrude "sudden mountings of the mind"
(1:20) that spontaneously overcome him. Literally inspired
(breathed into by the "creative breeze"), he feels possessed by
"trances of thought" (1:20) and becomes aware of an upsurge of
creativity. After doubling back to the experience of freedom's
rich promises, he arrives at the fullest expression of his inspired
state, the fullest formulation of the metaphor of the reticular
breeze:

> For I, methought, while the sweet breath of Heaven
> Was blowing on my body, felt within
> A corresponding mild creative breeze,
> A vital breeze which travell'd gently on
> O'er things which it had made, and is become
> A tempest, a redundant energy
> Vexing its own creation.
>   (1:41–47)

In the analogy of "sudden mountings of the mind" and na-
ture's "gentle breeze" engendering a tempest, this passage in-
corporates the earliest surviving draft of the preamble, which
may indeed be the earliest fragment of the entire *Prelude*:[8]

> a mild creative breeze
> a vital breeze that passes gently on
> Oer things which it has made and soon becomes
> A tempest a redundant energy
> Creating not but as it may
> disturbing things created.—
>   (MS JJ, *1799 Prelude*, p. 123)

In the manuscript Wordsworth hesitates between the terms "in-
spiration" and a "vital breeze," as if he were unsure about the
emphasis on the naturalistic image. But in both the manuscript
and the 1805 version, Wordsworth completes the equation be-

tween the breeze that blows from the fields and the speaker's heightened creativity. To inspire, as M. H. Abrams has reminded us in his article "The Correspondent Breeze," once meant " 'to blow or breathe into,' and when a man received the divine 'afflatus' he received, literally, the breath or wind of a god or muse" (45). The physical and spiritual meanings were undivided in the Latin *spiritus* and *anima*, as well as in the Greek *pneuma* and the Hebrew *ruach*—all of which signified wind, breath, and soul (44–45). In his creative breeze, Wordsworth no doubt also remembered that Milton conflated the heavenly Urania and the spirit that brooded over the face of the waters. And he may further have remembered that in the Old Testament world this mysterious breath, which was present at the creation, stormed into the world and inspired the prophets.

Wordsworth condenses Judeo-Christian associations in his root metaphor of the vital breeze that generates a tempest; moreover, that tempest, which is both palpable and impalpable, emerges as a synecdoche for the power that inspirits nature and naturalizes spirit, a "redundant energy," a "rushing power" that sweeps across the external world and bursts into the speaker's soul.[9] Only such disturbing, disordering, disrupting energy, only such a pentecostal storm, can release the poet from the "long-continued frost" (1:49) of his wintry bondage and revive in him the "holy life of music and verse" (1:54). In the manuscript draft the poet is quick to harness this tempestuous energy, lest it overwhelm him. He seems to rejoice in and yet to fear the creative power that must, in Coleridge's view, dissolve, diffuse, dissipate, in order to re-create. The draft moves quickly to the reassuring comment that the tempest, in "disturbing things created," brings nothing more horrifying than "lights and shades," "loveliness and power" (MS JJ, *1799 Prelude*, p. 123). In other words, this storm is the kind of nonrevolutionary, beneficent storm that the speaker longs for in Coleridge's *Dejection* when he prays that the swelling gusts of wind,

> Those sounds which oft have raised me, whilst they awed
> And sent my soul abroad,

> Might now perhaps their wonted impulse give,
> Might startle this dull pain, and make it move and live!
> (17–20)

Wordsworth's speaker has undergone a similar ordeal of spiritual dessication from which the pentecostal breeze has released him as it stirred his "quickening virtue" (*Prelude* 1850, 1:36) and sent his soul abroad.

The narrative focus throughout Wordsworth's hymnal preamble is clearly on the teller and the telling, rather than on the listener or reader. As we discover later, the speaker has been singing his "prelusive songs" among "the silence of the woods and hills"—to borrow phrases from *Home at Grasmere* (273–75). Although he becomes increasingly introspective, disregarding society, he never shuts out the external world of fields and valleys or the physical sensation of the invigorating breeze. He focuses on a prolonged present ("this hour"), a present alive with forward-looking "vernal promises" of future activity—the hope

> Of active days, of dignity and thought,
> Of prowess in an honorable field,
> Pure passions, virtue, knowledge, and delight,
> The holy life of music and of verse.
> (1:50–54)

Even though he makes no vows, the speaker seems at the end of this hour to come close to relinquishing his personal freedom, his "uncontroul'd enfranchisement" (1:34, MS M, *apparatus criticus*, p. 4), ready to exchange drifting with the wind for steering a deliberate course. Possibly that is the gist of the "prophecy" he told to the open fields.

Wordsworth begs the question when suddenly, as with a magic wand, without transition or explanation, his narrative shifts from celebrating a "present joy" to re-viewing the same experience from a distance; it shifts from present to past tense, from direct to indirect discourse, from lyric immediacy to rhe-

torical meditation. The poet's role changes also, from that of a
participant finding words for a revelatory experience in which
he is intensely immersed to that of a spectator *ab extra* interpret-
ing a past event. Wordsworth speaks as commentator on his own
text:

> Thus far, O Friend! did I, not used to make
> A present joy the matter of my Song,
> Pour out, that day, my soul in measur'd strains
> Even in the very words which I have here
> Recorded: to the open fields I told
> A prophecy. . . .
>   (1:55–60)

Why did Wordsworth "record" the "very words" that he had
spontaneously spoken to the open fields? And why, having
recorded them as a "present joy," is he now reviewing them as
past utterance? If nature was a fit audience for the spoken
"prophecy," for whom was the written record intended? For
those future disciples to whom he addressed the narrative of
Michael, who in his native hills will carry on his poetic mission
as his "second self" when he is gone? (*Michael* 38–39) Or are we
to understand the transposition from oral to written prophecy
in the light of Old Testament prophets such as Isaiah or Jere-
miah, who transmitted God's word orally but also reduced it to
writing? Jaweh explicitly instructs Isaiah: "Now go, write it be-
fore them in a table, and note it in a book, that it may be for the
time to come for ever and ever" (Isaiah 30:8). (Notably, on this
occasion the prophet is not asked to go out and speak to his
people but to go into his house and write "for the time to
come.") Unfortunately, Wordsworth is less explicit about his
intention and enlightens his audience only obliquely. Indeed,
in his persona of narrator-commentator he demands extreme
nimbleness as he puts his reader through some mental acrobat-
ics. First he asks his reader to imagine an unwritten scenario in
which the poet, alone in the fields, spontaneously burst into
poetic prophecy, voicing his sense of joyful liberation and inspi-

ration. This is the oral *Urtext* that the poet later reduced to writing and still later deployed as preamble to the *Prelude*.

The *Prelude*'s opening passage of fifty-four lines, together with the exegesis of this passage that immediately follows, generates almost as many unexpected permutations of meaning as the perplexing dream of the Arab in Book 5. Recently critics have interpreted the dream of the "Semi-Quixote" who carries a stone and a shell as a series of metaphoric displacements, revealing Wordsworth to be in effect a true Derridian without knowing it. According to Hillis Miller, "the dream may be described as a complex system of displacements, displacement within displacements, displacements added in chain fashion to previous displacements, displacements interwoven with other displacements" ("Stone and Shell" 134–35).[10] Miller argues further that this process of displacement is "not only the form but also the theme of the dream of the Arab, which is to say that its theme is the book, defining a book as the replacement of a reality which always remains at a distance from its printed image. To put this another way, the theme of the dream is language or the sign-making power. The essence of this power is in this text affirmed to be that naming of one thing by the name of another which puts in question the possibility of literal naming and suggests that all names are metaphors, moved aside from any direct correspondence to the thing named by their reference to other names which precede and follow them in an endless chain" (139–40).

Miller's involuted interpretation of the dream of the Arab is suggestive for interpreting the opening passage of the *Prelude*. Wordsworth's commentary on the opening invocation of the "gentle breeze" displaces the spontaneous overflow of powerful feelings by retrospective, thoughtful meditation. His gloss displaces the theme of poetic inspiration by that of poetic hermeneutics. Disrupting the linear progression of the poem before the narrative proper even gets under way, the gloss demonstrates that only by such disruptive displacements of thematic structures can the poet make us attend to the "general truths," the "Under-Powers" (1:163) that both generate the narrative and are generated by it. The poet must disrupt the sequential flow of his autobiographical thoughts to uncover, by circling back, the truths behind the words he has written, the imageless truths in his "underconsciousness" (13:71, MS variant, *apparatus criticus*, p. 484). His words both conceal and reveal. Heidegger's philosophy elaborates on this paradox: "It is art which enacts the dialectical reciprocity of cloture and radiance. The essence of 'thereness' and of meaning which a great painting or sculpture reveals, exhibits, makes sensible, is, obviously, 'within it.' It is embodied in the substance of the thing. We cannot externalize it, we cannot extract it from the work's specific mass and configuration. In this sense, it is a hiddenness. But such embodiment is, at the very same instant, a making manifest, a deployment, an articulate and radiant projection" (Steiner, *Heidegger*, 128).[11]

Wordsworth's remarkable poetic commentary on his opening invocation of the *Prelude* discloses, makes manifest, some of the creative undercurrents at work in his hymnal celebration of the liberating breeze.[12] Whereas the invocation is presented as artless expression of a revelatory experience, the commentary artfully elaborates and restructures the original words. The preamble creates the illusion of spontaneous song; the postscript, the sense of "slow creation" by "considerate and laborious work."[13] The lyric "I" pouring forth a song to nature has given way to the exegetical "I" recollecting and unfolding the spoken and unspoken implications of the *Urtext*. The latter persona literally translates the original song into a different language, reformulating the original experience:

> poetic numbers came
> Spontaneously, and cloth'd in priestly robe
> My spirit, thus singled out, as it might seem,
> For holy services: great hopes were mine;
> My own voice chear'd me, and, far more, the mind's
> Internal echo of the imperfect sound;

To both I listen'd, drawing from them both
A chearful confidence in things to come.
     (1:60–67)

   Wordsworth's reflection on his words, attending to his mind's "internal echo," produces a tautological poetics, a poetics of self-reference, of "the mind reflecting on its own operation by means of its own operation" (Colie, "Rhetoric," 147). The tautology of a speaker commenting on his own poetry by means of poetry, reviewing how he heard what he said, creates its own difficulties. As in mirror images, "self-reference begins an endless oscillation between the thing itself and the thing reflected, begins an infinite regress" (Colie, *Paradoxia Epidemica*, 355). Even though poetry cannot fully express these oscillating mirror images, self-referential poetry can generate intriguing results. Wordsworth's poet speaking of the "internal echo" of words composed by him invites the reader to enter the creative and re-creative process much as Vermeer does in his *Artist in His Studio* (also known as *The Painter and His Model*).[14] Vermeer painted a painter seated at his easel painting a young model crowned with laurel leaves, looking down at a trumpet she holds in one hand and a great book she holds in the other—emblems of fame and history. The painting teases the spectator into entering the scene, playing the role of the implied, unseen figure who has lifted the heavy embroidered curtain to disclose the room in which the painting is in process. Vermeer draws the spectator into the artist's dialogue with himself about his wager on immortality. But in whose dialogue are we participating? That of the depicted painter—Vermeer's double—who is filling in details of the laurel crown on his canvas? Or that of Vermeer, who has presented us with a finished but ambiguous allegory of fame? Is Vermeer asserting that the artist's painting will outlive himself and bring him fame, or is he glancing ironically at artists who entertain such illusions?
   Just as Vermeer draws the spectator into the mental debate that is evoked by self-referential painting, Wordsworth draws the reader into the mental process of the poet's attending to

reverberations of his own words. He makes the reader attend to these words as what Valéry, in "Poetry and Abstract Thought," calls a "language within a language" in order to distinguish the poetic use of language from ordinary discourse. In the ordinary discourse, Valéry argues, the words with which, for example, I ask for a light are abolished when the person I asked gives me a light. The words vanish when they have done their job; they are negated when they are understood. But when the words that have been understood continue to echo in the listener's mind, continue to exist and to create the need to be heard again, then "we are on the threshold of the poetic state" (*Collected Works* 7:64).

When Wordsworth's autobiographical speaker comments on his own echoing words, he attends to words that do not vanish when their meaning is understood. Their echo generates new ramifications of the core meanings. The speaker's self-referential commentary echoes some of the preamble's characteristic lexicon of inspiration (joy, great hopes, holy life) in order to bring two submerged themes into sharp focus. First, he highlights the religious language about a prophet chosen for a holy task; second, he focuses sharply on the inspiring word, condensing the broad cluster of allusions in the synecdoche of the creative breeze. From two lines in the preamble—"this hour / Hath brought a gift that *consecrates* my joy," the promise of the "*holy* life of music and of verse" (1:39–40, 54; my italics)—the poet-commentator distills the sense of religious vocation. He translates his original concern with *choosing* where to settle, what direction to give his future life, into his *having been chosen*, his being a spirit "singled out" for "holy services" (1:62–63).

Wordsworth's revision of his *Urtext* brings out an interesting analogy between his sense of being singled out and a prophet called to office. "The prophetic call," according to the distinguished theologian Gerhard von Rad, "in fact gave rise to a new literary category, the account of a call" (2:54). Such an account was typically in the first person and phrased not in cultic formulas but in intensely personal language. The speakers in these accounts "were men who had been expressly called upon to abandon the fixed orders of religion which the majority of the people still considered valid—a tremendous step for a man of the ancient east to take—and because of it the prophets, in their new and completely unprecedented situation, were faced with the need to justify themselves both in their own and in other people's eyes" (2:54–55). The parallel with Wordsworth's persona immediately springs to mind. He, too, felt called upon to abandon literature's fixed canons, which the majority of the public still considered valid. Every author, Wordsworth said, "as far as he is great and at the same time *original*, has had the task of *creating* the taste by which he is to be enjoyed" (*Prose* 3:80).[15] And it is not surprising that this task brings with it the doubts and uncertainties that the poet dramatizes in the *Prelude* as he seeks to justify his novel poetics, both in his own and in his readers' eyes.

Suggestive for Wordsworth's comments on his own epic invocation is von Rad's further observation that the prophet's account of his call involved a distinction between the event of receiving the call and its reduction to written form: "The event of which the prophet tells burdened him with a commission, with knowledge and responsibility which placed him in complete isolation before God. It forced him to justify his exceptional status in the eyes of the majority. This makes clear that the writing down an account of a call was something secondary to the call itself, and that it served a different end than did the latter. The call commissioned the prophet: the act of writing down an account of it was aimed at those sections of the public in whose eyes he had to justify himself" (2:55). This analysis of Old Testament accounts of a prophet's call suggests a possible explanation of Wordsworth's rhetorical intention in his exegetical postscript to the preamble of The Prelude. He may have sought to authenticate his experience of receiving the call in order to justify himself in his own eyes as an exceptional being, and to call upon his patron-friend-addressee (and on later readers as well) to bear witness to his being a true prophet of nature. Like Israel's prophets, he felt his vocation at times as an awful burden from which he was tempted to take refuge (1:235–36).

Moreover, Wordsworth, like the prophets, felt isolated in his vocation and felt the burden of forging a language that could authenticate and communicate his private convictions. In fact Wordsworth faced the problem that Paul Ricoeur has characterized as central in modern religious experience: "How can one communicate to another and to oneself the meaning of the kerygma in such a way as to develop something approaching a comprehensible discourse?" (*Philosophy* 223).

The series of questions with which Wordsworth plunges into a radical self-examination at the beginning of the *1799 Prelude* suggests just such a struggle to account for and communicate to others the poet's sense of himself as a "favored being" (1:70) who yet feels uncertain over the means by which he will redeem nature's "dim earnest" (1:14). The two-part *1799 Prelude* opens abruptly:

> Was it for this
> That one, the fairest of all rivers, loved
> To blend his murmurs with my Nurse's song,
> And from his alder shades, and rocky falls,
> And from his fords and shallows, sent a voice
> That flowed along my dreams?
> (1:1–6)

Our only clue for the antecedent of the demonstrative pronoun "this" in the opening line—and for the repetitions of the "Was it for this" formula throughout the passage—is the draft fragment of the preamble apostrophizing the creative breeze and the corresponding "mountings of the mind," which, as Stephen Parrish has recently suggested in his introduction to the *1799 Prelude*, would equate "this" with the "powerful disturbance of mind occasioned by a superabundant flow of inspiration" and would establish the tone of the passage not as "ironic or regretful, but wondering, perhaps confused even perhaps quietly exultant" (6).

Wordsworth's enigmatic questions in the opening passage probe, on the one hand, his earliest memory of nature's language subliminally influencing—literally "flowing into"—his thoughts and dreams. The questions also address, on the other hand, the poet's adult consciousness of having not yet fulfilled his calling as well as his awareness of the desultory nature of inspiration. "For this," he asks of the Derwent River that flowed past his "sweet birthplace,"

> didst thou beauteous Stream
> Make ceaseless music through the night and day,
> Which with its steady cadence tempering
> Our human waywardness, composed my thoughts
> To more than infant softness, giving me,
> Among the fretful dwellings of mankind,
> A knowledge, a dim earnest of the calm
> Which Nature breathes among the fields and groves?
>   (*1799 Prelude* 1:8–15)

Thus the poet sees in his threshold experience of nature's wordless cadences the roots of an organic bond, the promise of the calm "which Nature breathes among the fields and groves," a "dim earnest" which years later he comes to match with a correlative, spontaneous pledge:

> I made no vows, but vows
> Were then made for me; bond unknown to me
> Was given, that I should be, else sinning greatly,
> A dedicated Spirit.
>   (4:341–44)

To authenticate for himself and for others the primal sources of such unknown, unexpressed bonds is central to the speaker's self-exploration, the self-interrogation, of the opening passage of the *1799 Prelude*:

> The mind of man is fashioned and built up
> Even as a strain of music: I believe

That there are spirits, which, when they would form
A favored being, from his very dawn
Of infancy do open out the clouds
As at the touch of lightning, seeking him
With gentle visitation. . . .
   (1:67–73)

Thus in 1798–99 Wordsworth embodies in the spirits of nature
—the "Beings of the hills" (1:130) and "Genii of the springs"
(1:186)—a mysterious solicitation, a call, a kerygma, addressed
to him, shaping him as inobtrusively as harmonic notes forming
a "strain of music." The kerygma flares up at the threshold of
consciousness, the threshold of being, as he is sought out by
"gentle visitation," which in the 1805 *Prelude* he transforms into
the seminal image of "eolian visitations" (1:104)—an image that
he evolves, as we have seen, into a dynamic repertory of inspira-
tion. But only in his exegetical probing, articulating, and trans-
forming do the echoing reverberations of the external and
internal, objective and subjective "creative breeze" (1:43) fully
emerge.

   In seeking to account for the inspiriting visitations, the exe-
getical speaker shifts the emphasis from the inspiring breeze to
the inspiring word—literally the breath of his own voice. In the
extemporaneous salutation to the breeze, the hymnal poet did
not speak self-consciously about his craft. Only as he reflects on
his own utterance does he speak of having poured out his soul
in "measur'd strains," (1:57) in spontaneously created "poetic
numbers" (1:60). Apparently he notices only retrospectively
that he has been speaking to the fields in blank verse! But that
is not all he notices retrospectively. His comments on his earlier
utterance notably conflate sacred and profane texts, as indeed
exegetes have done since the days of Dante and Boccaccio. But
his conception of the logos is unprecedented. Picking up the
thread of the two corresponding breezes, he reconstructs the
earlier interplay of external and internal, physical and spiritual
inspiration. In his revision, not the "sweet breath of Heaven"

but his own utterance breathed into his own mind inspires him. Not God's voice coming out of the whirlwind but his own natural-supernatural breath, his own logos, animates and elects him:

> poetic numbers came
> Spontaneously, and cloth'd in priestly robe
> My spirit, thus singled out, as it might seem,
> For holy services. . . .
>   (1:60–63)

Notably, the poet's own words invest him with "priestly robe," the visible sign of his call to the prophetic office. He invents a sacrament, administers it, and receives it! But the self-circling energies of the root metaphor of the breeze-logos are not yet exhausted. The poet-commentator's kerygmatic exegesis entails a dialectic of reflection that resembles the hermeneutic circle of faith described by Ricoeur: "to believe is to listen to the call, but to hear the call we must interpret the message. Thus we must believe in order to understand and understand in order to believe" (*Freud* 525). Wordsworth must believe that he was singled out from the very dawn of his infancy in order to understand his poetic mission, and he must understand the promise of his call in order to believe in the "holy life of music and of verse" (1:54). He attends to his own words in order to gain kerygmatic certainty:

> great hopes were mine;
> My own voice chear'd me, and, far more, the mind's
> Internal echo of the imperfect sound;
> To both I listen'd, drawing from them both
> A chearful confidence in things to come.
>   (1:63–67)

This egocentric confidence in things to come, which echoes the hopeful "vernal promises" (1:50) of the oral *Urtext*, is grounded in a hypostatized "I" who listens to the recollected spoken words and their "internal echo" at the same time. As the speaker tries to mediate between these internal echoes, this internal language, and the reader's understanding, he exposes layers of consciousness within consciousness like the receding images in Blake's crystal cabinet. His poetic exegesis becomes what Coleridge called an "orphic song" in his poem written on the occasion of hearing Wordsworth recite parts of *The Prelude*:

> An Orphic song indeed,
> A song divine of high and passionate thoughts
> To their own music chaunted!

To describe these prophetic revelations, Coleridge has recourse to Wordsworthian language:

> Of a Human Spirit thou has dared to tell
> What may be told, to the understanding mind
> Revealable; and what within the mind
> By vital breathings secret as the soul
> Of vernal growth, oft quickens in the heart
> Thoughts all too deep for words!—

And Coleridge recognizes Wordsworth's revelation of "moments awful"

> Now in thy inner life, and now abroad
> When power streamed from thee, and thy soul received
> The light reflected, as a light bestowed. . . .
> (*To William Wordsworth* 45–47, 6–11, 17–19)

Clearly, Wordsworth succeeded in communicating the primal, orphic power that he read in nature's oracular text; he felt

> whate'er there is of power in sound
> To breathe an elevated mood, by form
> Or image profaned; and I would stand,
> Beneath some rock, listening to sounds that are
> The ghostly language of the ancient earth,

Or make their dim abode in distant winds.
Thence did I drink the visionary power.
(*Prelude* 2:324–30)

Coleridge was the first critic to recognize this distinctive Wordsworthian reading of nature: "The superscription and the image of the Creator still remain legible to him" (*BL* 2:150), just as the "ghostly language of the ancient earth" still remained audible. And Coleridge knew that the source from which Wordsworth drew this orphic power was self-reflection, as an interesting notebook entry of 1804 reveals: "Mem. To write to the Recluse that he may insert something concerning *Ego* / its metaphysical Sublimity—& intimate Synthesis with the principle of Co-adunation—without *it* every where all things were a waste-nothing" (*CN* 2:2057f24).[16] In Coleridge's view such egotistical sublimity was not self-serving but was the source of all knowledge: "That, which we find in ourselves, is (gradu mutato) the substance and the life of *all* our knowledge. Without this latent presence of the 'I am,' all modes of existence in the external world would flit before us as colored shadows" (*Lay Sermons* 78).

By way of the *Prelude*'s hymnal preamble and kerygmatic exegesis, Wordsworth invents a hermeneutics of inspiration that begins with the Book of Nature and ends with the "latent presence of the 'I am'" in the mind's self-reflection. This hermeneutics informs Wordsworth's root metaphor of the creative breeze with such powerful meanings that it approaches the kind of sensuous language of nature, which, according to Boehme's *De Mysterio Magno*, is man's only way of recovering the holistic universal language man lost with the destruction of the tower of Babel. Adam understood the language of nature, according to Boehme, as the manifest, informed word. He knew each creature's essence and gave each its essential name (5:104). In Adam's language, the word perfectly expresses the essence, the soul, of the thing named, for, as Vico explained, God granted him "divine onomathesia, the giving of names according to the nature of each" (86). Just as Adam knows the invisible spirit concealed in the visible creation, so his words both reveal and conceal the invisible being. Thus Boehme says all that is visible and comprehensible derives from the invisible and incomprehensible: "The expression or exhalation of the invisible power becomes the visible creature; the divine power's invisible, spiritual word is coefficient in and through the visible being as the soul is in and through the body" (5:1)[17]

What was the grammar and vocabulary of this mysterious holistic language? In the late eighteenth century, mythologists and philosophers, theologians and poets found this a favorite topic of speculation. Some sought clues in Hebrew, Phoenician, or Amonian for the recovery of the Adamic universal language. Others linked this *Ursprache* to the metaphoric language of poetry, whatever its national character. Thus Herder asked: "What was *this first language other than an anthology of the elements of poetry?* Imitation of sonorous, active, living Nature!" Herder called this *Natursprache* a "dictionary of the soul, [*ein Wörterbuch der Seele*] which is at once a mythology and a marvelous epic of the actions and utterances of all beings! . . . What else is poetry?" (35–36) Herder's "dictionary of the soul" bears more than a hint of the occult tradition that transmitted the belief in a primal universal language which enabled man to communicate with God and man alike with perfect understanding. This prelapsarian metaphoric language, as George Steiner states, "bodied forth, to a greater or lesser degree, the original Logos, the act of immediate calling into being whereby God had literally 'spoken the word.'" And Steiner goes on to say that the "vulgate of Eden contained, though perhaps in a muted key, a divine syntax—powers of statement and designation analogous to God's own diction, in which the mere naming of a thing was the necessary and sufficient cause of its leap into reality" (*After Babel* 58). Thus each time man spoke, he reenacted this divine syntax, since in the Garden of Eden the word of man was significantly "given precedence over the world of objects. It was only when man gave the animals their names that they existed for him and were available for his use" (von Rad 2:81).

Wordsworth's rhetoric and hermeneutics of inspiration reenact such creative naming in man's internal Eden, where nature's inspiration calls into being the poetic word that generates revealed and concealed reverberations. Wordsworth's root metaphor of the correspondent breeze, like the Edenic *Ursprache*, resists all distinction between spiritual and physical, internal and external, feeling and thought, word and object. His language aspires to the presentational language of nature that Coleridge called the "subordinate Logos, that was in the beginning, and was with the thing it represented" (*Shakespearean Criticism* 1:185). This is the divine syntax which, according to the Church Fathers, was revealed in God's Book of Nature and in Holy Scripture. As Thomas Aquinas expresses the point in his *Summa Theologia*, the "author of Holy Scripture is God, in Whose power it is to signify His meaning, not by words only (as man also can do), but also by things in themselves. So, whereas in every other science things are signified by words, this science has the property that the things signified by words have themselves signification" (1:16). Thus the divine word is charged with symbolic meaning within symbolic meaning. There are no letters, no objects, devoid of meaning. The divine hieroglyphics were readily decipherable in Eden.

Many Romantics subscribed to the view that in the postlapsarian world only the poet comes close to such Edenic expressivity. According to Schiller, the poet-genius remains a custodian of such ideal coordination of meaning and form, thought and expression, for the true genius must be naive (*NA* 20:424). The naive poet's ideas, he says, are the inspiration of a god; his words are divine oracles out of the mouths of babes—"Göttersprüche aus dem Mund eines Kindes" (20:426). Schiller argues that the genius's naive mode of thought necessarily begets a naive mode of expression. He contrasts the genius's inspired words with the language of school learning and logic chopping that "crucifies words and concepts upon the cross of grammar and logic" in order to avoid ambiguity. Whereas in such scholastic language "the sign will always be heterogeneous and alien to the signified," in the genius's poetic language "the sign disappears totally within the signified. It is so indissolubly one with the thought from which it springs that the language leaves the expressed thought naked, leaves the spirit unveiled, disclosed under its corporeal husk" (20:426).[18]

Wordsworth's ideal of language is close to Schiller's—an immaculate conception begetting an incarnation of thought: "If words be not . . . an incarnation of the thought but only a clothing for it, then surely will they prove an ill gift" (*Prose* 2:84). Wordsworth's own language in the "glad preamble" to the *Prelude* recaptures the synecdochic resources of Edenic language that eighteenth-century metonymic poetry had abandoned, as he complained in his second essay *Upon Epitaphs*: "Energy, stillness, grandeur, tenderness, those feelings which are the pure emanations of nature, those thoughts which have the infinitude of truth, and those expressions which are not what the garb is to the body but what the body is to the soul, themselves a constituent part and power or function in the thought—all these are abandoned for their opposites" (*Prose* 2:84).

Wordsworth's root metaphor of the correspondent breeze brilliantly solves the problem of how to restore to poetic language the expressive power of nature's pure emanations, to make it disclose the invisible interior world of the human spirit, to make the body the visible sign of the invisible soul. But because his readers were all too habituated to seeing language as "the dress of thought" (Pope 2:118), Wordsworth added to his preamble a poetic exegesis, an exegetical poetics, to show his readers the way, illuminating the spiritual energy that joins mind and nature, disclosing nature's kerygmatic solicitation and visitation as well as the poet's inspired and inspiring response to his call. Only by forging an Arcadian rhetoric and hermeneutics could he speak to his lapsed readers of the incommunicable powers that lie "far hidden from the reach of words." His invocation to the correspondent breeze enlarges their—and our—conceptual boundaries. It is the kind of poetics, the kind of venture of which T. S. Eliot speaks:

Trying to learn to use words, and every attempt
Is a wholly new start, and a different kind of failure
Because one has only learnt to get the better of words
For the thing one no longer has to say, or the way in
    which
One is no longer disposed to say it. And so each venture
Is a new beginning, a raid on the inarticulate. . . .
    (*East Coker* 5:3–8)

Wordsworth's rhetoric of inspiration is truly "a new beginning, a raid on the inarticulate."

5

WORDSWORTH'S PASTORAL COVENANT

"There have been greater poets than Wordsworth," A. C. Bradley noted at the beginning of this century, "but none more original. He saw new things, or he saw things in a new way" (100). Among the things Wordsworth saw in a new way was the authentic experience of both human solitude and human community. Although Bradley is right in saying that "no poet is more emphatically the poet of community" (143), Wordsworth's *Home at Grasmere* does not succeed, as I have argued in a previous chapter, in realizing the poet's "sublime retirement" (*Home* 723) as being also the "true community, the noblest Frame / Of many into one incorporate" (819–20). From the perspective of the economic and social dilemmas of our own time, Raymond Williams is able to throw fresh light on Wordsworth's difficult choices: "Wordsworth saw that when we become uncertain in a world of apparent strangers who yet, decisively, have a common effect on us, and when forces that will alter our lives are moving all around us in apparently external and unrecognisable forms, we can retreat, for security, into a deep subjectivity, or we can look around us for social pictures, social signs, social messages, to which, characteristically, we try to relate as individuals but so as to discover, in some form, community" (*Country and City* 295). We might say that *Home* shows us the poet's response to dislocating forces as a retreat into deep subjectivity, whereas *Michael* shows his search for social signs that affirm his relation to true community; it presents an "almost visionary mountain republic" (*Prose* 2:207) that is accessible to all who hold fast to the pastoral ethos.

Michael answers the question posed in *Home*:

> Is there not
> An art, a music, and a stream of words
> That shall be life, the acknowledged voice of life?
> Shall speak of what is done among the fields,
> Done truly there, or felt, of solid good
> And real evil, yet be sweet withal,
> More grateful, more harmonious than the breath,
> The idle breath of sweetest pipe attuned
> To pastoral fancies?
> (*Home* 620–28)

With *Michael* Wordsworth attempts just such an art, speaking with the voice of life to tell of the real sweetness and real terror of a Westmorland shepherd's lot. The poem surpasses traditional pastoral by bypassing "Arcadian dreams, / All golden fancies of the golden age" (*Home* 829–30). Whereas in *The Prelude* he draws on pastoral tradition from Theocritus to Milton, in *Michael* Wordsworth rigorously excludes classical allusions and most traditional motifs, such as singing contests and love debates between shepherds. Probably he shared Southey's opinion that English neoclassic pastoral was remarkable chiefly for the "servile dulness of imitated nonsense." Sillier than their sheep, Southey suggested in the preface to his *English Eclogues*, pastoral writers have, "like their sheep, gone on in the same track one after another" (411). When Wordsworth subtitled *Michael* "A Pastoral Poem," he wished not to associate it with but to dissociate it from this sheepish tradition. With extraordinary restraint for someone steeped in the classics, he even steered clear of all traditional names—"from Tityrus and Corydon down to our English Strephons and Thirsisses," to quote Southey once more (*Poems* 411)—doubtless because he feared they would "unrealize" his narrative.[1]

In place of classical tradition, Wordsworth invokes the authority of local dalesmen who have handed down stories such as Michael's from one generation to the next. In fact, local oral tradition is Wordsworth's alternative to what he sees as eighteenth-century writers' "hackneyed and lifeless use" of classical mythology (*PW* 4:423).[2] Subtly he transposes and translates into the realistic topicality of Michael's history those few traditional pastoral motifs that he finds congenial: the pastoral pleasance in a mountain valley, the moral superiority of country over city, the bond between shepherds who cherish their freedom and independence. He uses these motifs to portray a real sheepfarmer, living at a specific time and in an identifiable place, confronting his arduous, even dangerous, daily tasks. He further uses the traditional motifs to show that this Westmorland shepherd is also the pastor of a traditional spiritual patrimony:

> He feels himself
> In those vast regions where his service is
> A Freeman; wedded to his life of hope
> And hazard, and hard labour interchang'd
> With that majestic indolence so dear
> To native Man.
> (*Prelude* 8:385–90)

Michael attests to what Hartman calls Wordsworth's "supreme gift to purge the factitious and restore the elemental situation—in his poetry every convention, figure or device is either eliminated, simplified or grounded in humanity" ("Wordsworth, Inscriptions" 403). Wordsworth simplifies and grounds in humanity the traditions of both "soft" and "hard" pastoral, combining them in fresh ways, bringing together the delights of freedom and the teachings of adversity.[3] His realism makes him dwell on the shepherd's physical hardships, while his idealism makes him emphasize the shepherd's spiritual gratification, his joys and hopes. His poem particularizes the ideal and idealizes the particular.

Central to Wordsworth's achievement of the "acknowledged voice of life" is his persona of pastoral narrator.[4] The "I" who tells Michael's story is spiritually anchored in both Michael's region and his ethos. He might well say to Michael what a similar narrator says to the shepherd in *Hart-Leap Well*: "Small difference lies between thy creed and mine" (162). The autobiographical persona in the preamble to the narrative of Michael is attuned to all who share Michael's values, which are also the values of such other typical autobiographical personae as the poet of *The Prelude* and the Wanderer of *The Excursion*. At the same time the preamble distances the narrator from the unsympathetic and uninitiated listeners who would pass unnoticed the ruins of Michael's sheepfold and who might call the pastoral poet's visionary attachment to his native valley a "shadow" and a "delusion." To them he might say, with the poet in the *Prelude*,

> Call ye these appearances
> Which I beheld of Shepherds in my youth,
> This sanctity of Nature given to Man
> A shadow, a delusion, ye who are fed
> By the dead letter, not the spirit of things. . . .
> (*Prelude* 8:428–32)

Only those who feed not on the dead letter but on the living spirit of nature could be as receptive to Michael's story as the narrator himself was. He recalls that the story was the first

> Of those domestic tales that spake to me
> Of Shepherds, dwellers in the valleys, men
> Whom I already loved;—not verily
> For their own sakes, but for the fields and hills
> Where was their occupation and abode.
> (22–26)

Thus the narrator was able to respond to the story of Michael's life because the "gentle agency / Of natural objects" led him, even as a boy, "to feel / For passions that were not my own, and think / . . . on Man, the heart of man, and human life" (29–31, 33). Furnished by nature with the kind of "prepossession without which the soul / Receives no knowledge that can bring forth good" (*Prelude* 8:460–61), the narrator, through imaginative identification with the tale of the shepherd, was able to enlarge the circumference of his feeling and understanding.

Wordsworth has used an intriguing opening gambit: he has presented his narrator first as an auditor responding in exemplary fashion to the cautionary tale he is about to retell for the "delight of a few natural hearts" (36). He thus plays the double role of listener and teller as he inducts the chosen few into his pastoral microcosm that reverberates with influential meaning. Implicitly he suggests a paradigmatic chain reaction of listening and telling, as his listeners or readers become future tellers, the future poets "who among these hills, / Will be my second self when I am gone" (38–39). Only through such a magnetic chain can Michael's legacy be passed on from generation to generation, and the legacy can only be passed on in the hills and valleys that are the shepherd's abode. In *Michael*, as in traditional pastoral, the natural domain, rather than the city or the court, is truly civil and civilizing. But the poem goes beyond that tradition when the pastoral landscape is imbued with the seminal power to shape the individual's disposition toward the pastoral ethos. The *locus amoenus* in *Michael* is no mere backdrop for a symposium or a singing contest, no mere pleasance distancing life's distressing events. It emblematically embodies the "sense of dim similitude which links / Our moral feelings with external forms" (*1799 Prelude* 2:164–65) that is so characteristic of Wordsworth's pastoral bias:

> To every natural form, rock, fruit or flower,
> Even the loose stones that cover the high-way,
> I gave a moral life, I saw them feel,

Or link'd them to some feeling.
(*Prelude* 3:124–27)

Beginning his narrative with the scene that nourishes the narrator's and the shepherd's soul, Wordsworth quickly limns the landscape and the ethos, the physical and the spiritual context, of Michael's life:

> If from the public way you turn your steps
> Up the tumultuous brook of Green-head Ghyll,
> You will suppose that with an upright path
> Your feet must struggle; in such bold ascent
> The pastoral mountains front you, face to face.
> But, courage! for around that boisterous brook
> The mountains have all opened out themselves,
> And made a hidden valley of their own.
> (1–8)

This first of a series of landscape sketches borrows a motif from epitaphs as the poet directs the traveler-reader to locate a "straggling heap of unhewn stones" (17) whose meaning his narrative unfolds.[5] His reassurance that we may bypass the "bold ascent" up a steep mountain and follow an easy path into a secluded valley suggests that he will conduct us not on an arduous heroic exploit but on a restful pastoral excursion, a promise that the poem eventually leads us to review as paradoxical.

Having traced the traveler's path, Wordsworth arrests his forward movement to view the "hidden valley": a stylized tableau of quiet seclusion, a schematized still life in which the "boisterous brook" is the only dynamic feature, linking this insulated scene with the world beyond. In this valley

> No habitation can be seen; but they
> Who journey thither find themselves alone
> With a few sheep, with rocks and stones, and kites
> That overhead are sailing in the sky.

It is in truth an utter solitude. . . .
    (9–13)

As the identifiable topography of the path leading along Green-head Ghyll subtly changes into a schematized emblem of "utter solitude," we recognize that Wordsworth's pastoral will involve both a realistic and a conceptualized mimesis.

In his own comments on the poem, Wordsworth primarily stressed its truth to verifiable observation: the ruins of the sheepfold still exist, the circumstances of Luke's life derive from a family in whose house the poet himself has lived, and he knows of a house in the Grasmere Valley actually called the Evening Star.[6] Wordsworth's minute details about the shepherd's occupations during the changing seasons confirm his fidelity to observed truth—even occasionally at the expense of artistic economy, as when, descending into what Coleridge called "*matter-of-factness*,"[7] the poem specifies the items of the "cleanly supper-board" (99). But if Wordsworth dwells on Michael's "mess of pottage and skimmed milk" (100) to achieve realism, he also, though more sparingly, emphasizes symbolic details to point up his *pastor bonus* as a conceptual ideal. In the secluded valley, in the protective circle of their household, the shepherd's family are "as a proverb in the vale / For endless industry" (94–95). And the lamp, which illuminates the household's communal life following upon the day's solitary hardships and pleasures, beams its light across the valley as a "public symbol of the life / That thrifty Pair had lived" (130–31):[8]

> And from this constant light, so regular,
> And so far seen, the House itself, by all
> Who dwelt within the limits of the vale,
> Both old and young, was named THE EVENING STAR.
>   (136–39)

Although Wordsworth does not set the continuity and coherence of the way of life symbolized by the Evening Star in the mythic past of a golden age, his paradigm is unmistakably a retreat from the dominant ways of the modern world. Those who travel on the "public way" do not even suspect the pastoral valley's existence. Protective mountains shut out the whole world of commerce, with its getting and spending, its competitive acquisitiveness, and all the fallout of its dehumanization of labor.[9] The mountain refuge replaces this increasingly industrialized world with a pastoral microcosm that temporarily advances the illusion that the only reality is this sanctuary, which Abbie Potts notably identifies with Bunyan's Delectable Mountains.[10] A rejected manuscript passage develops this sense of temporal and spatial seclusion even more fully than the published poem. The poet discovers a spot "Shut out from man," a region that seems "the whole / Of nature and of unrecorded time"; in such a spot the poet looks into "past times as prophets look / Into futurity" (*PW* 2:479–80).[11]

Wordsworth thus initially places his shepherd not in the world of agricultural modernization, with its economic impact on small landowners, but displaces this contemporary rural scene by a mythical spot, an autonomous region insulated from what in *Home* he called "all remembrance of a jarring world" (836)—an exemplary *locus amoenus*. In the published version of *Michael* he dwells more briefly on this archetypal scene, observing it as a distant prospect, then shifting his focus to the realistic topography (though not the realistic demography) of Michael's native valley. The multiple planes of Wordsworth's landscape recall Claude Lorrain's schematized landscapes—much admired at the end of the eighteenth century for their Arcadian mood—in which a large dark scene on one side typically merges into a central foreground dominated by human figures, which, in turn, leads to a luminous distant vista. But for neither the painter nor the poet is the formal schema merely a formula.[12] Wordsworth's schema is distinguished from Claude's by its shifting perspectives in which the distant view of the steep mountains narrows to a close-up of the cliffs that now clearly show the access to the secluded valley. And the valley, which first appeared like Claude's luminous distant plane, becomes the foreground from which the human observer looks up at the steep mountains, which now form the backdrop. At the end of the poem Wordsworth narrows his focus to the single spot within the valley where Michael's house once stood. Like Claude, who uses some single landscape feature to link the different planes of his canvas, Wordsworth unobtrusively uses the "tumultuous brook of Green-head Ghyll" (322) as a continuous dynamic motif to link his shifting landscapes and underline the beginning, middle, and end of his narrative.[13]

The central action takes place against the background of the "green valleys, and the streams and rocks" (63) among which Michael has pursued his lifelong "shepherd's calling" (46). Although this landscape is not adorned by "an air of piety to the Gods," as Pope recommended in his "Discourse on Pastoral Poetry" (26), Michael's human, eventful or uneventful deeds imbue the fields with a patriarchal spirit. The scene is pervaded by an inexpressible sense of divine presence, elevating the grazing meadows into a sanctified abode.[14] Wordsworth finds in these native fields the patriarchal air that Goethe sought in his imaginary excursion to the Orient, to a time when God's teaching was still heard on earth in *Erdesprachen*.[15] "Those fields, those hills," exclaims Wordsworth's pastoral narrator,

> what could they less? had laid
> Strong hold on his affections, were to him
> A pleasurable feeling of blind love,
> The pleasure which there is in life itself.
>   (74–77)

For Michael, nature's awe-inspiring forms reverberate with "tragedies of former times"—to use the language of *The Prelude* —"of which the rocks / Immutable and everflowing streams" were "speaking monuments" (1850, 8:169–72). They shape nothing less than "a religion in his heart," as Wordsworth said in a manuscript fragment of *Michael* (*PW* 2:482). Human experiences and nature's forms, transitory feelings and immutable monuments are so firmly interwoven in this shepherd's life that "we infer what he is from where he is" (Murray 70). The hills impress upon Michael's mind many incidents of "hardship, skill or courage, joy or fear" (69) that his memory preserves "like a book" (70). The shepherd reads traces of human events imprinted on nature's forms and he records them in nature's primal language in the pages of his silent memory. Dangers and hardships do not disrupt this organic harmony; they play their part in the shepherd's free collaboration with nature:

> The elements, and seasons as they change,
> Do find a worthy fellow-labourer there—
> Man free, man working for himself, with choice
> Of time, and place, and object. . . .
> (1850 *Prelude* 8:102–5)

Thus the Wordsworthian rural retreat is a *concordia discors*, uniting repose and labor, pastoral *otium* and unpastoral *negotium*, pleasure and stress. While its green recess may not be a bower of bliss, it yet affords the "pleasure which there is in life itself." That pleasure is not incompatible with the Hesiodic emphasis on hard work, as Wordsworth's shepherd performs tasks for which he must marshal all his strength in order to survive nature's buffeting.[16] His reward is independence and dignity:

> Yet is it something gained—it is in truth
> A mighty gain—that Labour here preserves
> His rosy face, a Servant only here
> Of the fire-side or of the open field,
> A Freeman, therefore, sound and unenslaved.
> (*Home* 439–43)

Such labor creates human bonds, not inhuman bondage. Intent on essential needs rather than on luxuries, Michael gains the self-sufficiency and self-reliance that guarantee his freedom. Wordsworth shares Rousseau's sentiment: "What yoke, indeed, can be imposed on men who have no need of anything?" (4).

Following Virgil rather than Theocritus, Wordsworth focuses his pastoral poem on a small landowner, a sheepfarmer for whom economic independence is the essential foundation of moral strength, a belief "inconceivable by those who have only had an opportunity of observing hired labourers, farmers, and the manufacturing Poor," as Wordsworth explained to the Whig leader Charles James Fox, warning against the encroaching industrialization that threatened the last remnants of a way of life enshrined in *Michael* (*EY* 314). Industrialization threatened Michael's "patrimonial fields" (224), which had sustained him throughout his long life, just as they had sustained his parents and their parents before them. These fields represented far more than mere property, as Wordsworth emphasized to Fox: the small landowners' "little tract of land serves as a kind of permanent rallying point for their domestic feelings, as a tablet upon which they are written which makes them objects of memory in a thousand instances when they would otherwise be forgotten. It is a fountain fitted to the nature of social man from which supplies of affection, as pure as his heart was intended for, are daily drawn" (*EY* 314–15).

This "little tract of land" symbolizes the hope that human community can endure beyond a single life, just as the country house served for an earlier age as custodian for traditional aristocratic values. In fact Wordsworth seems to transpose from the country-house tradition to his egalitarian pastoral the emphasis on a symbolic structure that embodies stable, permanent values. Michael's Evening Star is the humble counterpart of Sidney's grand Penshurst, embodying the virtue of frugality rather than liberality. Both houses, both estates symbolize a long family tradition, a timeless ideal transmitted in a process well summarized by Mary Ann McGuire: "The community renews itself biologically, but also morally, as each new generation of Sidneys is taught to fulfill their responsibilities as aristocrats to their fellow men and to God and to repeat traditional patterns of life" (97). Even though Michael has no patronymic privilege to transmit to the next generation, he has a patronymic ethos to transmit, a coherent pattern of life rooted in the patrimonial fields of a hard-working farmer. He represents the "humble sons of the hills" of whom Wordsworth said, in his *Guide to the*

Lake District, that many "had a consciousness that the land, which they walked over and tilled, had for more than five hundred years been possessed by men of their name and blood" (*Prose* 2:206).

Wordsworth's appeal to save the independent "proprietors of small estates, which have descended to them from their ancestors" is urgent: "This class of men is rapidly disappearing" (*EY* 314–15). They are to Wordsworth the only remaining model of a true human community. His distress at seeing this community disappear before his eyes as a result of what Raymond Williams calls "the familiar process of engrossing and enclosing" (*Country and City* 43) colors Wordsworth's pastoral perspective. The narrator of Michael's story is not a neutral spectator but a deeply involved participant who watches the ideals of his youth vanish; he makes real for us what has become a sentimental literary convention. Raymond Williams has shown how, during the last two hundred years, writers in every age have claimed to witness the dying out of the timeless values of rural life, the rural life they knew in their childhood. He has himself witnessed it. Born in a village on the Welsh border, Williams notes how his feelings for that village were attached both to its landscape—the green meadows etched against the red earth of the ploughland—and to its inhabitants—the men who worked the fields and built the cottages. But now a wide highway runs through the village, right past the cottage in which he lived as a boy. Thus he has seen the Old England of his childhood disappear, just as Lawrence, Hardy, George Eliot, Wordsworth, Crabbe, and Goldsmith all witnessed the disruption of the rural stability and tranquility of their childhoods. Nostalgia, Williams concludes, "is universal and persistent; only other men's nostalgias offend. A memory of childhood can be said, persuasively, to have some permanent significance" (3–12).[17]

Wordsworth endowed such memory, symbolized by the sheepfold, with the pastoral virtues of independence, equality, justice, and tranquility. The moral climax of his narrative is the forging of the covenant between Michael and Luke, just at the moment when they come to a parting of the ways. On the eve of Luke's departure for London, Michael walks with him deep into the valley, to the site of his projected sheepfold near the lively brook of Green-head Ghyll, to offer him an anchor and a shield against all temptation.[18] The "links of love" (401) of their covenant join father and son, link both to former generations, and guarantee future continuity. In this spirit Luke lays the sheepfold's cornerstone—a cornerstone of patrimonial bonds, moral integrity, and lasting faith in the pastoral ethos. Their covenant embodies the kind of religious value described by Erich Kahler as seen at work in Chinese and Hindu sages, the Jewish prophets, and religious poets and thinkers from Plato to Pascal. All passionately care for values that "do not appear as fixed, external impositions, as mere commandments or obligations. They are embedded in life. . . . This gives them their freshness and vital seriousness. Here we can hardly make out whether values are the very blossoms and fruits of life or the guiding principles that bring life to fruition" (194).

In Wordsworth's pastoral narrative it is indeed impossible to make out whether Michael's daily tasks shape his moral values or whether his values direct his daily acts. It is clear, however, that his guiding ethos is reinforced as he beholds in his son a second self, who "more than all other gifts / That earth can offer to declining man, / Brings hope with it, and forward-looking thoughts" (146–48).[19] "Why should I relate," asks the pastoral narrator,

> That objects which the Shepherd loved before
> Were dearer now? that from the Boy there came
> Feelings and emanations—things which were
> Light to the sun and music to the wind;
> And that the old Man's heart seemed born again?
>   (198–203)

In a rejected draft for *Michael*, Wordsworth amplified these reciprocal feelings and emanations between father and son that render inviolate the psychosocial integrity of the human life-cycle:

> And thus it is
> That in such regions, by the sovereignty
> Of forms still paramount, to every change
> Which years can bring into the human heart
> Our feelings are indissolubly bound
> Together, and affinities preserved
> Between all stages of the life of man.
>   (*PW* 2:481)

In a prelude to their covenant, Michael reminds his son of these indissoluble feelings as he recapitulates the course of their lives governed by their forefathers' ethos. Michael's story within a story might be entitled "emotion recollected in anxiety," seeking to anchor the future in the past. In their covenant they pledge to struggle for the continuity of their way of life, Luke by going to the city, Michael by carrying on the sheepfarm's work alone. "I will begin again" (391), he assures his son, even in his old age, to resume alone the tasks that they had come to share, maintaining the hope that "both may live / To see a better day" (388–89). The cornerstone of the sheepfold, which Luke lays at Michael's request, formally seals their mutual bond, their commitment to their tract of land, and their trust in the sustaining power of this spot of time. The Old Testament overtones reinforce the pathos of this moment in which a patriarchal shepherd and his son bind themselves to the continuity of the old ways.

If ownership of a small tract of land sustains the pastoral values, desire for wealth in the city disrupts cohesive ties. The "dissolute city" (444) in Wordsworth's narrative evokes the traditional Christian implications of the lures of worldly pleasure and gain. To send his son into this world of temptation, even temporarily, is for Michael a desperate remedy for the threatened loss of his land. The mere thought of London proves corrupting. To fortify Luke against its evil snares, Michael impresses on him the memory of pastoral innocence:

> ". . . amid all fears
> And all temptation, Luke, I pray that thou
> May'st bear in mind the life thy Fathers lived,
> Who, being innocent, did for that cause
> Bestir them in good deeds."
> (408–12)

Such warning becomes necessary only as industrialization encroaches upon the secluded pastoral valley. Neither Michael nor anyone else in his family even mentioned London until they received the "Distressful tidings" (209) that they must forfeit half their land. Michael's desperate plan to send Luke to London to redeem the land stirs his wife's imagination not only with visions of her son's successful mission but also with fantasies of grandeur and wealth. Even the pure of heart are not proof against the evil snares of the metropolis. She recalls how a parish boy grew "wondrous rich" (267) in a London enterprise, though she tempers her worldly fantasy by thoughts of the young man's Christian charities. Wordsworth dwells in greater detail on Isabel's memories of the parish boy's success story than on Luke's inevitable failure. He sketches Luke's career in its barest outline: he slackened in his duty, gave himself to "evil courses," and was forced to flee overseas (443–47).

Wordsworth's primary concern is not with Luke and the "dissolute city" but with Michael and his resolute pastorate. His focus is on the disastrous impact of Luke's failed mission on Michael: the rupture of the cohesiveness of his life both in the fields and in his domestic household, the erosion of his ties to the past and future. Having lost his "comfort and his daily hope" (206), he can no longer actively engage in his daily tasks or believe that through them lasting values can come to fruition. Yet even if he cannot fulfill his pastoral mission and complete the covenantal sheepfold, he lacks neither compassion for his prodigal son nor fortitude in bearing the inevitable loss of his land. Although Abbie Potts's identification of the story of Michael and Luke with Milton's "conflict between obedient and disobedient angel" in *Paradise Lost* is farfetched, it leads to an apt insight: "The great war against evil which Milton's Michael could not quite win, Wordsworth's Michael cannot quite lose. The operation of love is not less authentic than the operation of justice" (310–11).

And yet Wordsworth's poem raises the question whether love or justice can inform, moment by moment, lives governed by capitalistic industry rather than by egalitarian nature. In the concluding passage of the poem, Wordsworth epitomizes Michael's tragic loss in a final still life: the cottage has been razed, the land ploughed over,

> yet the oak is left
> That grew beside their door; and the remains
> Of the unfinished Sheep-fold may be seen
> Beside the boisterous brook of Green-head Ghyll.
> (479–82)

Unlike the tableau of the secluded valley at the beginning of the poem, this schematic scene is not a refuge from the world of commerce and technological advance: it represents all that is left *after* the industrial changes have engulfed Michael's village, leveling the Evening Star, the valley's symbol of constancy. The tableau of the oak and the heap of stones suggests the vanity of pastoral covenants in a rapidly changing world in which only one oak tree, once the shepherd's shearing tree, remains an emblem of nature's immutability, powerless to preserve Michael's moral heritage.[20] The old covenant has been destroyed, but there are no signs of a new dispensation.

Wordsworth here etches sparingly the bleak picture of despoiled nature that he painted more profusely in 1808, in his unfinished poem *The Tuft of Primroses*. It too shows the ravage of Grasmere, which once "had a holy grace, / That incommunicable sanctity / which Time and nature only can bestow" (116–18; *PW* 5:351). It too shows a "Patriarch of the Vale" (171), a "Planter, and a Rearer from the Seed" (175), a "Man of Hope, a forward-looking Mind" (177), who perishes along with his cottage and all his family's works that "round that Dwelling covertly preserved / The History of their unambitious lives" (189–90). The rapacious forces of economic progress triumph over the "incommunicable sanctity" of human community. In Michael Friedman's words, "sacramental value is being replaced by calculable value" (216).

Much of the *Tuft of Primroses* is the kind of elegiac lament that Schiller criticized because it is enervating rather than animating, backward rather than forward looking, captivating the reader's heart without nourishing the mind.[21] *Michael*, on the contrary, offers an image of an idyllic counterworld that Wordsworth depicts as having really existed in his own time. It is a realized ideal. *Michael* is, as Humphry Davy recognized, a poem "full of jus[t] pictures of what human life ought to be," a remark that Coleridge countered by saying, "believe me, that such scenes & such char[acters] really exist in this county—the superiority [of] the small Estatesman, such as W. pain[ts in] old Michael, is a God compared to our Peasants & small Farmers in the South: & furnishes important documents of the kindly ministrations of local attachment & hereditary descent" (*CL* 2: 663–64). Both Davy and Coleridge were right. *Michael* offered Wordsworth's readers what Schiller urged poets to provide: "Work for your contemporaries," he advised, "but create what they need, not what they praise." He further urged that the poet surround his contemporaries with the "symbols of perfection, until Semblance conquer Reality, and Art triumph over Nature" (*AL* 9:7).

To allow his symbols of perfection to work on the reader's imagination, Wordsworth, with utmost restraint, minimizes the pathos of Michael's fate by dwelling only briefly on the total eradication of all traces of his existence. And with equal restraint Wordsworth eschews satiric invective against the new captains of industry, whose application of mass production to agriculture was rendering independent farmers like Michael redundant. With brilliant understatement Wordsworth brings home his critique of the economic development that, in Marx's words, "put an end to all feudal, patriarchal, idyllic relations . . . and has left remaining no other nexus between man and man than naked self-interest, than callous 'cash payment'" (337). The ploughshare that has been through the land on which Michael's cottage stood heralds the age of combines and bull-dozers. The "stranger's hand" that seized Michael's land and demolished the Evening Star clearly symbolizes impersonal industrial power against the personal "life of eager industry" (122) for which Michael's family was "a proverb in the vale" (94).[22] It pits the new goal of productivity for the sake of accumulating wealth against the old value of work for the sake of independence and stability. Adam Smith, one of the first writers to use the term *industry* in its modern sense, denoting the manufacturing institution rather than the personal attributes of perseverance and diligence, was also one of the first to recognize that it brings with it a way of life that "does not fix or realize itself in any permanent subject which endures after [its] labour is past" (in Arendt 117). Michael's industry, in contrast, is aimed at making permanent beyond his lifespan the fruit of his labor. This aim was thwarted by the economics of commercial farming, which created a "growing surplus of the rural poor" (Hobsbawm 79).

The stark ending of *Michael* departs from Wordsworth's habit of mitigating the impact of such desolate scenes by ending with the narrator's consoling thoughts. In *Hart-Leap Well*, for example, the pastoral narrator chances upon a row of pillars on a dark hilltop ("More doleful place did never eye survey" [114]), but he assures the shepherd whom he addresses that he faces "no common waste, no common gloom" (170), for nature shall restore all beauty:

"She leaves these objects to a slow decay,
That what we are, and have been, may be known;
But at the coming of the milder day
These monuments shall all be overgrown."
(173–76)

And in a related manuscript fragment, Wordsworth speaks of the "intimation of the milder day / Which is to be, the fairer world than this" when the blessedness that in "these unhappy times" can only be gained by "seceding from the common world" will be enjoyed by "all the vales of earth and all mankind" (*PW* 2:515).[23]

Michael offers no such promise of a restored Eden. Although it opens with the narrator's autobiographical induction, it leaves the frame uncompleted at the end. The poet does not share his final thoughts; he offers no consolation. Yet, despite the narrative's unconciliatory ending, the final tableau of the oak and heap of stones in the midst of a wasteland evokes not only a tragic response but also a meditative mood. The concluding details of the sheepfold and the "boisterous brook of Greenhead Ghyll" lead us back to the poem's beginning to view the narrative not in its linear unfolding but in its circular completeness. For Wordsworth's poem well exemplifies what Coleridge describes as the creative effect of all poetry: "The common end of all *narrative*, nay, of *all*, Poems is to convert a *series* into a *Whole*: to make those events, which in real or imagined History move on in a *strait* Line, assume to our Understandings a *circular* motion—the snake with it's Tail in it's Mouth" (*CL* 4:545).

In the retrospective view of the poem's total pattern, we recognize that the pastoral way in *Michael* is after all a strenuous and precarious "upright path," and that the poet's task, though it lacks heroic scope, approaches heroic purposiveness.[24] The landscape of the "hidden valley" invites us in the end to share not a relaxing excursion but a rigorous choice: to bear witness to one man's fortitude in facing disastrous upheaval and to re-create his vanishing way of life. Thus Michael's tragedy emerges not only as an individual's loss but also as a threat to what Johan Huizinga calls a historical ideal of life (*Levens-ideal*), "any concept of excellence [which] man projects into the past" but which has the power to influence future aspirations (80). Whereas Michael's personal tragedy is irreversible, his pastoral ethos remains as an example to be imitated, even though the poet finds it difficult to demonstrate its virtue to an industrial society, just as he finds it difficult to transform a meaningless rubble of stones into a meaningful form, to turn a senseless fragment of existence into a sensible microcosm. But without the power of the poet's words, "Even of the good is no memorial left," as the Pedlar observes in *The Ruined Cottage* (330; *PW* 5:389). The poet's words are "too awful an instrument for good and evil to be trifled with: they hold above all other external powers a dominion over thoughts" (*Prose* 2:84). In pastoral, as in other literary genres, they constitute an instrument for communion or alienation. Whereas Michael's history ends in alienation from his world, Wordsworth's poem as a whole communicates a sense of heroic achievement, according to William James's description of heroism. When life "turns up its dark abysses to our view," writes James, "then the worthless ones among us . . . either escape from its difficulties by averting their attention, or . . . collapse into yielding masses of plaintiveness and fear." He contrasts such failure to face dreadful events with the heroic man's capacity to face them without losing his hold on life. "The world thus finds in the heroic man its worthy match and mate; and the effort which he is able to put forth to hold himself erect and keep his heart unshaken is the direct measure of his worth and function in the game of human life. He can *stand* this Universe" (2:578–79).

Wordsworth's ability to "stand this Universe" rests on the bedrock of shared values, of mutuality between himself, his protagonist, and the local community that has preserved his history. His art of verisimilitude establishes the pastoral ethos not as a golden age ideal but as a real, attainable way of life. And as destructible. The poet invokes witnesses who have felt the poignancy of Michael's fate:

> 'Tis not forgotten yet
> The pity which was then in every heart
> For the old Man—and 'tis believed by all
> That many and many a day he thither went,
> And never lifted up a single stone.
> (462–66)

Thus the poet attributes the expression of pathos (in the line that Matthew Arnold praised as Wordsworth's best single line of poetry) to one of the valley's inhabitants.[25] His formal role as poet focuses on preserving the oral heritage of Michael's life, aware that

> These Dalesmen trust
> The lingering gleam of their departed lives
> To oral record, and the silent heart;
> Depositories faithful and more kind
> Than fondest epitaph: for, if those fail,
> What boots the sculptured tomb?
> (*Excursion* 6:610–15)

Wordsworth attempts to create for a "few natural hearts" (*Michael* 36) a poetic depository that is "faithful and more kind / Than fondest epitaph." Yet he has no illusion about making converts: he is preaching to the faithful, who, like himself in his boyhood, have felt nature's civilizing power. And he is forging a covenant between himself and future poets "who among these hills, / Will be my second self when I am gone" (38–39). At a time of social and economic dislocations, he affirms his moral legacy, his belief in community, even as he tells of a shepherd's unsuccessful struggle to live out his life according to his guiding principles. Clearly the poet expects his word to be more durable than Michael's tract of land.

In his third edition of *Lyrical Ballads* (1802), Wordsworth changed the title to *Lyrical Ballads, with Pastoral and Other Poems* to call attention to *Michael* and *The Brothers*, which contained his most important beliefs.[26] And in his expanded Preface he strengthened his claim for the poet's responsibility for preserving the human community: The poet is "the rock of defence for human nature; an upholder and preserver, carrying everywhere with him relationship and love" (*Prose* 1:141).[27] Wordsworth's staunch optimism counters his almost Chekhovian awareness of the changing currents of society that were leaving behind as dying forms the ideals of life he valued most. Implicitly if not explicitly, his finest pastoral poem asserts that only the poet's words can restore the pastoral covenant in an iron age.

6

COLERIDGE IN SICILY:
A PASTORAL INTERLUDE IN *THE PRELUDE*

Toward the end of Book 8 of
The Prelude, when Wordsworth sums up what London, the "Pre-
ceptress stern" (678), contributed to his self-education, he
paints a picture of external and internal *concordia discors*. "In
presence of that vast Metropolis" (746), he tells us, his belief
in man's inherent nobility was severely tested yet remained
unshaken:

> Neither guilt nor vice,
> Debasement of the body or the mind,
> Nor all the misery forced upon my sight,
> Which was not lightly passed, but often scann'd
> Most feelingly, could overthrow my trust
> In what we may become, induce belief
> That I was ignorant, had been falsely taught,
> A Solitary, who with vain conceits
> Had been inspired, and walk'd about in dreams.
> (8:802–10)

By alluding to Milton's Adam cast out of paradise, Wordsworth
intensifies the contrast between outward decadence and inward
vision:

When from that awful prospect overcast
And in eclipse, my meditations turn'd,
Lo! everything that was indeed divine
Retain'd its purity inviolate
And unencroach'd upon, nay, seem'd brighter far
For this deep shade in counterview, that gloom
Of opposition, such as shew'd itself
To the eyes of Adam, yet in Paradise,
Though fallen from bliss, when in the East he saw
Darkness ere day's mid course, and morning light
More orient in the western cloud, that drew
'O'er the blue firmament a radiant white,
Descending slow with something heavenly fraught.'
    (8:811–23)

Wordsworth's Miltonic passage here epitomizes the Romantic pastoral vision that defines itself through tension between an internalized paradise, an inviolate heritage, and its "counterview," a postlapsarian reality, a questionable present that intertwines good and evil. The Miltonic echoes emphasize that only when man stands at the threshold of exile from Eden does he fully recognize its radiant bliss, etched against the encroaching darkness. For Wordsworth, as for Theocritus and Virgil, his classical models, both pastoral poet and reader are located in the jarring world of commerce while contemplating the tranquility of the pastoral bower. And like Virgil, he frequently frames his pastoral excursions by discordant historical events, pitting pastoral virtues against the stresses and distresses of modern life. The task of the pastoral imagination is not, as Renato Poggioli suggests, "to exalt the pleasure principle at the expense of the reality principle" (14) but to chart a course that will coalesce the values of both principles.

    Drawing on the rich classical and Renaissance heritage of pastoral motifs—a heritage deliberately expunged from his repertoire in the process of writing *Michael*—Wordsworth proves himself (in Coleridge's words) a "free imitator, who seizes with a strong hand whatever he wants or wishes for his own purpose and justifies the seizure by the improvement of the material or the superiority of the purpose to which it is applied" (*Miscellaneous Criticism* 176). He seizes pastoral motifs to deploy them for their psychological, moral, and aesthetic import. A pastoral ethos and pastoral rhetoric permeate *The Prelude* as a whole; in the unpastoral books about London and the French Revolution, however, the pastoral strain is contained in interludes, rather than in the central narrative.

As early as Theocritus's *Idylls*, pastoral was an eclectic form which, according to Gilbert Lawall, combined the resources of mime, popular folk song, Homeric epic, and Aeschylean tragedy (2).[1] All through its literary history it has readily assimilated themes and images from other literary kinds while also effectively intruding its presence into comedies and romances, epics and novels. Poggioli was the first critic to call attention to the importance of pastoral interludes in long works, ranging from the *Aeneid* to *Don Quijote* and *Gerusalemme liberata*. "Pastoral poetry," he wrote, "makes more poignant and real the dream it wishes to convey when the retreat is not a lasting but a passing experience, acting as a pause in the process of living, as a breathing spell from the fever and anguish of being." He went on to suggest that the *topos* of the *locus amoenus*, the landscape which forms the appointed resting place, functions in epic or romance to signal the "unexpected apparition of a bucolic episode, which breaks the main action or pattern, suspending for a while the heroic, romantic, or pathetic mood of the whole. Accordingly the topos itself is but an idyllic prelude to a bucolic interlude, where the characters rest from their adventures or passions" (9).

Among the pastoral interludes which suspend the central autobiographical narrative that authenticates Wordsworth's mission as poet-prophet, the concluding passage of Book 10 (Book 11 in the 1850 edition) most richly assimilates the classical heritage of Theocritus and Virgil to the poet's personal theme. This pastoral conclusion to the unpastoral book about the French Revolution and its aftermath opens with a conventional address to Coleridge, the traditional epic patron of

Wordsworth's poem.[2] But on this occasion Wordsworth invokes Coleridge's presence at unconventional length to meditate on his sojourn in Sicily, an event contemporaneous with Wordsworth's composing Book 10 of *The Prelude* in December 1804.[3] Another instance of Adam fallen from bliss, the distant friend poses for Wordsworth a central question: In the face of encroaching inner and outer darkness, how can the poet re-collect paradisal "purity inviolate" and prophesy its redemptive power for his time?

> Thus, O Friend!
> Through times of honour, and through times of shame,
> Have I descended, tracing faithfully
> The workings of a youthful mind, beneath
> The breath of great events. . . .
> (10:941–45)

Thus Wordsworth begins his summation of Book 10, which has traced his hopes and despairs during the decade following the French Revolution. In his "descent" into the times of shame, his inner turmoil mirrored the political turmoil of revolutionary France at war with reactionary England. And he resorted to pastoral associations fully to dramatize the warfare in his inmost being, as he felt

> The ravage of this most unnatural strife
> In my own heart; there lay it like a weight
> At enmity with all the tenderest springs
> Of my enjoyments.
> (10:251–54)

Articulating his inner change through the metaphor of the green leaf, the poet identifies the "tenderest springs" of his former carefree self with the blessed state of concord—both within the self and between himself and his native land—which suddenly turns into tempestuous discord:

> I, who with the breeze
> Had play'd, a green leaf on the blessed tree
> Of my beloved country; nor had wish'd
> For happier fortune than to wither there,
> Now from my pleasant station was cut off,
> And toss'd about in whirlwinds.
> (10:254–59)

The metaphors poignantly recall the poem's opening invocation, "Oh there is blessing in this gentle breeze / That blows from the green fields" (1:1–2). There the poet sanctifies the breeze as a "sweet breath of Heaven" (1:41) and celebrates a "corresponding mild creative breeze" (1:43) within himself that quickly mounts into a "tempest, a redundant energy / Vexing its own creation" (1:46–47). In his secure pastoral state, the sudden outbreak of tempestuous energy brings welcome release from wintry dormancy. Breeze and tempest, spring and winter, creativity and passivity, hope and distress, form the pulsating rhythm of the "holy life of music and of verse" (1:54), the binary tension of *concordia discors*.

But the poet cannot so readily harmonize the pastoral breeze of poetic inspiration and the overpowering whirlwinds of war. Despairing over the disastrous turn of France's "mighty renovation" (10:557), the poet needs to exercise heroic efforts in order to restore a green world in the recesses of his mind, even as he relinquishes the corresponding harmony between the inner microcosm and the political macrocosm. Never again will he use the organic images of breeze, leaf, and tree for the self's integration with *both* the natural and the political worlds. In his painful alienation from paradisal harmony, cut off from the "blessed tree" of England's green and pleasant land, his pastoral associations turn sour. Dwelling on the bitter truths of England's unholy war against France, Wordsworth (uncharacteristically, for him) turns the shepherd into a satiric image in the vein of Milton's denunciation of the corrupt clergy in *Lycidas*:

Our shepherds . . . at that time
Thirsted to make the guardian Crook of Law
A tool of Murder . . .
   (10:646–48)

while the rulers of the state perfidiously sought to undermine
justice and liberty. Wordsworth sees them as

Giants in their impiety alone,
But, in their weapons and their warfare base
As vermin working out of reach. . . .
   (10:653–55)

In vain Wordsworth searches the face of Europe, scarred by
Napoleon's armies, for a haven for liberty. As Schiller noted in
his poem *Der Antritt des neuen Jahrhunderts* (*The Advent of the New
Century*), freedom had fled from life's tumult into the sanctu-
ary of the human heart and was preserved only in dreams and
poems.

    Reconstructing the ravages of a Europe engulfed in war and
a France also engaged in "domestic carnage" (10:330), Words-
worth addressed Coleridge's finely attuned conscience to speak
of these atrocities as if speaking to him alone in "private talk"
(10:373). Even at the beginning of his narrative, as he charted
his way through the hallowed landscape of his childhood, cele-
brating the "union betwixt life and joy" in "our dawn of being"
(1:584–85), he found Coleridge's audience indispensable. His
cancelled draft of the opening of Book 2 testifies to his trans-
formation of Coleridge's role from that of formal patron to
symbiotic partner in his quest:

Friend of my heart and genius we have reach'd
A small green island which I was well pleased
To pass not lightly by for though I felt
Strength unabated yet I seem'd to need
Thy cheering voice or ere I could pursue

My voyage, resting else for ever there.
(*Apparatus criticus*, p. 42)

If Wordsworth needed Coleridge's cheering voice to help him reach the green islands of his paradisal childhood, how greatly must he need this voice to sustain him in his perilous mental journey through spiritual self-exile, cut off momentarily from all saving ideals? Only as private confession to his friend can he reveal his nightmarish visions of "treachery and desertion" witnessed not only in the streets but also within himself, "in the place / The holiest that I knew of, my own soul" (10:380–81). To moderate his distress Wordsworth charts his way circuitously, returning to green islands of memory of the Revolution's golden days when "the whole earth / The beauty wore of promise" (10:702–3), before anatomizing his illusions and probing the "crisis of that strong disease / This the soul's last and lowest ebb" (1850, 11:306–7). In his dark night of the soul, Wordsworth found in his "most precious friend" (10:906) and his beloved sister the "living help" (907) to maintain a "saving intercourse" with his "true self" (915–16). Yet they could not relieve the "over-pressure of the times / And their disastrous issues" (11:47–48), could not sustain the hope that "future times would surely see / The Man to come parted as by a gulph, / From him who had been" (11:58–60).

Pausing in his reflections on this self-division, this desperate war against the self, Wordsworth turns to address his friend and confidant, who now in turn is undergoing a spiritual trial. In a long envoy of nearly a hundred lines, he assimilates Coleridge's fate to his own fateful story of hope and disillusionment:

A Story destined for thy ear, who now,
Among the basest and the lowest fallen
Of all the race of men, dost make abode
Where Etna looketh down on Syracuse,
The city of Timoleon!
   (10:947–51)

With this rhetorical turn, Wordsworth displaces his autobiographical persona by his fellow poet as protagonist. The phrase "A Story destined for thy ear" reminds us of the formal role Coleridge plays throughout *The Prelude* as the narrator's patron, muse, comforter, ideal auditor, fellow pilgrim, and moral guide. By punctuating his narrative with such apostrophes as "O Friend! O Poet! Brother of my soul" (5:180), Wordsworth underscores the shared task of speaker and auditor in his epic journey:

> A Traveller I am,
> And all my Tale is of myself; even so,
> So be it, if the pure in heart delight
> To follow me; and Thou, O honor'd Friend!
> Who in my thoughts art ever at my side,
> Uphold, as heretofore, my fainting steps.
>   (3:196–201)

Of course Coleridge figures in the envoy to Book 10, as in the whole *Prelude*, not only as the attendant spirit timelessly present in the narrator's mind, but also as a historical person, the friend who has left England and who abides "Where Etna looketh down on Syracuse" (10:950). Coleridge's interlocking roles of formal patron-addressee and historical person parallel the complex roles of Wordsworth's own persona. When Wordsworth presents himself as a traveler literally journeying across the Alps, through France, or across Wales, the actual scenes "modulate easily into symbolic landscapes traversed by a metaphorical wayfarer" (Abrams, *Natural Supernaturalism*, 285). As in Coleridge's persona, historical-biographical and formal-literary roles interact as the narrator "figures his own imaginative enterprise, the act of composing *The Prelude* itself, as a perilous quest through the uncharted regions of his own mind" (285).

In the envoy to Book 10, the narrator suspends his own larger quest while engaging in a miniature enterprise, an imaginary voyage to Sicily to restore Coleridge to full health and creative vigor, presumably so that he will return to his role as

the narrator's comforter and guide. It is a curious rhetorical
ploy in an epic poem. It is hard to imagine Dante stopping his
journey through hell to worry about Virgil's state of mind and
to devise a cure for his distress before trusting him to lead on.
But Wordsworth's guide is a more fallible alter ego whose fall
and recovery directly affect the poet in the act of composing *The
Prelude*:

> Thou wilt not languish here, O Friend, for whom
> I travel in these dim uncertain ways
> Thou wilt assist me as a Pilgrim gone
> In quest of highest truth.
>   (11:390−93)

Clearly, while his meditation on Coleridge in Sicily allows
Wordsworth's persona a holiday from his own arduous and
painful self-exploration, it also bears directly on the psychologi-
cal and political issues of his own crisis, the story of which
frames this pastoral interlude. He can replay features of his
own drama in a distanced scenario. In fact, in this interlude
Coleridge figures significantly as Wordsworth's double, in a way
that is best illuminated by Freud. Freud discusses the implica-
tions of the double in one of his rare excursions into the realm
of aesthetics, his essay *Das Unheimliche* (*The Uncanny*). Analyzing
the fantastic tales of E. T. A. Hoffmann, Freud calls attention to
the recurrent theme of the identification of the self with an-
other, of "a doubling, dividing, and interchanging of the self"
—"Ich-Verdopplung, Ich-Teilung, Ich-Vertauschung." He notes
with approval Otto Rank's recognition that the double as mirror
image or guardian spirit serves as "insurance against the extinc-
tion of the self, an energetic denial [*Dementierung*] of the power
of death." While this role of the double originates in infantile
narcissism, it need not be eliminated, according to Freud, when
this narcissism has been surmounted. In this later stage of
psychic development, the double may embody those infantile
fantasies that the self has learned to criticize and to censor.
Further, the double may come to embody "all the aspirations of

the self [*Ich-Strebungen*] that external adversities have crushed, as well as all the suppressed acts of the will [*Willensentschei-dungen*] that result in the illusion of free will" (12:246–48).

The figure of Coleridge as Wordsworth's double can be seen to assume the psychological functions that Freud specified. Above all Wordsworth invests Coleridge with the power to save him from the radical discontinuity between his prelapsarian and his postlapsarian self. The threat of discontinuity was present from the start in his poetic enterprise of mapping a territory that constituted the self. As early as the *1799 Prelude*, Wordsworth had noted the void opening up between the poet narrating the tale of himself and the younger self who was the subject of his narration:

> so wide appears
> The vacancy between me and those days
> Which yet have such self-presence in my heart
> That sometimes when I think of them I seem
> Two consciousnesses, conscious of myself
> And of some other being.
> (1799, 2:26–31; 1805, 2:28–33)

Thus even before Wordsworth needed to confront the wider gulf that opened in his inner self at the time of the French Revolution, he needed his double as a repository of a continuous self, a permanent self immune from the assaults of time. Coleridge is the friend who in his "ample mind" has "stationed" the authentic Wordsworthian self "for reverence and love" (3: 324–25).

Even more urgently does Coleridge figure as the double that canonizes the Wordsworthian inviolate self when, in Books 9 through 11 of the *Prelude*, Wordsworth confronts the scene of "revolutionary Power" tossing "like a Ship at anchor, rock'd by storms" (9:48–49). Reconstructing these dire events, he does not dare to brook such storms; he no more revives fully the violence that assaulted his inmost core of being than Goethe dared to reenter the catastrophic Werther episode of his life when writing his autobiography, *Dichtung und Wahrheit*. Goethe said to Eckermann in 1824 that he had reread *Werther* only once since its publication and would take care never to read it again, since it was full of incendiary rockets (*Brandraketen*) (*GA* 24: 545). Like Goethe, Wordsworth transposed his personal crisis into fictional form. He tells it as the "tragic Tale" (9:550) of Vaudracour and Julia, a tale rescued from obscurity, he says, and told in *The Prelude* (1805) as a "memorial" (9:552) to the events of the revolutionary period, replacing what Wordsworth will not speak of: "the emotions wrought / Within our minds by the ever-varying wind / Of Record and Report which day by day / Swept over us" (9:546–49).[4] Rather than descending into the abyss of his guilt over deserting Annette Vallon and of his divided loyalties in the conflict between England and France, Wordsworth displaces his discontinuous self from the center of his narrative at a crucial point and replaces it by his double, to whom "the unity of all has been reveal'd" (2:226). Through this strategy he can salvage the hopes nourished by his sacramental childhood experiences, enshrining them in his double. His double thus embodies the unfulfilled aspirations of which Freud speaks, the possible futures to which Wordsworth's ego wishes to cling in order to preserve his belief in free will as well as his faith in his mission as poet-prophet. Yet even invested with the displaced Wordsworthian ethos, Coleridge remains in Wordsworth's crisis books of the *Prelude* not merely a static symbol but also a developing, searching, historical persona, himself affected by contemporary events and vicissitudes. Like Blake's Milton, Wordsworth's Coleridge must enter the temporal flux and regain his own unified self in order to redeem his alter ego's prophetic quest.

In the envoy to Book 10 of the *Prelude*, Wordsworth supplants his anatomy of the repercussions of the French Revolution for himself by a digressive narrative of Coleridge's less catastrophic confrontation with an oppressed Sicily, on the one hand, and with personal, inner distress (his opium addiction and unhappy marriage) on the other—a distress that remains unspecified, like Wordsworth's guilt in relation to Annette Vallon. Wordsworth's own despair over France's (and his own) betrayal of lofty ideals is displaced by his double's disillusionment over Sicily's decadence. As in displacements in dreams, in which, as noted by Freud, the dreamer transfers the physical intensity from actual content to a manifest content, Wordsworth transfers his psychic conflict to Coleridge. Seeing Sicily's decadence through Coleridge's eyes, Wordsworth observes,

> If for France I have griev'd
> Who, in the judgment of no few, hath been
> A trifler only, in her proudest day,
> Have been distress'd to think of what she once
> Promised, now is, a far more sober cause
> Thine eyes must see of sorrow, in a Land
> Strew'd with the wreck of loftiest years, a Land
> Glorious indeed, substantially renown'd
> Of simple virtue once, and manly praise,
> Now without one memorial hope, not even
> A hope to be deferr'd; for that would serve
> To chear the heart in such entire decay.
>   (10:955–66)

Coleridge's decline mirrors Sicily's. He, too, is but a shadow of his gloriously gifted self, "without one memorial hope," an outcast, as he said of himself in response to the *Prelude*,

> whose hope had seem'd to die
> A wanderer with a worn-out heart
> Mid strangers pining with untended wounds.
> (*To William Wordsworth*, MS variant, *Complete Poetical Works* 1:406–7)

In short, Coleridge in Sicily presents an *Et in Arcadia ego* tableau in which not only spiritual death invades Arcadia, but idyllic Sicily itself also becomes a moral and political *memento mori*.[5]

Far more explicitly and extensively than in tracing his own recovery from deepest despair, Wordsworth invokes for Cole-

ridge's (and Sicily's) restoration a full array of pagan and bibli-
cal, classical and Renaissance pastoral associations. Out of this
rich tradition, he constructs a ladder for Coleridge's spirit to
"reascend / To health and joy and pure contentedness" (10:
979–80). In urgent supplication for his friend, he introduces
the first series of pastoral allusions:

> Oh! wrap him in your Shades, ye Giant Woods,
> On Etna's side, and thou, O flowery Vale
> Of Enna! is there not some nook of thine,
> From the first playtime of the infant earth
> Kept sacred to restorative delight?
>   (10:1002–6)

Thus Wordsworth begins his imaginary therapeutic quest by
first transmuting Coleridge's setting from bleak decadence into
green pleasance. He calls on Etna's green valleys to "interpose a
little ease"—to borrow Milton's phrase that Wordsworth adapts
for his invocation of Book 11:

> And you, ye Groves, whose ministry it is
> To interpose the covert of your shades,
> Even as a sleep, betwixt the heart of man
> And the uneasy world, 'twixt man himself,
> Not seldom, and his own unquiet heart.
>   (11:15–19)

Wordsworth converts the Sicilian *memento mori* into a *locus
amoenus*, invoking the Theocritean *topos* for its tranquilizing
ministry and for its invigorating powers. He seeks its baptismal
secret in a mountainside nook kept "sacred to restorative de-
light" (10:1006), a rejuvenating source surviving from the "first
playtime" of the "infant earth" (10:1007). The actual place of
Coleridge's sojourn in Sicily near Mt. Etna merges impercepti-
bly with Theocritus's pastoral bower and with Ovid's Sicilian
fields where Pluto abducted Proserpina. And Wordsworth's Mil-
tonic echo synthesizes the pagan myth with the biblical para-

digm of man's expulsion from paradise, as his "flowery field /
Of Enna" (1850, 11:419–20) brings to mind

> Not that fair field
> Of *Enna*, where *Proserpin* gath'ring flow'rs
> Herself a fairer Flow'r by gloomy *Dis*
> Was gather'd, which cost *Ceres* all that pain
> To seek her through the world, not that sweet Grove
> Of *Daphne* by *Orontes*, and th' inspir'd
> *Castalian* Spring might with this Paradise
> Of *Eden* strive. . . .
>   (*Paradise Lost* 4:268–75)

Milton's Eden wins this contest with other pastoral bowers, but
not without dark forebodings that man's wrong choice will
transform eternal spring into changing seasons, and that, like
Proserpina, he must dwell half in light and half in darkness. In
Wordsworth's context of Book 10 of *The Prelude*, the Miltonic
Eden reverberates with the French Revolution's initial promise
of the "golden times" of a restored Eden, a promise that wrong
human choices turned into a grim nightmare. On this cosmic
stage of man's first and man's most recent fall, Wordsworth
places the self-tormented, self-exiled Coleridge, for whom he
seeks the secret of a redemptive "counterview." He addresses
himself to the task of re-creating, through the power of the
word, the "breath of Paradise" (11:11) that once animated his
spirit. Only by recapturing such eolian visitations through his
poem can he hope to restore his languishing friend.

Glancing back at his own Edenic childhood, Wordsworth ex-
plains his deep-rooted affinity for all things Sicilian:

> Child of the mountains, among Shepherds rear'd,
> Even from my earliest school-day time, I lov'd
> To dream of Sicily. . . .
>   (10:1007–9)

He refrains from setting up a pastoral contest with Coleridge
"reared / In the great City, pent 'mid cloisters dim" (*Frost at
Midnight* 51–52). He does not brag of his better fortune. Echo-
ing Coleridge's self-characterization several times in *The Prelude*,
he reconciles their country-city rivalry in the concord of their
shared poetic mission. In Book 2, for example, having cele-
brated nature's sustaining support and blessing, Wordsworth
turns to address Coleridge:

> Thou, my Friend! wert rear'd
> In the great City, 'mid far other scenes;
> But we, by different roads at length have gain'd
> The self-same bourne.
> (2:466–69)

So firmly were their efforts joined in a common "quest of
highest truth" (11:393) that meditating on Coleridge's exile in
Sicily induces in Wordsworth a corresponding visionary gloom.
He ingeniously adapts the classical *topos* of nature's echoing
lament, exemplified in Thyrsis's lament for Daphnis in Theoc-
ritus's *Idyll* 1 and in Milton's *Lycidas*, where the woods and caves
"and all their echoes" not only mourn the dead shepherd but
themselves reflect the loss:

> The Willows and the Hazel Copses green
> Shall now no more be seen,
> Fanning their joyous Leaves to thy soft lays.
> (42–44)

In Wordsworth's elegiac lines not the natural scene itself but its
image in the speaker's memory mourns the friend's absence.[6]
His landscape of the mind takes on a sober coloring:

> My own delights do scarcely seem to me
> My own delights; the lordly Alps themselves,
> Those rosy Peaks, from which the Morning looks

> Abroad on many Nations, are not now
> Since thy migration and departure, Friend,
> The gladsome image in my memory,
> Which they were used to be. . . .
>   (10:990–96)

A "vital promise" (10:1010) wafted from pastoral Sicily suffi-
ciently assuages the speaker's grief that he can carry on his
poetic quest for his friend's recovery. Casting an eye on Sicilian
poets, philosophers, and scientists for guidance, he settles on
Theocritus as the most efficacious. For does not Theocritus
report that a man's own gifts prevail on the powers of heaven
and earth to work miracles? Wordsworth finds in the *Seventh
Idyll* the perfect prescription for Coleridge's cure, guaranteed
by Coleridge's own gifts and effected by Wordsworth's creative
words. "O Theocritus," he addresses his powerful precursor,

>   not unmov'd,
> When thinking of my own beloved Friend,
> I hear thee tell how bees with honey fed
> Divine Comates, by his tyrant lord
> Within a chest imprison'd impiously
> How with their honey from the fields they came
> And fed him there, alive, from month to month,
> Because the Goatherd, blessed Man! had lips
> Wet with the Muse's Nectar.
>   (10:1020–28)

From the way the narrator "hears" Theocritus's story of
Comatas's imprisonment, one would never guess that it forms
part of the most involuted narrative in the Theocritean corpus.
Set not in Sicily but in Cos, the *Seventh Idyll* opens with the
poet's first-person narrative of his excursion from town to coun-
try and closes with his participation in a luxuriant harvest festi-
val on a friend's farm. Within this frame the poet dramatizes a
song contest between Simichidas (usually taken as Theocritus's
persona) and Lycidas, whom his challenger acknowledges as the

best piper among herdsmen and reapers. Lycidas's song in turn opens with an autobiographical frame, his prayer for a beloved friend's safe voyage to Mytilene, followed by an imaginary celebration of his anticipated safe arrival. At this projected feast Lycidas depicts himself as entertained by Tityrus's songs, which rapidly shift from the cowherd Daphnis's pining away for love to an unnamed goatherd's imprisonment in a chest by the "impious presumption of a king" (which Wordsworth conflates with the Comatas story) and his remarkable survival because "bees came from the meadows to the fragrant chest of cedar and fed him on tender flowers because the Muse had poured sweet nectar on his lips." Only at this point in the Idyll does Theocritus introduce Comatas, when Lycidas sings of the unidentified cowherd and relates him to the mythical goatherd: "Ah, blessed Comatas, thine is this sweet lot; thou too wast closed within the coffer; thou too, on honeycomb fed, didst endure with toil the springtime of the year" (83–85). Thus the song that Wordsworth quotes in his address to Coleridge in Sicily is, in *Idyll* 7, a song within a song performed in a pastoral contest set within an autobiographical frame in Cos.

The Idyll offers many suggestive parallels to the Wordsworth-Coleridge relationship of Book 10 of *The Prelude*. Lycidas's farewell song for his beloved friend as well as Lycidas-Tityrus's lament for Daphnis's sorrow parallels Wordsworth's sympathetic involvement in Coleridge's perilous voyage in search of physical health and spiritual hope. Wordsworth probably steers clear of alluding to Lycidas's and Daphnis's suffering because of its erotic emphasis. He designs a more complex poetic role for Coleridge, the "beloved friend" to whom he presents the poem as the "Offering of my love" (13: 427). Just as he bypasses the *Seventh Idyll's* vicissitudes of love, Wordsworth also bypasses the suggestive singing contest between the acknowledged rustic master, Lycidas, and the city poet, Simichidas. Wordsworth displaces such rivalry by friendly reciprocity; for him the prize at stake is not a shepherd's staff but nothing less than vatic powers for both contestants. He turns to the story of Comatas for his perfectly fitting analogue.

Brilliantly exploiting the details from Theocritus's *Idyll*, Wordsworth casts the exiled Coleridge in the role of the imprisoned Comatas and presents his own poem as the life-saving nourishment. The image of imprisonment combines the personal motif of Coleridge's self-torment by "viper thoughts" coiling around his mind with the political reminder of Italy's subjugation—Napoleon acting like the "tyrant lord" who impiously shut up the "Divine Comatas" in a coffer. Wordsworth easily intertwines Coleridge's and Europe's ordeals:

> A lonely wanderer, art gone, by pain
> Compell'd and sickness, at this latter day,
> This heavy time of change for all mankind.
>   (10:984–86)

Before thinking of Syracuse as the city that once harbored Pindar, Theocritus, Aeschylus, and Archimedes, Wordsworth identified it as the "City of Timoleon," the city that was oppressed by tyrants and that found a powerful liberator in the Corinthian general and statesman. Timoleon reestablished democracy in Syracuse. As Napoleon was expanding his empire over the map of Europe, was Wordsworth hoping that another Timoleon would oust this latest tyrant?

If Wordsworth clearly casts Coleridge as the imprisoned Comatas, his own persona assumes the role of the life-giving bees who cull their honey from flowering groves. Thus he transfers the power of paradisal "restorative delight" (10:1006) sought earlier in a sacred nook of Mt. Etna to his own "Hyblean murmurs to poetic thought"—to quote Coleridge's phrase from his tribute to *The Prelude* (*To William Wordsworth* 21).[7] Wordsworth seems unconcerned about a possible ironic echo of Socrates's version of poetic inspiration as irrational chain reaction. "The poets tell us, don't they," Plato's Socrates argues, "that the melodies they bring us are gathered from rills that run with honey, out of glens and gardens of the Muses, and they bring them as the bees do honey, flying like the bees? And what they say is true, for a poet is a light and winged thing and holy, and never able to compose until he has become inspired, and is beside himself" (*Ion* 534a–b). Inspired but not beside himself, Wordsworth's speaker identifies himself with the "light and winged" poet-bees. A courier of the Muses, he brings his honeyed words to the anguished Coleridge-Comatas, whose own poetic gift magnetically attracts this redemptive offering. Wordsworth's Theocritean allegory compliments himself and Coleridge: both redeemer and redeemed are blessed by the Muses. And it compliments Theocritus as well for his timelessly applicable tale.

Like the speaker of Keats's *Ode to Psyche*, the poet in *The Prelude* sings by his own eyes inspired. He has not merely uttered a prayer for Coleridge's consolation and recovery, but he has also imaginatively directed and acted out the means of its realization. "Our prayers have been accepted," he announces confidently, changing his own role from elegist to hymnist, from supplicant to prophet-seer. He speaks "no dream but things oracular" (12:252) as he foretells a triumphant Coleridge standing on Mt. Etna's summit "Not as an Exile but a Visitant" (10:1033).

Wordsworth painstakingly formulated and reformulated his vision of the captive turned conqueror, the paralyzed poet turned inspired vates, until he arrived at these finely tuned pastoral-prophetic modulations:

> thou wilt stand
> On Etna's summit, above earth and sea,
> Triumphant, winning from the invaded heavens
> Thoughts without bound, magnificent designs,
> Worthy of poets who attuned their harps
> In wood or echoing cave, for discipline
> Of heroes. . . .
> (1850, 11:453–59)

Comatas's miraculous cure, won from the "Powers of heaven and earth" (10:1017), pales beside the "magnificent designs" that the enraptured Coleridge will win "from the invaded heavens." Wordsworth here requires the higher mood of Virgilian messianic prophecy for his brief vision of the bardic Coleridge who shall be a mentor to heroes. Perhaps he can reawaken the spirit of Timoleon in Sicily.

Through his alter ego Wordsworth's persona briefly allows himself the first attenuated confirmation of his own ultimate mission since his crisis annihilated all designs for a *paideia*. He is able to believe again in his own vocation since he has freed himself from self-division and self-torment. Through participating in his double's pilgrimage to Sicily, he has resolved the paralysis of his spirit that threatened to block his development into poet-prophet. He has regained momentum in his life and in his art, has cast off (in Schiller's terms) the state of determinacy (*Bestimmung*) and regained a measure of indeterminacy (*Bestimmbarkeit*) (*NA* 20:416). His pastoral interlude has revived in him the human ideal embodied in the infinite potentiality of the child, an ideal that he can again project as a future goal. And he has regained for himself the kind of equilibrium that Schiller saw as characteristic of aesthetic excellence. Experiencing such aesthetic moments leaves us "master in equal degree of our passive and of our active powers, and we shall with equal ease turn to seriousness or to play, to repose or to movement, . . . to the discursions of abstract thought or to the direct contemplation of phenomena" (*AL* 22.2). Through the meditation on Coleridge's persona, Wordsworth can communicate the kind of "lofty equanimity and freedom of the spirit, combined with power and vigour" that forms the "mood in which a genuine work of art should release us" (22.3).

As he resumes his autobiographical journey after his long address to Coleridge, Wordsworth doubles back to recount his hours of agony and regained integrity (11:42–120). Apparently only such "backward wanderings along thorny ways" (1850, 14:138) can purge him of the paralyzing poison of despair. His dramatic scenario for Coleridge's triumphant ascent from dejection to godlike creativity marks a turning point in his own struggle to invigorate his imagination and to clarify his task as poet-teacher. The cathartic identification with Coleridge leads him to discover the path to his own visionary mountaintop. He is himself refreshed by the supreme consolation he offers Coleridge:

> And thou, O Friend! wilt be refresh'd. There is
> One great Society alone on earth,
> The noble Living and the noble Dead:
> Thy consolation shall be there, and Time
> And Nature shall before thee spread in store
> Imperishable thoughts. . . .
>   (10:968–73)

Coleridge echoed this Platonic consolation as he returned the compliment, placing Wordsworth in the timeless pantheon of the wise and the noble:

>   The truly great
> Have all one age, and from one visible space
> Shed influence! They, both in power and act,
> Are permanent, and Time is not with them,
> Save as it worketh for them, they in it.
>   (*To William Wordsworth* 50–54)

Thus both Coleridge and Wordsworth replace revolutionary hopes for an egalitarian society by the elitist fraternity of "One great Society" that enshrines in its timeless archives the master-pieces—which presumably include *The Prelude*—of the "truly great." The contrast between the two conceptions of a great society is vividly brought home by Wordsworth's placing both the temporal and the atemporal versions in Book 10 of *The Prelude* (1805). His annunciation of the political reality of a new society occurs in the book's best-known passage, in which Wordsworth recaptures his enthusiasm for the French Revolution: "Bliss was it in that dawn to be alive, / But to be young was very heaven" (10:693–94). And he ends his paean to revolutionary change by rejoicing that its work was going forward

Not in Utopia, subterraneous Fields,
Or some secreted Island, Heaven knows where,
But in the very world which is the world
Of all of us, the place in which, in the end,
We find our happiness, or not at all.
(10:724–28)

Wordsworth, however, revokes this powerful affirmation of his past revolutionary expectations in order to invoke his present faith in the spiritual polity of the chosen few: "There is / One great Society alone on earth, / The noble Living and the noble Dead" (10:968–70). He even restates this conviction in the political context of his tract on *The Convention of Cintra* (1809): "There is a spiritual community binding together the living and the dead; the good, the brave, and the wise of all ages" (*Prose* 1:339).

What has happened to the "world / Of all of us" where "in the end, / We find our happiness, or not at all"? Its circumference has contracted to encompass only the realm of nature, the domain of "a pastoral Tract" (8:325) which ennobles the shepherd and consecrates "his service" as the work of a "Freeman" (8:386–87). The larger world embodies for Wordsworth only the harsh lesson that "men return to servitude as fast / As the tide ebbs" (13:433–34), especially to the servitude of self-delusion. Yet Wordsworth holds fast to his belief in man's divine spark and commits himself to the poet's redemptive task of nourishing the creative "under-presence" that constitutes the individual's power to restore Eden within his soul. He believes with Coleridge that works of art "excite the minds of the spectators to active thought, to a striving after ideal excellence. The soul is not stupefied into mere sensations, by a worthless sympathy with our own ordinary sufferings" (*BL* 2:184–85). In the final words of *The Prelude* Wordsworth speaks with one prophetic voice for both poets, "united helpers" working toward a day of "firmer trust," "joint labourers" working for their fellowmen's restoration:

> Prophets of Nature, we to them will speak
> A lasting inspiration, sanctified
> By reason and by truth. . . .
>   (13:442–44)

Although his long epilogue on Coleridge in Sicily prepares for this ultimate testament of Wordsworth's creed, Book 10 concludes not with a strenuous ascent to prophetic vision but with a relaxing turn to pastoral holiday. The narrator envisions Coleridge wandering among ruined yet inspiring temples, "served by sapient priests, and choirs / Of virgins crowned with roses" (1850, 11:460–61). Playfully he imagines Coleridge himself performing priestly rites on top of Mount Etna:[8]

> . . . by pastoral Arethuse
> Or if that Fountain be in truth no more,
> Then near some other Spring, which by the name
> Thou gratulatest, willingly deceived,
> Shalt linger as a gladsome Votary. . . .
>   (10:1034–38)

His creative power revived, Wordsworth's Coleridge can afford to dally with false surmise, to be "willingly deceived," when, through his joyful act of naming, he hallows an ordinary Sicilian spring as the returned Arethusa. He thus becomes a *genius loci* inspiriting the landscape, just as Milton's Lycidas becomes the "genius of the shore." And just as Wordsworth foretold:

> . . . the Place itself [shall]
> Be conscious of thy presence, and the dull
> Sirocco air of its degeneracy
> Turn as thou mov'st into a healthful breeze
> To cherish and invigorate thy frame.
>   (10:973–77)

Coleridge becomes a restorative presence, a "gladsome Votary" where he once was a dispirited exile. The narrator's parting glimpse of Coleridge as a happy wanderer suggests that he is setting out for "fresh Woods, and Pastures new."

From this final perspective Coleridge emerges not only as Wordsworth's personal muse, a humanly fallible attendant spirit, but also as the type of redeemable auditor or reader who can rise to the level of "joint-labourer" in the task of bringing about humanity's renovation. That pastoral *topoi* provide a fitting medium for communicating this ideal is demonstrated by a rejected variant of the Arethusa passage of Book 10. In the process of redrafting his 1805 text, Wordsworth elaborated on the curative powers of his Theocritean allusions. Such images, he claims, teach our souls

> to flow, though by a rough
> And bitter world surrounded, as, unting'd
> With aught injurious to her native freshness,
> Flowed Arethusa under briny waves
> Of the Sicilian Sea.
> (*Apparatus criticus*, p. 426)

Thus Wordsworth appropriates the classical myth of the chaste nymph who fled from the river god Alpheus. Her reemergence in Sicily as a hallowed spring had become a cliché in pastoral verse. Wordsworth invests the Arethusa myth with fresh import, making it symbolize the "fructifying virtue" (*1799 Prelude* 1:290) of his pastoral prophecy, which, even if driven underground by bitter adversity, can vivify those readers who have kept undefiled their "native freshness" in the recesses of their souls. Arethusa becomes a synecdochic trope for the poet's pastoral resources, expressing an affirmative answer to his earlier question addressed to Sicily: "is there not some nook of thine, / From the first playtime of the infant earth / Kept sacred to restorative delight?" (10:1004–6). Without minimizing the power of the ruthless world to corrupt the native freshness of the human soul, Wordsworth has come to believe that the poet, speaking in pastoral symbols, can teach

How Life pervades the undecaying mind,
How the immortal Soul with God-like power
Informs, creates, and thaws the deepest sleep
That time can lay upon her. . . .
   (4:155–58)

In the final book of *The Prelude*, Wordsworth once more
has recourse to the synecdoche of the underground river—not
naming Arethusa this time—to figure the all-pervading, renew-
ing, and integrative current of the imagination, which is "but
another name for absolute strength / And clearest insight, am-
plitude of mind, / And reason in her most exalted mood" (13:
168–70). Having gained confidence in the redemptive current
of the imagination through his Theocritean interlude, Words-
worth can retrospectively see that the same current has sus-
tained him through all the vicissitudes of his poetic voyage,
through the dark caverns and bright surfaces of his inner
world. He can triumphantly claim that the imagination has
been, for himself and for his fellow pilgrim, the "moving soul"
of their "long labour" (13:171–72):

                    we have traced the stream
     From darkness, and the very place of birth
     In its blind cavern, whence is faintly heard
     The sound of waters; follow'd it to light
     And open day, accompanied its course
     Among the ways of Nature, afterwards
     Lost sight of it, bewilder'd and engulph'd,
     Then given it greeting, as it rose once more
     With strength, reflecting in its solemn breast
     The works of man and face of human life. . . .
        (13:172–81)

THE "GOLDEN THEME" OF APOLLO:
A PASTORAL INTERLUDE IN *HYPERION*

In October 1818, the month in
which he began *Hyperion*, Keats described the centrifugal en-
ergy of his imagination: "I feel more and more every day, as my
imagination strengthens, that I do not live in this world alone
but in a thousand worlds. . . . According to my state of mind I
am with Achilles shouting in the Trenches or with Theocritus in
the Vales of Sicily" (*Letters* 1:403–4). Such shifting moods called
up the overlapping worlds of Homer, Theocritus, Milton, and
Wordsworth as Keats pursued his precarious excursion into
heroic enterprise. Like Wordsworth's dark vision of man's fall
into psychological dissociation and political alienation during
the aftermath of the French Revolution, Keats's vision of the
Titans' fall into sterile divisiveness contains a pastoral interlude.
That interlude serves as a focus in which the divergent rays of
universal questions about man's fall and redemption and his-
torical questions about social progress converge, as in Words-
worth's interlude, toward the single issue of the poet's identity
and vocation. In the years since Wordsworth had begun *The
Prelude* in 1798, the role of exemplary art in the exploitative
realm of industrial England had become increasingly problem-
atical. Keats's epic rejects as its social sphere an England dedi-
cated to the religion of money whose God, as Blake pointed out,
"Creates nothing but what can be Touched & Weighed & Taxed

& Measured" (659), and instead situates its heroic enterprise in the mental space of Greek myth.

The protagonist of Keats's pastoral interlude in *Hyperion* is Apollo. His pastoral microcosm, the island of Delos, is a lush *locus amoenus*, a type of earthly paradise. According to the tradition that derives from the Homeric hymns to Apollo, Delos was a rocky, barren island until Apollo, nursed on nectar and ambrosia, burst his golden swaddling bands. As his foot touched the earth, the desolate island was transformed into a blossoming paradise. This paradisal Delos is the scene to which Keats's *Hyperion* shifts rather abruptly at the beginning of Book 3, but not without earlier intimations of the emerging "golden theme" (3:28). In the council scene of the fallen Titans in Book 2—a scene modeled on Milton's council in hell in Book 2 of *Paradise Lost*—Keats interrupts the increasingly vituperative debate with the introduction of a totally incongruent voice. From impotent Saturn undergoing a cosmic identity crisis, to Stoic Oceanus advocating hopeful acquiescence in the advent of a superior race, to the wrathful Encedalus preaching all-out war, the Titans are trapped in inner strife, wounded pride, frustrated anger, fraternal conflict, and prevaricating argument. Their setting, a secluded den "where no insulting light / Could glimmer on their tears" (2:5–6), resembles the Cave of Quietude in *Endymion*, "Where pale becomes the bloom / Of health by due; where silence dreariest / Is most articulate; where hopes infest" (4:538–40). The Titans' dark retreat fittingly mirrors their festering souls.

In this council of despair only Clymene is capable of visions of a bright paradise. She marches to the music of a different drummer. And she speaks timorously after Oceanus's presentation of the "eternal law / That first in beauty should be first in might" (2:228–29), a consolation for their fall that he asks the assembled Titans to receive as the truth and their balm (243). The Titans receive it in silence:

> none answered for a space,
> Save one whom none regarded, Clymene;

And yet she answered not. . . .
(2:247–49)

Clymene's non-answer does not address the subject of the de-
bate. She alone is not locked into the linear thinking of gen-
erational strife. She is as unconcerned with pride as she is
unregarded; she is indifferent to political, military, or philo-
sophical strategies to alleviate the Titans' defeat. The other
Titans speak from the perspective of a painful present over-
shadowed by an idealized past, and they speak as deposed pow-
ers. Clymene, on the other hand, has had no power to lose.
Thus her speech, her non-answer, differs rhetorically from the
speeches of her male brethren. Theirs are designed to arouse,
exhort, persuade; hers is uncalculatedly, unselfishly spoken to
recall and transmit images, impressions, feelings of joy and
sorrow. "I am here the simplest voice" (2:252), she says self-
deprecatingly, "Yet let me tell my sorrow, let me tell / Of what I
heard, and how it made me weep, / And know that we had
parted from all hope" (259–61). She offers herself as a me-
dium, not as a mentor, leaving it up to her combative fellow
Titans to interpret her observations and to react to her impres-
sions. They receive them as foolish "baby-words" (314).

Clymene's timid narrative begins by limning the setting of her
experience, which signals a shift to pastoral discourse. She wan-
dered away from the "covert drear" (2:33) which harbored the
gloomy Titans and "stood upon a shore, a pleasant shore, /
Where a sweet clime was breathèd from a land / Of fragrance,
quietness, and trees and flowers" (2:262–64). Having physically
and psychologically distanced herself from the Titans' cave of
despair, her soul is open to a different climate and receives
a breath of paradise. Significantly, the blissful fragrance and
sweet tranquility that move her originate not from the pleasant
shore on which she has found a green refuge, but from an
unseen pleasance across the water. The breath of spring, with
its promise of "soft delicious warmth" (2:266) and joyful re-
newal, contrasts sharply with her inward grief, her empathy
with the fallen Titans' wintry gloom. To express this experience

of dissonance, she takes a "mouthèd shell," murmurs into it, and makes a melody (270–71). Although she describes herself as uninspired and singing "with poor skill" (273), she receives an inspired response. Her song of discord, cast upon the breeze through the "dull shell's echo" (274), is echoed back to her mysteriously as a song of concord.

Keats thus intriguingly reinterprets the traditional pastoral *topos* of a song being sung to nature, which evokes an echoing response. Clymene, however, is unaware of this pastoral tradition when she spontaneously murmurs her melody into a shell, singing simply to relieve her discomfort and anxiety. Her song's unexpected echo does not resound her melody but superimposes its own enchanting counterpoint, carried by the shifting wind from the "bowery strand" of an "island of the sea" (2:274–75) opposite her shore. Like the strings of a windharp set in motion by the breeze, Clymene's soul vibrates with "that new blissful golden melody" (2:280).[1] She is overcome by joy and grief at once: "A living death" was in each strain of "rapturous hurried notes" (2:281–82). This inscrutable melody recalls Coleridge's description of the music produced by the "desultory breeze" sweeping across the windharp:

> And now, its strings
> Boldlier swept, the long sequacious notes
> Over delicious surges sink and rise,
> Such a soft floating witchery of sound
> As twilight Elfins make, when they at eve
> Voyage on gentle gales from Fairy-Land. . . .
> (*Eolian Harp* 17–22)

In fact this music, which for Coleridge becomes emblematic of cosmic harmony, can just as fittingly be emblematic of Apollonian music, the music of the god of order, light, and harmony: "A light in sound, a sound-like power in light, / Rhythm in all thought, and joyance every where" (28–29)—a world so animated that "the breeze warbles, and the mute still air / Is Music slumbering on her instrument" (32–33).

The Apollonian music in Keats's *Hyperion* contains an admixture of Dionysian agony not present in Coleridge's eolian melody celebrating the "one Life within us and abroad" (26). In Apollo's melody,

> A living death was in each gush of sounds,
> Each family of rapturous hurried notes,
> That fell, one after one, yet all at once,
> Like pearl beads dropping sudden from their string;
> And then another, then another strain,
> Each like a dove leaving its olive perch,
> With music winged instead of silent plumes,
> To hover round my head, and made me sick
> Of joy and grief at once.
>   (2:281–89)

Hearing this music, Clymene is torn between joyful promise of a new world and fearful grief over the passing of the old order. She flees this Apollonian-Dionysian witchery of sound, only to be pursued by a voice "sweeter than all tune," crying "Apollo! Young Apollo! / The morning-bright Apollo!" (292–94).

Narrating this mysterious experience, speaking as the "simplest voice" (252) among her brethren, her words flowing on like a "timorous brook" (300), Clymene suggests a naive narrator addressing jaded, defeated, sentimental listeners. Although she empathizes with their misery, she speaks a language that comes close to nature's. She alone is attuned to the birth of "new tuneful wonder" (3:67). She feels intimations of an Apollonian concord that transcends the discordant emotions that move her. The fact that Clymene's is a purely passive sensibility suggests that the way out of the deposed Titans' predicament lies not in charting a rationally determined course. Instead, her sensibility suggests the way of intuitive indirection that Schiller mapped in his *Aesthetic Letters*. Schiller argued that at times man needs to take a step back from one-sided, goal-directed activity and return momentarily to a kind of childlike potentiality, to pure determinability (*Bestimmbarkeit*), before making the transition to a different goal-directed activity (*AL* 20.3–4).[2] To initiate such a movement backward toward open-minded indeterminacy seems to be Clymene's role among the fallen Titans, who are suffering the inexorable ravages of time. Clymene also suffers, but passively, enduring without struggling to break out of the web of entanglement. Her characteristic way of being-in-the-world is a state of reverie, much like that explored by Rousseau. Poggioli calls Rousseau's reverie "a state of passive introspection, by which the pastoral psyche reflects its shadow in nature's mirror, fondly and blissfully losing its being within the image of itself" (22). In such a state of reverie Clymene's pastoral psyche reflected its shadow in nature's mirror and found its shadowy image forming itself into the image of Apollo.

Keats's Apollo is a specialist in reverie. In fact, Book 3 of *Hyperion*, the book centered on Apollo, might fittingly be entitled *Les rêveries du promeneur solitaire*. Keats's Apollo is decidedly not the mighty Python-slayer whom Byron celebrated in *Childe Harold*:

> the Lord of the unerring bow,
> The God of life, and poesy, and light,—
> The Sun in human limbs array'd, and brow
> All radiant from his triumph in the fight;
> The shaft hath just been shot—the arrow bright
> With an immortal's vengeance; in his eye
> And nostril beautiful disdain, and might
> And majesty, flash their full lightnings by,
> Developing in that one glance the Deity.
> (4.161:1–9)

Instead of this triumphant god of light and poetry, Keats introduces the reader to a maudlin Byronic hero like Harold— "He of the breast which fain no more would feel, / Wrung with the wounds which kill not but ne'er heal" (3.8:4). Desolate and dispirited, Apollo wanders about the groves of olives and poplars, palms and beeches of his island paradise. Thus Keats fails to fulfill the wonderful expectations set in motion by Clymene's narrative of discovering the golden melodist blissfully embowered on Delos, the "chief isle of the embowered Cyclades" (3:23) —the central jewel within the circle of Aegean islands.[3] The god of music is out of tune with his Edenic recess, where he is privileged to taste creation's plenitude. Not Apollo but only the narrator luxuriates in the sensuous sounds and sights of this island pleasance where the thrush's song succeeds the nightingale's melody. Throughout the island,

> There was no covert, no retirèd cave,
> Unhaunted by the murmurous noise of waves,
> Though scarcely heard in many a green recess.
> (3:39–41)

Self-absorbed, unresponsive to this paradise's tuneful harmony, Apollo wanders "Full ankle-deep in lilies of the vale" (3:35), a solitary, melancholy youth who resembles Byron's lovesick Juan:

> Young Juan wander'd by the glassy brooks,
>   Thinking unutterable things; he threw
> Himself at length within the leafy nooks
>   Where the wild branch of the cork forest grew. . . .
>   . . . .
> He pored upon the leaves, and on the flowers,
>   And heard a voice in all the winds; and then
> He thought of wood-nymphs and immortal bowers,
>   And how the goddesses came down to men. . . .
>   (*Don Juan* 1.90:1–4; 94:1–4)

Unlike Juan, the youthful Apollo is suffering not from unrecognized pangs of illicit love but from an undefined *Weltschmerz*. He is not so much the Apollonian god of poetry as the Romantic *poète maudit*, feeling "cursed and thwarted," as he tells Mnemosyne, the mother of the muses:

I strive to search wherefore I am so sad,
Until a melancholy numbs my limbs;
And then upon the grass I sit and moan,
Like one who once had wings. Oh, why should I
Feel cursed and thwarted, when the liegeless air
Yields to my step aspirant? Why should I
Spurn the green turf as hateful to my feet?
   (3:88–94)

We find it difficult to recognize in this weary pilgrim weeping amidst his "grassy solitudes" (3:57) the prophetic author of the blissful golden melody that enchanted Clymene. And why should the reader not be puzzled, when even the all-seeing Mnemosyne, the sponsor of his musical gift, is baffled by his autumnal gloom in springtime Eden? "Is't not strange," she asks, "that thou shouldst weep, so gifted?" (3:67–68). She finds it perplexing that, although she has been his attendant Genius since his infancy, he has not matured to "bend that bow heroic" (3:75) as she expected, but instead he moans and raves about the Edenic grove. His total absorption in a misery he does not understand seems peculiarly ironic in Apollo, to whom two precepts were attributed that were inscribed on his temple in Delphi: "Know thyself" and "Nothing in excess." Keats's young Apollo is not on the road to Delphi. His poetic temperament exemplifies that tendency toward the elegiac *Empfindungsweise* which Schiller insisted "must ultimately unnerve the character and submerge it in total passivity, from which nothing real can emerge, either for the external or internal life" (*NA* 20: 460). Like the "nerveless," "listless," "realmless" Saturn (*Hyperion* 1:19–20), the impotent Apollo wonders,

                 Where is power?
Whose hand, whose essence, what Divinity,
Makes this alarum in the elements,
While I here idle listen on the shores
In fearless yet in aching ignorance?
   (3:103–7)

Nothing short of an apotheosis can enable Apollo to grasp the reality of cosmic upheavals—"dire events, rebellions, / Majesties, sovran voices, agonies / Creations and destroyings" (3:114–16). Trying to engorge godlike knowledge of cosmic agonies, Apollo experiences in himself mortal agony, undergoes a *sparagmos*, and is reborn as a god:

> Soon wild commotions shook him, and made flush
> All the immortal fairness of his limbs—
> Most like the struggle at the gate of death;
> Or liker still to one who should take leave
> Of pale immortal death, and with a pang
> As hot as death's is chill, with fierce convulse
> Die into life.
>   (3:124–30)

Critics have generally seen this whole episode as the weakest section of *Hyperion*, as Keats's lapsing into the sentimental mode of *Endymion* after achieving an austere, heroic tone in the first two books. According to Bate, for example, the conception of Apollo is maudlin and the depiction of his deification "sways dangerously on the brink of the grotesque. The all-important evolution from 'aching ignorance' to knowledge is being attained by something close to hypnotism . . ." (*Keats* 404–5). While this criticism is certainly just, Van Ghent's comments on the nature of Keats's Apollo are far more illuminating. "Keats called this character Apollo," she writes, "but the emotional attributes and the activities of the character—his craving to enter into everything that is, his undergoing ritual death and rebirth—are those of the mystery god Dionysos and all Keats's heroes." She comments further that it is the mission of this Dionysian protagonist "to *become* Apollo by rebirth" (194). That is to say: the poet whose frantic suffering "venoms all his days" (*Fall of Hyperion* 1:175), who is a "fever" of himself (1:169), must transform himself into the poet of Apollonian calm, order, and foresight. Keats himself, according to Van Ghent, is here dramatizing the two poles of his psyche. He wanted to be "not the

Dionysian poet writing out of the *dynamis* of the instinctive libido, out of dreams and images welling from the unconscious, but the Apolline poet writing the 'ordered paean' under a 'sober Muse.'" She concludes that Keats "drew on the fevered Dionysian temperament for the personality of his heroes, but he had them seek, as the goal of their quest, the immortal calm and 'identity' of Apollo" (195).

What role do pastoral *topoi* and values play in this Keatsian quest? We have already seen that in *Hyperion* Keats reinterprets the traditional pastoral *topos* of the *locus amoenus* as the island setting that is inharmonious rather than harmonious with his Dionysian Apollo's sensibility. This Dionysian dreamer is also out of tune with the annunciation heard by Clymene of the "morning-bright Apollo!" (2:294). Even though Keats offers only the barest hints of what ideal this new dawn, this "morning-bright" poet heralds, these hints suggest a pastoral model: they allude to Virgil's famous *Fourth Eclogue* with its celebration of a new birth that will inaugurate a golden age, a new *Saturnia regna*, and enthrone Apollo:

> The last great age the Sibyl's song foretold
> Rolls round: the centuries are born anew!
> The Maid returns, old Saturn's reign returns,
> Offspring of heaven, a hero's race descends.
> Now as the babe is born, with whom iron men
> Shall cease, and golden men spread through the world,
> Bless him, chaste goddess: now your Apollo reigns.
> (4–10, Alpers's translation)

Here is surely the inspiration for Keats's rejoicing that "Apollo is once more the golden theme" (3:28) as he implores his Muse to leave the Titans "to their woes" (3:3) and to cease singing "such tumults dire" (4); he asks her instead to "touch piously the Delphic harp" (10) and sing of the "father of all verse" (13). While Keats does not call on the Sicilian Muse whom Virgil invokes, he calls on another pastoral Muse, the *genius loci* of Delos, to rejoice in his Apollonian theme:

> Rejoice, O Delos, with thine olives green,
> And poplars, and lawn-shading palms, and beech
> In which the zephyr breathes the loudest song,
> And hazels thick, dark-stemmed beneath the shade.
> Apollo is once more the golden theme.
>
> (3:24–28)

Yet it is ironic that, whereas Virgil invokes the Sicilian Muse to sing of higher matter ("Sicelides Musae, paulo maiora canamus"), Keats calls on his pastoral Muse to modulate from high epic narrative to elegiac introspection, "antheming a lonely grief" (3:6).

As Keats abandons epic objectivity for elegiac pastoral subjectivity, the poem gains in intensity and import. The shift in style brings with it a change in the implied auditor's role. In the first two books, the auditor remains an uninvolved spectator, watching the static tableau of the unsceptered Saturn confronting the other despondent Titans. He may feel fleeting moments of mild pity, but he remains largely unmoved by the gigantic static spectacle. Even the potential hero, the space voyager Hyperion, elicits little sympathy or admiration, since his action is as ineffectual and fragmentary as Saturn's inertia. Hyperion offers no glimpse of a new ethos that might lead to a restored *Saturnia regna*. Such a vista opens up briefly as Keats displaces his frozen epic with a more fluid pastoral interlude. Although the auditor may be disillusioned to discover that the promised golden theme turns out to be a solipsistic dream, he comes to empathize with the young poet-genius who is born into an unfavorable time. Apollo registers the upheavals of his age, though he has been insulated against them by being embowered on his island. How is he going to achieve what Saturn could not do, to "oppose to each malignant hour / Ethereal presence" (1:339–40)?

The problem for Keats is to show the young genius's capacity to generate a new ethos of wholeness from within himself when external reality offers him only signs of discord and disintegration.[4] How is Apollo to become a culture bearer who can be an exemplary model for his time or times to come? Mnemosyne reminds him of his special gift, since he has apparently forgotten that he is Apollo:

> 'Thou hast dreamed of me; and awaking up
> Didst find a lyre all golden by thy side,
> Whose strings touched by thy fingers all the vast
> Unwearied ear of the whole universe
> Listened in pain and pleasure at the birth
> Of such new tuneful wonder.'
>   (3:62–67)

That this "new tuneful wonder" was to constitute a Keatsian evangel is clear from Mnemosyne's further reminder to Apollo that she is an "ancient Power"

> Who hath forsaken old and sacred thrones
> For prophecies of thee, and for the sake
> Of loveliness new born.
>   (3:76–79)

Here Keats assimilates the Virgilian prophecy of a new golden age brought about by a new birth, the prophecy that Poggioli remarkably describes as the "instauration of the new order . . . conceived as the restauration of the happy state that mankind enjoyed under the rule of Saturn" (112). Keats's fallen Saturn impotently seeks to prophesy such regeneration: "Saturn must be King. / Yes, there must be a golden victory" (*Hyperion* 1:125–26). And Saturn elaborates on this fantasy: "there shall be / Beautiful things made new, for the surprise / Of the sky-children" (131–33). Although he has lost his "strong identity" (114) and is but a hollow shell of his once powerful self, Saturn deludes himself into believing that he can be the creator of a new world:

> 'But cannot I create?
> Cannot I form? Cannot I fashion forth

Another world, another universe,
To overbear and crumble this to naught?'
(1:141–44)

Clearly his vision of a newly created Saturnian realm is the
result of enervating nostalgia rather than of energizing commit-
ment to the future, but it nevertheless serves to anticipate the
positive ideal to be fashioned by Apollo. Saturn helps to gener-
ate the poem's vision of a new golden age to be inaugurated
when Apollo's vivifying word will reanimate the petrified world
of the Titans. His "new blissful golden melody" (2:280) will
herald a new age of peace and concord, just as Virgil's *Fourth
Eclogue* predicted a new Saturnian age to be ushered in by the
birth of a child who will become a hero. Putnam's comments on
the child's role in Virgil's eclogue also throw light on Keats's
conception of his poet-hero. "Though the boy's role may at first
appear unusual," Putnam writes, "the result is thoroughly 'pas-
toral': it is merely the idea of peace expanded to touch all
humanity. Nevertheless, Virgil assumes the imminence of fur-
ther war wherein *virtus*, that manly courage which distinguishes
the true warrior and raises a mortal to the level of the divine,
will bring about the peaceable reign of Apollo and the boy.
Hence, as if to summarize the broadened dialectic of bucolic
song in *Eclogue* 4, Virgil has reiterated his wish that, through his
magic *carmen*, woods and consul could be reconciled" (145).
Putnam concludes that "the most novel intellectual idea thus far
advanced by Virgil is not so much the rejuvenation of the ages,
happy dream though that be, but the combination of the golden
and heroic eras," reconciling "'woods' and consul, pastoral *otium*
and heroic *virtus*, in an ideal amalgam" (145).

Such an ideal amalgam of the contemplative and active life
must surely have appealed to Keats, just as it appealed to Shel-
ley and to Wordsworth. All three, however, explicitly locate the
heroic *virtus* exclusively in the poet's visionary and verbal power
to renew a truly human community. Shelley strikes the note of
Virgilian prophecy to embody his goal of a regained paradise in
the final chorus of *Hellas*:

The world's great age begins anew,
  The golden years return,
The earth doth like a snake renew
  Her winter weeds outworn. . . .
    (1060–63)

Another Athens shall arise,
  And to remoter time
Bequeath, like sunset to the skies,
  The splendour of its prime. . . .
    (1084–87)

After his further affirmation of the return of Saturn and Love, concluding his prophecy of the new age of happiness (for which he cites the authority of Isaiah and Virgil), Shelley modulates to a bitter final speculation that displaces the golden-age myth:

O cease! must hate and death return?
  Cease! must men kill and die?
Cease! drain not to its dregs the urn
  Of bitter prophecy.
The world is weary of the past,
O might it die or rest at last!
    (1096–1101)

Shelley's lines show how problematical the Romantic poet found the prophetic vision of a happier world, if it was to be uttered as inevitable futurity rather than as conditional subjunctive. Shelley explains his own dilemma in a note to the final chorus: "Prophecies of wars . . . may safely be made by poet or prophet in any age, but to anticipate however darkly a period of regeneration and happiness is a more hazardous exercise of the faculty which bards possess or feign" (*Oxford Shelley* 479). Messianic eclogues splinter into fragments. Keats could readily envision a state of disintegration, disunion, or demoralization among the Titans, but he found it a hazardous exercise indeed to chart the path to regeneration. His myth pointed the way toward making Apollo into the redemptive poet-prophet who can bring about the "blissful hour" so confidently announced by Wordsworth in his *Prospectus* for *The Recluse*, when man's paradisal renewal could be celebrated as a "simple produce of the common day" (*Prose* 3:7). But Keats's experience undermined his myth. "Even a Proverb is no proverb to you till your Life has illustrated it" (*Letters* 2:81), he wrote, and he no doubt believed the same about myths. In March 1819, shortly before he abandoned *Hyperion*, he wrote that "there is an ellectric fire in human nature tending to purify—so that among these human creature[s] there is continully some birth of new heroism." But he added immediately, "The pity is that we must wonder at it: as we should at finding a pearl in rubbish" (*Letters* 2:80). His speculations about the birth of new heroism turn to Socrates and Jesus, as he found himself "straining at particles of light in the midst of a great darkness" (2:80). In due course his speculations crystallized into the question of redemption: "The most interesting question that can come before us is, How far by the persevering endeavours of a seldom appearing Socrates Mankind may be made happy. . . . But in truth I do not at all believe in this sort of perfectibility—the nature of the world will not admit of it" (2:101).

Keats may have been more skeptical about the possibility of human perfectibility than Schiller was, but he shared Schiller's imperative to project an Elysian goal rather than retreat to an Arcadian ideal. And his Apollo fragment suggests intriguing similarities to Schiller's projected idyll on the subject of Hercules. Both schemes deal with the transition from man to god. Both poets ground their heroes in the human world while they also attain immortal knowledge and serenity. And both poets confront the crucial problem of how to give human individuality to their mythic figures while also universalizing them as mortal beings. Neither poet, moreover, in the completed section of his fragment successfully counters his hero's elegiac mode of seeing reality as a world of pain and sorrow, without transcending human limits. Schiller's speaker in the *Reich der Schatten* typically struggles to free himself from earthly suffering by leaving behind the temporal world of the senses while aspiring to the atemporal realm of pure thought.[5] Keats's Apollo similarly seeks to free himself from the confines of his anguished existence by gleaning deific "Knowledge enormous" from Mnemosyne's silent face (3:113). And yet neither Schiller nor Keats solves the problem of how to coalesce godlike wisdom with human suffering in his hero, or how to unite idyllic and elegiac moods in his pastoral perspective.

Given this impasse, it is surprising to find Keats making a fresh start at recasting his *Hyperion* instead of abandoning it for good. Possibly his Apollo episode had shown Keats the end toward which he wanted his hero to evolve without his being able to devise either the specific means toward the end—an all-knowing god—or the authentic actions for his deified Apollo. What convincing experiences could transform the fevered Dionysian sufferer into an Apollonian "foreseeing God"? Despite his stated intentions, Keats's Apollo on Delos remained an alter ego of Endymion, instead of emerging as his antitype. Endymion "being mortal," Keats had explained to Haydon in 1818, "is led on, like Buonaparte, by circumstance; whereas the Apollo in Hyperion being a fore-seeing God will shape his actions like one" (*Letters* 1:207). It is fair to say that, in writing *Hyperion*, Keats was himself led on by unforeseen circumstances, whereas in his *Fall of Hyperion* he tried through his frame narrative to give the poem a clearer direction. His pastoral interlude of *Hyperion* seems to have led him to redefine the central issue of his poem. The myth of the Titanomachy and the possibility of the restoration of a Saturnian age become the cosmic hornbook through which the poet will presumably discover his proper sphere of action. But can he also thus discover his identity? Can he discover how to combine the strengths of Dante and Shakespeare, Milton and Wordsworth, and, most basically, Dionysus and Apollo?

In his new start Keats seeks a fresh way to reconcile pastoral *otium* and heroic *virtus*, as well as Dionysian suffering and Apollonian tranquility. He presents his narrative as a dream vision in which the protagonist is no longer a mythological figure but

an autobiographical persona. The poet's time-bound conscious-
ness becomes interwoven with timeless events. His own feelings
and reactions to the mythological events are now more fore-
grounded than the events themselves.[6] Revealingly, Keats pre-
faces the first scene of the *Fall of Hyperion*, which shows the poet
in an earthly paradise, by an induction that comments on the
relation of dreams to poetry. Dreams by themselves—including
the dreams of religious enthusiasts—can enchant us with visions
of paradise, but they are merely ephemeral apparitions. Only
poetry, as Shelley says, "arrests the vanishing apparitions which
haunt the interlunations of life, and veiling them, or in lan-
guage or in form, sends them forth among mankind. . . . Poetry
redeems from decay the visitations of the divinity in Man"
(*Critical Prose* 32). By telling his dreams, the poet arrests and
objectifies them, gives them an aesthetic form that makes their
felt meaning accessible to others. Moreover, by his "fine spell
of words" (*Fall* 1:9) the poet can free himself from the dark
dreams and imaginings whose poisonous charm paralyzes Sat-
urn. The poet can counteract the "sable charm / And dumb
enchantment" (1:10–11) by the more powerful charm of words.
Instead of submitting to a savage god within, he becomes a
godlike artificer, a Prospero, who uses white magic to order the
forces of darkness. Yet, having made this charming claim for
the superiority of the poet's dreams over those of ordinary
enthusiasts, Keats leaves it an open question "Whether the
dream now purposed to rehearse / Be poet's or fanatic's" (1:16–
17). Does he after all doubt whether the poet's "fine spell of
words" can give permanence and substance to visions of human
life that originate in paradisal dreams? Is he alerting the reader
to both the potency and delusiveness of the poet's verbal elixir?
    The first act of poetic alchemy in the *Fall of Hyperion* places
the poet-dreamer in a timeless paradisal pleasance that recalls
Apollo's island paradise as well as Milton's Eden:

> Methought I stood where trees of every clime,
> Palm, myrtle, oak, and sycamore, and beech,
> With plantain, and spice-blossoms, made a screen—

In neighbourhood of fountains, by the noise
Soft-showering in my ears, and by the touch
Of scent, not far from roses.
   (1:19–24)

Within this larger sensuous pleasance, the dreamer discovers a
fragrant arbor, a secluded bower that forms a natural temple:

I saw an arbour with a drooping roof
Of trellis vines, and bells, and larger blooms,
Like floral censers swinging light in air. . . .
   (1:25–27)[7]

The anticipatory hint of religious ceremony in the simile "like
floral censers swinging light in air" is confirmed by the subse-
quent descriptive details of a mound of moss that forms a
natural altar, on which the dreamer discovers "a feast of sum-
mer fruits" that on closer inspection turns out to be the "refuse
of a meal / By angel tasted, or our Mother Eve" (29–31). This
refuse, the leftovers of offerings to the gods, is yet more plenti-
ful than the mythical cornucopia. And as if he were himself a
god or priest, the dreamer participates in the ritual feast. He
eats "deliciously" and drinks a "full draught" from a "cool vessel
of transparent juice" (40, 42). As he sinks into a "cloudy swoon"
among the remnants of the divine feast, "Like a Silenus on an
antique vase" (55–56), we seem to be once more confronting a
Dionysian poet in the guise of the autobiographic persona of
the dreamer. The scene recalls Apollo in his Dionysian convul-
sion, dying into life, as horrendous knowledge pours "into the
wild hollows" of his brain, as if he had drunk "some blithe
wine / Or bright elixir peerless" (*Hyperion* 3:117–19).
   It is worth noting that Keats offers this first dream sequence
with psychological verisimilitude, presenting the sensuous de-
tails of the dream fabric without commentary, allowing the im-
ages themselves to work on the reader's imagination without
bullying him, as he accused Wordsworth of doing, into accept-
ing his interpretation. "Every man has his speculations," Keats

wrote, "but every man does not brood and peacock over them till he makes a false coinage and deceives himself" (*Letters* 1:223). Keats's dream imposes no palpable design but invites the reader to enter his dream world and collaborate with the poet in completing the import of the sensuous scene.

This earthly paradise containing a natural shrine seems to signal the poet-dreamer's entrance into a process of initiation and transformation. It suggests the liminal state of rites of passage. The dreamer has detached himself from his ordinary, mundane way of life and has entered a deeper level of existence. By eating and drinking consecrated food and wine, he has participated in a symbolic death and rebirth. He stands at the threshold of a new life. He has in fact performed the kind of vital ritual that Victor Turner distinguishes from formal ceremony by its being a "transformative self-immolation of order as presently constituted, even sometimes a voluntary *sparagmos* or self-dismemberment of order, in the subjunctive depths of liminality" ("Social Dramas" 164). In the liminal phase of such ritual transformation, the "cognitive schemata that give sense and order to everyday life no longer apply but are, as it were, suspended—in ritual symbolism perhaps even shown as destroyed or dissolved. Gods and goddesses of destruction are adored primarily because they personify an essential phase in an irreversible transformative process" (165).

Keats himself recognized a liminal phase in his own development. "The imagination of a boy is healthy," he noted in his preface to *Endymion*, "and the mature imagination of a man is healthy; but there is a space of life between, in which the soul is in a ferment, the character undecided, the way of life uncertain" (*Poems* 119). A more intense entrance into such a "space of life between" is dramatized in the *Fall of Hyperion* by the dreamer's interval in the paradisal arbor, an interval that ends with his sinking into a timeless sleep ("How long I slumbered 'tis a chance to guess" [57]), a symbolic death of his mundane self. He awakens within a transformed landscape: the lush, flowery grove has turned into a stony, vast, "eternal domèd monument" (1:71), an unfathomable primeval sanctuary presided over by

Saturn's image. Keats here inverts the traditional pastoral *topos* of the magical transformation of a harsh landscape into a recreative pleasance, usually effected by the power of love. Thus, for example, Asia's "transforming presence" invests a desolate scene of exile with the "fair flowers and herbs," "sweet airs and sounds" of paradise as love triumphs over hate in Shelley's *Prometheus Unbound* (1:827–32). In a similar pastoral transformation, Faust's love for Helena magically changes a fortress into an Arcadian grove. By weaving the fine spell of words, Faust obliterates the past, reclaims for Helena the golden age, and offers her a bower of bliss:

> Nicht feste Burg soll dich umschreiben!
> Noch zirkt in ewiger Jugendkraft,
> Für uns zu wonnevollem Bleiben,
> Arkadien in Spartas Nachbarschaft.

> Gelockt, auf selgem Grund zu wohnen,
> Du flüchtetest ins heiterste Geschick!
> Zur Laube wandeln sich die Thronen:
> Arkadisch frei sei unser Glück![8]
>   (*Faust* 2.3:9566–9573)

Keats inverts this well-established tradition of pastoral transformation as his protagonist's ritualistic eating and drinking irreversibly propels him out of his timeless Edenic retreat into the consciousness of historical time and place, when his blissful bower metamorphoses into the stony vastness of Saturn's sanctuary.

Here the protagonist enters another stage of the liminal suspension between his previous way of life and his future vocation. If the first stage in the blissful arbor that drugged his senses was a state of soft pastoral *otium*, a state of being "blissfully havened both from joy and pain" (*Eve of St. Agnes* 240), this second stage in Saturn's august temple promises an initiation into a hard pastoral of strenuous discipline. Keats is now devoting himself—as he said of Milton—"rather to the Ardours than the pleasures of Song, solacing himself at intervals with cups of old wine" (Forman 5:292). For a second time, the protagonist undergoes a ritual death, a kind of Dionysian self-immolation. This second dream sequence not only focuses on further ritualistic actions—the dreamer's arduous ascent of "these immortal steps" (1:117)—but also introduces verbal dialogue, which was totally absent in the pastoral grove. Keats now creates a psychomachia in which the protagonist debates his fears and hopes about his vocation as poet. That is to say: I think Moneta can be seen as an inner voice that counters the poet's darker self by admonishing him to justify his poetic ambition, to clarify his role in the world by enlarging his perspective. One part of him is the dreamer who revels in the incense that spreads "Forgetfulness of everything but bliss" (1:103–4), but the other part of his psyche finds expression through empathizing with the "giant agony of the world" (1:157) and aspires to be a poet who is "a sage, / A humanist, physician to all men" (189–90).

In the debate between these two opposite selves emerge the poet's deep-seated doubts about his identity. "What am I then?" he asks Moneta. "Thou spakest of my tribe: / What tribe?" (1:193–94). He cannot accept her mocking answer:

> 'Art thou not of the dreamer tribe?
> The poet and the dreamer are distinct,
> Diverse, sheer opposite, antipodes.
> The one pours out a balm upon the world,
> The other vexes it.'
>   (1:198–202)

Like the deposed Saturn who has lost his "strong identity," his "real self" (*Hyperion* 1:114), like the Dionysian Apollo who feels "painful, vile oblivion" seal his eyes (3:87)—like them, Apollo's alter ego, the poet (the "I") of the *Fall of Hyperion* confronts what Coleridge calls the great questions that interest the best and noblest minds: "Where am I? What and for what am I? What are the duties, which arise out of the relations of my

Being to itself as heir of futurity, and to the World which is its present sphere of action and impression?" (*CN* 3:3593). Coleridge does not answer his existential questions but offers a simile: "I would compare the human Soul to a Ship's Crew cast on an unknown Island." After playing with this simile a bit, Coleridge comments further on this process of soul-making, in remarks that show remarkable affinity with Keats's speculations on the subject.[9] Coleridge writes: "The moment, when the Soul begins to be sufficiently self-conscious, to ask concerning itself, & its relations, is the first moment of its *intellectual* arrival into the World—its *Being*—enigmatic as it must seem—is posterior to its *Existence*—" (*CN* 3:3593).

Keats's protagonist in the *Fall of Hyperion* is sufficiently self-conscious to search for the answers to these crucial questions that will lead him, in Coleridge's terms, from Existence to Being, and from accepting oblivion to assuming the duties of his being-in-the-world as "heir of futurity." His process of initiation that began in the Edenic grove takes him to seeing through Moneta's eyes the cosmic events of the Titanomachy. Even though he is privileged to witness these events free of pain, he enters so intensely into Saturn's calamity that he finds the "load of this eternal quietude, / The unchanging gloom" unbearable and prays that death would take him "from the vale / And all its burthens" (*Fall* 1:390–91, 397–98). In the face of giant suffering, the poet has difficulty maintaining his distance and commanding an aesthetic response:

> Methought I heard some old man of the earth
> Bewailing earthly loss; nor could my eyes
> And ears act with that pleasant unison of sense
> Which marries sweet sound with the grace of form,
> And dolorous accent from a tragic harp
> With large-limbed visions.
>   (1:440–45)

The poet is thus unable to marry his tragic vision to a graceful form creating an aesthetic *concordia discors*. What then does

he derive as an artist from his private viewing of the Titans'
sorrowful fate, which breaks off just as the Titans' only hope,
Hyperion, rushes onto the stage? Keats completes neither the
rehearsal of cosmic upheavals nor the poet's identity crisis. We
assume that the knowledge gained through his vicarious suffer-
ing deepens the poet's moral and social commitment. Keats
seems to be dramatizing the process by which the imagination
serves to intensify moral responsiveness. He had long believed
in the authenticity of the imagination—"What the imagination
seizes as Beauty must be truth" (*Letters* 1:184)—but in the *Fall of
Hyperion* he seems to be probing the way it can function morally,
even when it is enthralled by myth. Shelley eloquently formu-
lated this view in his *Defense of Poetry*: "The great secret of
morals is love; or a going out of our own nature, and an
identification of ourselves with the beautiful which exists in
thought, action, or person, not our own. . . . The great instru-
ment of moral good is the imagination. . . . Poetry enlarges
the circumference of the imagination by replenishing it with
thoughts of ever new delight, which have the power of attract-
ing and assimilating to their own nature all other thoughts, and
which form new intervals and interstices whose void for ever
craves fresh food" (*Critical Prose* 12–13). While Keats could
embody in *The Fall* the initial stages by which mythic events
enlarge the circumference of the poet's imagination, he left us
with a large void when it came to the poet's assimilating the
myth into the question of his vocation and its practice in the
real world. Is he going to become an Apollonian "sage, / A
humanist, physician to all men" (1:189–90), or will he be a
Dionysian dreamer who "venoms all his days" (1:175)? And
what event in the Titanomachy would have a decisive effect on
the direction of his creative energy? Keats warns us at the end
of Canto 1 that he may be able to show only a glimpse of what
lies ahead without actually exploring the uncharted territory.
Moneta spoke on, he says,

> As ye may read who can unwearied pass
> Onward from the antechamber of this dream,

> Where even at the open doors awhile
> I must delay, and glean my memory
> Of her high phrase—perhaps no further dare.
>   (1:464–68)

"Perhaps no further dare": what arrested Keats's passage beyond the "antechamber of this dream"? Was it possibly his recognition of an abyss between what he could authentically imagine as the experiences shaping the poet's identity and what he glimpsed as a hoped for but not yet experienced coalescence of private dreamer and public vates, suffering Dionysus and calmly all-seeing Apollo?[10] Keats's *Hyperion* fragments remind us that, from Wordsworth and Coleridge to Hölderlin and Novalis, the phenomenon of fragmentation, as Thomas McFarland has recently demonstrated, is mirrored in the cultural iconology of Romanticism itself. "Incompleteness, fragmentation, and ruin," McFarland writes, "not only receive a special emphasis in Romanticism but also in a certain perspective seem actually to define that phenomenon" (7). Drawing on Hegel's *Philosophy of Art*, another critic, Tilottama Rajan, persuasively argues for an idealistic definition of this phenomenon as a gesture of triumph: "a new way of reading the literary fragment as something which stands as the formal equivalent of hope and potential. It becomes possible to see the breaking off of a poem as a high point, a moment of conversion in which the poem, by announcing its own finiteness, also makes known to the reader the infiniteness of that which it does not contain." She makes a case for such a reading of Shelley's *Epipsychidion* and Keats's *Hyperion* while also acknowledging the problems that make it difficult to decide whether Keats "meant the incompleteness of *Hyperion* to be read as a gesture of triumph or defeat" (180).

Given the fragmentary modality of Keats's two *Hyperion* versions, it becomes difficult to assess the importance of pastoral virtues for resolving Keats's doubts about the poet's role in a fragmented world. Not being able to re-view the narrative from the perspective of the ending, we cannot confidently assign a meaning to any of the segments. We cannot, for example, be certain about the import of Oceanus's speech beyond its dramatic role in the council of the Titans. Was his eternal law that "first in beauty should be first in might" (*Hyperion* 2:229–30) really intended to be the ultimate wisdom embraced by the poet after all mysteries were revealed to him? "Myths are the agents of stability, fictions the agents of change," writes Frank Kermode. "Myths call for absolute, fictions for conditional assent. Myths make sense in terms of a lost order of time . . . ; fictions, if successful, make sense of the here and now" (*Sense of an Ending* 39). Keats's fragments are his heroic attempts to create *both* myth and fiction, a fiction that through timeless myth was to make sense of the poet's role in the here and now. The hope of bringing a pastoral vision of wholeness to his fragmented world informs the Apollo theme of Keats's myth. But would it ultimately be a sufficiently authentic myth to shape the human poet's soul-making in a soulless world with which he was out of tune?

"SILENCE AND SLOW TIME":
PASTORAL *TOPOI* IN KEATS'S ODES

When· Keats abandoned *Hype-rion*, he scuttled with it the heavy load of classical myth that he had been unable to mold into his own shifting moods and perspectives. Yet, stymied though he felt in the spring of 1819 by the "over-powering idea of our dead poets" (*Letters* 2:116), he did not ruthlessly reject all literary precursors. He knew that (in Yeats's words) "A style is found by sedentary toil / And by the imitation of great masters" (*Ego Dominus Tuus* 65–66). Like other Romantics, Keats insisted on his right to enlarge the neoclassic canon of "great masters," to test a wide spectrum of masterpieces and to allow the masterpieces to test him. When he turned to experimenting with the Pindaric ode, he evolved both his own stanzaic form and his own repertoire of *topoi* by testing literary models, imprinting on them his own design. Like Schiller, he remained to the end of his life a romantic classicist who believed that he could find his "true voice of feeling" (*Letters* 2:167) and yet temper its Dionysian intensity with Apollonian knowledge and order. In some of his odes Keats the classicist deployed pastoral *topoi* to give allusive resonance to his personal debates, while Keats the romanticist exploited the tensions and dissonances that surfaced in his confrontations with literary tradition. Three of the spring odes —*Ode on Indolence, Ode to Psyche,* and *Ode on a Grecian Urn*—

most clearly illustrate the range of Keats's assimilation of pastoral *topoi*. In terms of Hayden White's progression of tropes, these odes move from a heavy reliance on metaphor and metonymy, which express simplistic or reductive relationships, to greater exploration of the integrative trope of synecdoche, and finally to experimentation with synecdoche shading off into irony, the "metatropological mode of self-critical thought".[1]

Praising the pleasures of "summer indolence" (16), Keats quickly evokes the pastoral *topos* of *otium* in his *Ode on Indolence*. *Otium*, the holiday from the world of *negotium*, as Thomas Rosenmeyer reminds us, means "escape from pressing business, particularly a business with overtones of death" (67–68). In the spring following his brother's death, Keats uses the opiate of the poetry of James Thomson's *Castle of Indolence* to dream himself into a world remote from the business of life and death, choice and strife, pleasure and pain. He takes his own advice on how someone might pass a carefree life: "let him on any certain day read a certain Page of full Poesy or distilled Prose and let him wander with it, and muse upon it, and reflect from it, and bring home to it, and prophesy upon it, and dream upon it. . . . How happy is such a 'voyage of conception,' what delicious diligent Indolence!" (*Letters* 1:231). In just such a mood of delicious indolence, in March 1819, he longs for a stanza or two of *The Castle of Indolence* to muse and dream upon:

> This morning I am in a sort of temper indolent and supremely careless: I long after a stanza or two of Thompson's Castle of Indolence—My passions are all alseep [asleep] from my having slumbered till nearly eleven and weakened the animal fibre all over me to a delightful sensation about three degrees on this side of faintness . . . —In this state of effeminacy the fibres of the brain are relaxed in common with the rest of the body, and to such a happy degree that pleasure has no show of enticement and pain no unbearable frown.
>
> (*Letters* 2:78–79)

In this mood of supreme indolence—*indolence* literally means freedom from pain—Keats's imagination turns to Thomson not only for a landscape of perfect ease but also for a temporal realm doubly distanced from contemporary reality by its status as a dream-world and by its translation into archaic Spenserian idiom:

> A pleasing Land of Drowsy-hed it was:
> Of Dreams that wave before the half-shut Eye;
> And of gay Castles in the Clouds that pass,
> For ever flushing round a Summer-Sky:
> There eke the soft Delights, that witchingly
> Instil a wanton Sweetness through the Breast,
> And the calm Pleasures always hover'd nigh;
> But whate'er smack'd of Noyance, or Unrest,
> Was far far off expell'd from this delicious Nest.
> (*Castle of Indolence* 1:6)

Echoing Thomson, Keats's *Ode on Indolence* presents a speaker addicted to the sweet delights of "drowsy noons, / And evenings steeped in honeyed indolence" (36–37). *Otium* for him does not mean recreative vacation but spiritual vacuity. Yet Keats was aware that the Epicurean tradition of *otium*, embodied in Theocritean pastoral, involved not a negative escapism but a positive repose, the peace of mind and enjoyment of an unchanging present, without nostalgia for the past or aspirations for the future. This was the priceless gift that Keats's Titans had lost and that Hyperion feared to lose:

> Am I to leave this haven of my rest,
> This cradle of my glory, this soft clime,
> This calm luxuriance of blissful light?
> (*Hyperion* 1:235–37)

This last representative of unperturbed, luxuriantly calm golden-age existence evokes a whole ethos of passionless contentment that the *Ode on Indolence* revokes. *On Indolence* contracts the macrocosmic myth into one persona's minimal consciousness. In *Hyperion* Keats figured an ideal of wise passiveness, but in the ode he depicted the folly of regressive quiescence. His biblical motto, "They toil not, neither do they spin," uses the letter of the Gospel ("Consider the lilies of the field, how they grow; they toil not, neither do they spin"— Matthew 6:28) to advance a holiday from the Christian spirit, to preach the triumph of the body over the soul. The same Scriptural maxim served Spenser's beguiling Phaedria to "allure fraile mind to careless ease" (*Faerie Queene* 2.6:13) and inspired James Thomson's enchanter to bewitch the unwary with false delights (1.10:1–6). But Keats's speaker needs no such false enchanters: he has enticed himself into such total indolence that he sees any activity at all, even that of writing poetry or making love, as seducing him from near oblivion. Thomson's enchanter, while banishing ambition, fame, and "those Passions that this World deform," nevertheless recommends the "soft Gales of Passions" (1.16:4,6) to enliven the monotonous calm of indolence. And he advises those who wish "a little Exercise" to "indulge the Muse" amid the pastoral groves (1.18:1,3). Keats's speaker, however, retires not merely from worldly existence but from existence as such, allowing only a state "about three degrees on this side of faintness." At the same time he lacks the Epicurean repose of mind that makes Thomson's enchanter so persuasive when he affirms:

> "Here nought but Candour reigns, indulgent Ease,
> Good-natur'd Lounging, Sauntering up and down:
> They who are pleas'd themselves must always please. . . ."
>   (1.15:1–3)

Keats's speaker is much more ambivalent about his realm of indulgent ease and those "shadowy Forms" that idleness produces "in her dreaming Mood" (*Castle of Indolence* 1.5:3,4). Though he protests that he is pleased with his drowsy indolence, he is both disturbed and fascinated by three figures that

his reverie generates: they pass "like figures on a marble urn, /
When shifted round to see the other side" (5–6). Their strange-
ness teases him out of his torpor into thought:

> How is it, Shadows, that I knew ye not?
>   How came ye muffled in so hush a masque?
> Was it a silent deep-disguisèd plot
>   To steal away, and leave without a task
> My idle days?
>   (11–15)

The word *idle* recalls him to the pleasures of *otium*, the joy of
being without a task:

>   Ripe was the drowsy hour;
>   The blissful cloud of summer indolence
>   Benumbed my eyes; my pulse grew less and less;
> Pain had no sting, and pleasure's wreath no flower:
>   Oh, why did ye not melt, and leave my sense
>   Unhaunted quite of all but—nothingness?
>   (15–20)

Keats's persona is an uneasy escape artist. He wishes to lan-
guish in his bower of indolence, "Blissfully havened both from
joy and pain" (*Eve of St. Agnes* 240), yet he accuses the three
intrusive figures of abandoning him to total idleness. And who
are these three muffled figures in their white robes and san-
dals, silently performing a masque? In his journal entry for
19 March 1819, which contains the prose sketch of the ode,
Keats describes his "state of effeminacy" as so benumbing "that
pleasure has no show of enticement and pain no unbearable
frown. Neither Poetry, nor Ambition, nor Love have any alert-
ness of countenance as they pass by me: they seem rather like
three figures on a greek vase—a Man and two women—whom
no one but myself could distinguish in their disguisement" (*Let-
ters* 2:78–79).[2] In both the letter and the ode, a state of supreme
idleness generates a poetic reverie whose slow, rythmic cadences

mirror the speaker's idling mind. In both Keats personifies the abstractions Poetry, Ambition, and Love and presents them ecphrastically as three figures carved on a marble urn. And in both letter and ode this emblematic figuration exhausts Keats's imaginative effort. There is, however, one striking difference between the two visions: in the journal Keats speaks of the figures as a man and two women, whereas in the ode all three are women. The man suggests the personification of poetry as Apollo, possibly as in Poussin's painting *The Inspiration of the Poet*, which shows Apollo with his lyre as the central figure flanked by two muses.[3] Apollo was of course much in Keats's thoughts early in 1819, when he found it impossible to complete *Hyperion*. "I have not gone on with Hyperion," he notes in his journal-letter for 14 February 1819, "for to tell the truth I have not been in great cue for writing lately—I must wait for the s[pr]ing to rouse me up a little" (*Letters* 2:62). Both Keats himself and his Apollo were in a state of acedia. "I have been very idle lately, very averse to writing," Keats confided to a friend in June. "You will judge of my 1819 temper when I tell you that the thing I have most enjoyed this year has been writing an ode to Indolence" (2:116).

When Keats incorporates the vision of his three compelling passions (love, ambition, and poetry) into his ode, he no longer accords poetry a prominent position in the visual tableau. Instead, he places poetry's prominence entirely in the speaker's mind. As the speaker watches the shapes pass by him for a third time, he recognizes them by a single aspect. Keats wastes no imaginative effort on Love, whom he pictures simply as a "fair maid" (25). He makes Ambition a bit more vivid: she is "pale of cheek, / And ever watchful with a fatiguèd eye" (26–27), apparently consumed with pursuing fame. He distinguishes the last figure by a surprising aspect: she is a "maiden most unmeek" (29). Yet this temptress is not Voluptas:

> The last, whom I love more, the more of blame
> Is heaped upon her, maiden most unmeek,

I knew to be my demon Poesy.
(28–30)

Recognizing and naming the shadowy shapes here is not Adam's creative act of naming that calls into being, but is instead the work of inertia that produces reductive tropes, minimizing the allegorical figures' mystery. The speaker can rouse himself briefly to express the only moment of intense emotion—"to follow them I burned / And ached for wings" (23–24)—but as the figures fade, his desire for action also fades. He does not have the energy to endow the phantoms with enough reality to engage them in debate. He cannot lend them existence by an "ardent pursuit," by a "greeting of the Spirit" (*Letters* 1:243). Although Keats surpasses Thomson in his nostalgia for "indulgent Ease," he reduces his precursor's debate between the virtues of *otium* and *negotium* to a plaintive soliloquy, narrowing his multiple perspectives—including an anti-illusionary, even satiric, view of the enchanting dream world—to the single perspective from within the state of numbing indolence. His repose totally lacks the equipoise that Schiller opposed to empty inertia and that stems from the fullness of human energy, evoking a sense of infinite potentiality (*NA* 20:473).

Although Keats's persona protests that his retirement is self-sufficient, his tone becomes increasingly plaintive as the three figures haunt his dreams for the last time:

A third time came they by. Alas, wherefore?
     My sleep had been embroidered with dim dreams;
My soul had been a lawn besprinkled o'er
     With flowers, and stirring shades, and baffled beams.
The morn was clouded, but no shower fell,
     Though in her lids hung the sweet tears of May. . . .
          (41–46)

The poet's limp imagination generates the decorative metaphor of his soul seen as a flowering meadow, suggesting the store of visions that make him self-sufficient. And yet, with the disturbing "stirring shades" and "baffled beams" immediately qualifying the affirmation, the mood becomes more elegiac than joyful. "Blissful clouds" give way to rainy ones. Keats here resorts to conventional personification as he depicts the morning whose eyelid trembles with "the sweet tears of May." Such pictorialism is common in Thomson and in the early Keats but is displaced by integrative tropes in the major odes of the spring of 1819. Here the details undercut the speaker's declared ease, as when, for example, he repeats the sentimental emphasis on tears in the concluding lines of the same stanza:

> O Shadows, 'twas a time to bid farewell!
> Upon your skirts had fallen no tears of mine.
> (49–50)

Why is it necessary to affirm that the poet has shed *no* tears over his dismissing Love, Ambition, and Poesy, if these are offensive intruders upon his paradisal lawns? The very denial gives substance to his regret and indulges an elegiac feeling that cannot generate idyllic visions. He cannot inspirit his pleasance and be inspired by it like the nightingale in its "melodious plot / Of beechen green" (*Ode to a Nightingale* 8–9), an Elysian refuge

> Where the nightingale doth sing
> Not a senseless, trancèd thing,
> But divine melodious truth,
> Philosophic numbers smooth,
> Tales and golden histories
> Of heaven and its mysteries.
> (*Ode* ["Bards of Passion and of Mirth"] 17–22)

In the human realm Keats doubted the possibility of participating in such cosmic harmony, just as he doubted the possibility of perfectibility or of lasting happiness. In his journal-letter of March 1819, in which he extolled the pleasure of indolence as the only happiness, Keats goes on to note that in this world "we

cannot expect to give way many hours to pleasure—Circum-
stances are like Clouds continually gathering and bursting—
While we are laughing the seed of some trouble is put into the
wide arable land of events" (*Letters* 2:79). A month later, in an
entry in the same journal-letter, Keats is willing to speculate
about "happiness carried to an extreme," but he concludes that
he cannot believe in it—"the nature of the world will not admit
it." Man can no more remove the ever-present threats to happi-
ness than he can control whirlpools and volcanoes: "Let men
exterminate them and I will say that they may arrive at earthly
Happiness." And in the same vein, he comments: "Let the fish
philosophise the ice away from the Rivers in winter time and
they shall be at continual play in the tepid delight of summer"
(2:101).

In his *Ode on Indolence* Keats created a speaker who is such a
philosophizing fish; he tries to make the "blissful cloud of sum-
mer indolence" screen his mind from wintry thoughts. Even
embowered as he is, he seeks to seal himself off still more tightly
from the outside world:

> Oh, for an age so sheltered from annoy
>   That I may never know how change the moons,
>   Or hear the voice of busy common-sense!
>   (38–40)

As he tries to philosophize away his awareness of mutability and
negotium, protesting his self-sufficiency—a sufficiency of dreams
but not of self-understanding—he is perhaps trying to still the
voice of a stern muse like the admonishing Moneta of the *Fall of
Hyperion*. Significantly, Keats does not follow Thomson's poem
as it modulates from the easy bliss of the Castle of Indolence to
a more arduous task for the poet:

> Come then, my Muse, and raise a bolder Song;
> Come, lig no more upon the Bed of Sloth,
> Dragging the lazy languid Line along,
> Fond to begin, but still to finish loth,

Thy half-writ Scrolls all eaten by the Moth:
Arise, and sing that generous Imp of Fame,
Who, with the Sons of Softness nobly wroth,
To sweep away this Human Lumber came,
Or in a chosen Few to rouse the slumbering Flame.
    (2.4:1–9)

For Keats's countervision that might rouse the "slumbering Flame," we must turn to his other spring odes. His *Ode on Indolence* has only one string to its bow, and Keats does not test its tension to the point of producing dissonant notes. Or, to change the musical analogy to a pictorial one more appropriate to Keats's ode, we might say that he leaves us with a static tableau resembling a triptych in which the center panel is missing. We see the comatose speaker ensconced on his bed of flowers on one side and the three seductive apparitions on the other, but we miss the central action that might transform the metonymic flatness into synecdochic richness.

For a "bolder Song," let us turn to the *Ode to Psyche*. It fills the triptych by promoting the poet-dreamer to the central panel, while relegating the figures in the dream to the side panels. In this ode, moreover, Keats overcomes the pastoral stasis of *On Indolence*: he animates his still life by dramatizing the internal complexities of the poet's mental workshop. In fact, it can be argued that "the main purpose of the poem is to re-present retrospectively the process by which the poet's mind has become animated and transformed by Psyche. Instead of poetic mind animating external object, the mythological Psyche enters his mind and animates it internally so that it becomes changed into a vast mental landscape" (Bunn 582). Like the persona of Marvell's *Garden*, Keats's poet-priest withdraws into the recesses of his mind to repeat there, in the finite mind, the eternal act of creation. Like Marvell, Keats refurbishes the classical *topos* of the *locus amoenus* with fresh vitality and wit, that he may consecrate it as the precinct in the mind within which he creates his temple to Psyche. In the process he engages the mysteries of inspiration and the labors of verbal expression. Thus his pleasance in the mind becomes a psychologically profound synecdoche.

Following the Pindaric tradition in his own fashion, Keats immediately announces the addressee and the occasion of his ode:

> O Goddess! Hear these tuneless numbers, wrung
>> By sweet enforcement and remembrance dear,
> And pardon that thy secrets should be sung
>> Even into thine own soft-conchèd ear.
>>> (1–4)

Keats surprises us by announcing his encomiastic occasion in an elegiac formula: "tuneless numbers" "wrung" from him by "sweet enforcement and remembrance dear." Even though he softens the pressure for writing, his lines resonate with Milton's "Bitter constraint, and sad occasion dear" of the opening stanza of *Lycidas*. And Milton's lines in turn recall Spenser's *Pastorall Aeglogue upon the Death of Sir Phillip Sidney*, in which a mourner reassures his uncouth fellow singer that art is unnecessary for the occasion when "Griefe will endite, and sorrow will enforce / Thy voice" (33–34). Couching his apostrophe to Psyche in the formulaic language of pastoral elegy, Keats keeps the elegiac note alongside the happier encomiastic strain, although he is not mourning a fellow poet. Keats's mourning is more ironic: his tribute to Psyche is wrung from him by the sad occasion of Roman neglect and modern spiritual hollowness. He is forced into song not only because Psyche was "too late for antique vows" (36), too late for participation in an animistic world in which "holy were the haunted forest boughs, / Holy the air, the water and the fire" (38–39), but also because Keats's own time was continuing the process of enlightenment that anatomized nature and obliterated all vestiges of "happy pieties" (41). Keats no doubt shared Wordsworth's response to the waste land of his time:

> Great God! I'd rather be
> A Pagan suckled in a creed outworn;
> So might I, standing on this pleasant lea,
> Have glimpses that would make me less forlorn;
> Have sight of Proteus rising from the sea;
> Or hear old Triton blow his wreathèd horn.
> (*The World is Too Much With Us* 9–14)

Keats makes himself feel less forlorn by projecting himself into the timeless world of myth and catching a glimpse of Psyche and Eros in a dream:

> Surely I dreamt to-day, or did I see
> The wingèd Psyche with awakened eyes?
>   I wandered in a forest thoughtlessly,
>   And, on the sudden, fainting with surprise,
> Saw two fair creatures, couchèd side by side
>   In deepest grass. . . .
>   (5–10)

Keats's surprised dreamer conjures himself a charming variation on Apuleius's marriage of Cupid and Psyche, granting the mortal lovers unalloyed happiness in their heaven on earth. Keats has totally discarded the macabre oracle at the beginning of Apuleius's narrative (predicting that Psyche will be wedded to a viper) and borrows only some felicitous details of her being magically wafted into a secluded valley and laid on a bed of soft grass and sweet flowers, a prelude to Cupid's first visitation.

In his comments on Raphael's series of paintings dealing with the story of Cupid and Psyche, Hazlitt captures Keats's verbal painting of the happy pair: Raphael "even surpassed himself in a certain swelling and voluptuous grace, as if beauty grew and ripened under his touch, and the very genius of ancient fable hovered over his enamoured pencil" (17:149).[4] The "very genius of ancient fable" hovers also over Keats's enamored pen and inspires him, ironically enough, to deconstruct the central myth of Cupid and Psyche, which he had pithily sketched in *I*

Stood Tip-Toe after lingering over the first love scene. He refers to Apuleius,

> . . . who first told how Psyche went
> On the smooth wind to realms of wonderment;
> What Psyche felt, and Love, when their full lips
> First touched; what amorous and fondling nips
> They gave each other's cheeks; with all their sighs,
> And how they kissed each other's tremulous eyes;
> The silver lamp—the ravishment—the wonder—
> The darkness—loneliness—the fearful thunder;
> Their woes gone by, and both to heaven upflown
> To bow for gratitude before Jove's throne.
>   (141–50)

This is the story of the soul's trials and love's ultimate triumph that inspired Raphael and his pupil, Giulio Romano, and that lent grist to the mill of allegorizers from Boccaccio to Thomas Taylor.

Keats, however, decenters the focus on Psyche's trials and torments which interested the painters and commentators. He displaces the distressing labors which the jealous Venus inflicted on the mortal Psyche with the poet's self-imposed labors of creating an authentic form of worship for the deified Psyche. For these labors he needs only the inspiring dream image that conflates Psyche and Eros's earthly union with their heavenly reunion. He strips away the layers of allegorical elaboration not to reduce Psyche to decorative prosopopeia but to invoke her encompassing presence as human and divine, the breath of life, the inspirer and the inspired. And Keats assigns to the mortal poet the ironic role of immortalizing the deity by singing his inspired human words into her divine ear.

A latecomer to Olympus, Psyche has neither temple nor cult. "You must recollect," Keats told the George Keatses when sending them his ode, "that Psyche was not embodied as a goddess before the time of Apulius the Platonist . . . and consequently the Goddess was never worshipped or sacrificed to with any of

the ancient fervour." Keats added playfully, "I am more ortho-
dox that [than] to let a hethen Goddess be so neglected" (*Letters*
2:106). Keats compensated for Psyche's neglect by devising his
own fervent worship.[5] Enchanted by his dream vision of the
"winged Psyche" in her paradise, he affirms: "I see, and sing, by
my own eyes inspired" (43). This self-referential rhetoric em-
phasizes the speaker's awareness that, in "these days so far
retired / From happy pieties" (40–41), the poet must create his
own religious subject as well as his religious syntax. He must
withdraw from the "material sublime," from which Keats once
preferred to draw the substance of all dreams (*To J.H. Reynolds,
Esq.* 67–69), to the internal sublime furnished by his own in-
spired visions. Through them he can fill the gap left by late
antiquity. As he contemplates Psyche's privations—no temple,
no altar, no choir, no priest—these lacunae ironically prove
productive, engendering a rich repertoire of negatives:

> [No] virgin-choir to make delicious moan
>   Upon the midnight hours—
> No voice, no lute, no pipe, no incense sweet
>   From chain-swung censer teeming;
> No shrine, no grove, no oracle, no heat
>   Of pale-mouthed prophet dreaming.
>   (30–35)

Immediately the poet translates these absences into pres-
ences, transforms his catalogue of negations into the language
of positive performance. He begins by matching the negative
syntax with a fervent exhortation:

> So let me be thy choir and make a moan
>   Upon the midnight hours—
> Thy voice, thy lute, thy pipe, thy incense sweet
>   From swingèd censer teeming;
> Thy shrine, thy grove, thy oracle, thy heat
>   Of pale-mouthed prophet dreaming.
>   (44–49)

The syntactical relations between the negative and positive for-
mulations underscore the poet's ability to fill the lacunae of
worship. His ardent pleas to let him be Psyche's votary inspire
him with firm resolve, and he replaces the auxiliary *let* with *will*
and *shall*:

> Yes, I will be thy priest, and build a fane
>   In some untrodden region of my mind,
> Where branchèd thoughts, new grown with pleasant pain,
>   Instead of pines shall murmur in the wind. . . .
>   (50–53)

The *shalls* and *wills* continue right into the final quatrain of the
ode. The poet has indeed become a prophet-priest who dedi-
cates all his visionary power and all his verbal art to authenticate
as an external animating divinity the psychic power he craves,
just as Psyche craves the embraces of Eros, who, even when he
is near her, must remain invisible.

Before the poet-priest can perform his rites, he must create a
sacred grove. He creates it in some "untrodden region" of his
mind, internalizing the paradisal arbor of his initial dream vi-
sion which he had presented as existing outside himself. His
grove is not dream work but brain work, not an illusion that
immediately engages the dreamer but an image that is labori-
ously crafted in the poet's workshop. The movement from the
first to the second *locus amoenus* entails a dramatic shift from
one rhetorical level to another. The first is the dream vision in
which the poet saw himself coming upon an idyllic scene:

> two fair creatures, couchèd side by side
>   In deepest grass, beneath the whispering roof
> Of leaves and trembled blossoms, where there ran
>   A brooklet, scarce espied.
>   (9–12)

This luxuriously appointed dream-pleasance is clearly intended
to be read as both a natural garden and a symbolic landscape,

both a happy place and a happy state of being. Pastoral poets from Theocritus to Wordsworth have taught us to read in this way their green arbors, earthly paradises, Arcadias, bowers of bliss, echoing greens, hollowed valleys.

The second *locus amoenus*—the grove in some untrodden region of the mind—surprises the reader by a different level of discourse and makes him question his naive acceptance of the dream convention with its glimpses of paradisal bliss. When, instead of presenting himself as wandering in a forest *thoughtlessly* (7), the poet proclaims himself as building a *thoughtful* temple in his mind, Keats has disturbed the delicate balance of the pastoral grove as figuring both an external and an internal reality. He explicitly displaces the external landscape by a mental space "Where branchèd thoughts, new grown with pleasant pain, / Instead of pines shall murmur in the wind" (52–53). Annihilating the traditional green arbor (to borrow Marvell's words) into a "green Thought in a green Shade" (*Garden* 48) liberates Keats's imagination to luxuriate in traditional mythical figurations:

> Far, far around shall those dark-clustered trees
>   Fledge the wild-ridgèd mountains steep by steep;
> And there by zephyrs, streams, and birds, and bees,
>   The moss-lain Dryads shall be lulled to sleep. . . .
> (54–57)

Keats can deploy his garden language because he has detached it from nature and made it refer to purely mental constructs. His secluded scene is the work of the poet's fertile mind and not of a gardener's green thumb. Keats's echo of Wordsworth's "steep and lofty cliffs, / That on a wild secluded scene impress / Thoughts of more deep seclusion" (*Tintern Abbey* 5–7) underscores his dissolution of the Wordsworthian external-internal interchange in order to dramatize the process that works in still deeper seclusion. His "working brain" (60) labors to bring forth in and through language all the accoutrements of a sacred grove and of the ceremonies of worship—temple, altar, liturgy, votive offering. In the mind's "wide quietness" (58) the poet can play all the roles from architect to priest as he creates his unique pastoral encomium to Psyche. The poet's winged words are synecdochically epitomized by Psyche, the winged spirit-soul who inhabits a mental sanctuary, a spiritual omnipresence whose center is in the poet's mind but whose periphery is nowhere. Keats attempts what Blake called the "great task": "To open the Eternal Worlds, to open the immortal Eyes / Of Man inwards into the Worlds of Thought . . . " (*Jerusalem* Plate 5:18–19).

Yet in the end, as the sovereign poet-priest loads every rift with green thoughts, his prodigality begins to call attention to the fragility of his mental constructs:

> And in the midst of this wide quietness
> A rosy sanctuary will I dress
> With the wreathed trellis of a working brain,
>> With buds, and bells, and stars without a name,
> With all the gardener Fancy e'er could feign,
>> Who breeding flowers will never breed the same. . . .
>> (58–63)

The fanciful artifice that collaborates with nature to produce infinite variety was a favorite pastoral *topos* in Renaissance literature, but it cannot work for Keats in its traditional role.[6] Keats has already taught his reader to construe gardening as exclusively the process of poetic thought which operates without the assistance of external nature. When he now superimposes on the verbal craftsmanship the further artifice of graftsmanship, the trope has the effect of dislocating external reality while simultaneously calling into question the solidity and validity of language's configurations. The speaker's final apostrophe to Psyche reinforces this sense of language's fragility:

> And there shall be for thee all soft delight
>> That shadowy thought can win,
> A bright torch, and a casement ope at night,

To let the warm Love in!
(64–67)

In the middle of this quatrain Keats is once more changing levels of discourse, returning to the naive dream mode of the first tableau. And yet just at this moment when he asks us to regard language as a transparent medium for "hieroglyphic visioning" (to borrow his term for Hazlitt's comment on *King Lear* [Forman 5:282]), he invites an ironic reading of his proffered gift to Psyche: in the rosy sanctuary erected and consecrated to her in the poet's mind, he will give her "all the soft delight / That shadowy thought can win." How can we resist ironic speculations about the shape such shadowy delights might take? In the midst of such ironic musing, Keats suddenly snatches us away from the deconstructive labyrinth into which he was leading us and quickly propels us into the mythic vision that displaces the verbal temple: we see a rosy sanctuary fit for Psyche as both inspiring goddess and beautiful mortal who relishes the "soft delights" of Eros. In the end both Psyche's and the poet's "Labour is blossoming or dancing where / The body is not bruised to pleasure soul" (Yeats, *Among School Children* 57–58). Keats's open-ended final stanza approaches the soft closure that Coleridge noted in Pindar's odes: they "seem by intention to die away by soft gradations into a languid Interest, like most of the Landskips of the great elder Painters. Modern Ode-writers have commonly preferred a continued Rising of Interest" (*CN* 2:2886). Keats's window open to the possibility of "soft delights" dispels the elegiac tone of his opening invocation, even as it leads us back to the speaker's initial dream vision of the two lovers pausing between embraces. Between these mythopoeic tableaux the poet has revealed not only the spiritual lacunae of his age but also the tenuousness of the poet's medium with which he has tried to fill them.

In his *Ode to Psyche* Keats devoted his visionary and verbal powers to reviving a pagan goddess. In his *Ode on a Grecian Urn* he used his poetic resources to animate a marble sculpture,

making mute antiquity speak to him and to his time. Whereas
the poet could provide for Psyche an immortal shrine, he con-
fronts in the marble urn a nearly immortal object that exposes
his own mortality. The two odes illustrate Keats's maxim "that
eve[r]y point of thought is the centre of an intellectual world—
the two uppermost thoughts in a Man's mind are the two poles
of his World he revolves on them and every thing is southward
or northward to him through their means" (*Letters* 1:243). In
both odes the thought at the center of the poet's intellectual
world is the question of the *Fall of Hyperion*: What is the poet's
role in the modern world? Keats sets out to explore the aes-
thetic and moral certainties and uncertainties of realms made of
language and of marble. He may have been inspired by a real
work of art, but I am not going to contribute to the conjectures
whether the Borghese Vase or the Townley or the Sosibios Vase
or the Holland House Urn or any other piece of chiseled mar-
ble was the prototype for Keats's urn.[7] Here I am concerned
only with his incorporation and reinterpretation of the classical
topos of the decorated cup awarded as a prize in a bucolic
singing contest.

Theocritus's prize cup in *Idyll 1* set the pattern for variations
on the theme by Virgil, Spenser, Milton, Pope, and Keats.[8]
Theocritus vividly presents the sculptured details. Encircled
by tendrils of ivy and framed by acanthus, the panels depict
nonpastoral scenes: a coy woman toying with two suitors, an old
fisherman sinuously gathering up his net, two foxes plundering
a vineyard and raiding the knapsack of the boy on guard, who is
absorbed in braiding a cricket cage. These panels contain (in
both senses of the word) the nonpastoral world of competition,
hardship, cruelty, and deception, as it intrudes on Theocritus's
pastoral arbor. What matters, as Thomas Rosenmeyer points
out, is that "these echoes of the world beyond the pleasance" are
stilled, "frozen into sculptured beauty, hemmed in by the ivy
frame that winds around the lip of the cup. Within the poem,
their life force is minimal" (91). Keats reverses Theocritus's
strategy: instead of stilling the disturbing forces of the world
beyond the pastoral bower, he freezes the pastoral world and

reduces it to a single sculptured panel on his imaginary urn. But if he thus miniaturizes the pastoral realm, he vastly enlarges the scope of the cup itself; it is no longer a prize awarded either for singing a specially requested song, as in Theocritus, or for winning a singing match, as in Virgil. Keats prunes away the pastoral setting, shepherd-poets, and the pastoral occasion of his predecessors to allow his cup to fill all the space and time of his poem. His poem is not an ameobean eclogue containing the ecphrastic motif of a prize cup but a lyric debate, an ode on a Grecian urn. The speaker stations the urn squarely on the center of his mental stage, never letting it out of his sight, speaking to it and for it. He sings by his own eyes inspired, carrying on a lyric dialogue with the imaginary carved figures and engaging in a friendly contest with the urn itself. Keats's persona is at once spectator and actor, distant observer and empathic participant in the scenes he visualizes. And of course he is first and foremost the poet who translates into his verbal medium the marble object that exists only in and through his words, just as Psyche's temple exists only as a verbal construct. Yet his pictorial skill is so fine that readers speak of the urn as if it existed solidly in space, as if they could actually turn it or walk around it to look at the different panels. The panels include both pastoral and nonpastoral scenes, yet even an image of Dionysian frenzy does not prevent Keats from making his urn as a whole the bearer of the pastoral and Apollonian ideals of tranquility and order, equanimity and immutability.

The urn immediately evokes a compliment from its apostrophizing beholder: silent historian though it is, it can "express /A flowery tale more sweetly" than the poet's rhyme (3–4). The speaker awards the palm to his sister art before even challenging it to a contest. Nevertheless, the agon between poetry and plastic art emerges as a quiet undercurrent in the poem, with the poet playing the roles of both contestants and of the umpire. Does he immediately pronounce the urn as superior to the poet as a teller of tales because it is more truly pastoral, more truly a naive mimesis of the Arcadian world of resonant *silvae*? The epithet "silvan" recalls Virgil's ubiquitous forests and thickets that form the echoing groves for pastoral singers: "non canimus surdis, respondent omnia silvae" (*Eclogue* 10:8). Virgil's "muse is *silvestris*," says Phillip Damon, "because the forest is one of the natural echo chambers which his conception of the pastoral genre seems to require. . . . Songs are badly sung outside the forest" (282). Even the prize cups staked in *Eclogue* 3 are made of beechwood (*fagina*), linking them closely to the forest setting of the singing contest. Keats's "Silvan historian" silently encodes these echoes of a naive pastoral mood, which are antithetical to the sentimental speaker's divided sensibility.

The sentimental poet is immediately provoked to myriad questions and speculations about the sensuous reality that the urn unquestioningly embodies:

> What leaf-fringed legend haunts about thy shape
>> Of deities or mortals, or of both,
>>> In Tempe or the dales of Arcady?
>> What men or gods are these? What maidens loth?
> What mad pursuit? What struggle to escape?
>> What pipes and timbrels? What wild ecstasy?
>>> (5–10)

Not the classical sculptor but only the modern poet is teased into distinguishing between gods and mortals. Only the poet feels the need to name the pastoral valleys as Tempe or Arcady. But has he named them appropriately, or has he imposed his own nostalgia for Arcadian tranquility on the marble landscape? And is the dissonant Dionysian intensity of the "mad pursuit" and "struggle to escape" his own or the urn's? He quickly dissolves his perception of such "wild ecstasy" into an Arcadian pleasance of eternal spring and a happy piper serenading his youthful beloved. The poet dwells far more exuberantly on this pastoral tableau than on either the Dionysian panel that precedes it or that of a religious procession that follows, yet the whole "Attic shape" (41) strikes the speaker as "Cold pastoral" (45). Apparently all the sculptured depictions of happy spring, with its boughs that never shed their leaves and the love

"For ever warm and still to be enjoyed" (26), are painful reminders that such serenity is available only as still life, existence frozen into art and not as lived experience. In this agon between life and art, the poet lends his imaginative resources to realizing unreality—the sweetness of unheard melodies and the happiness of unconsummated love:

> Fair youth beneath the trees, thou canst not leave
> Thy song, nor ever can those trees be bare;
> Bold lover, never, never canst thou kiss,
> Though winning near the goal—yet do not grieve:
> She cannot fade, though thou hast not thy bliss,
> For ever wilt thou love, and she be fair!
> (15–20)

For the moment the speaker's imagination is so fully absorbed by the pastoral scene on the urn that he offers the chiseled lover consoling advice. The contest between art and life, sculpture and poetry, has reached a moment of equipoise. But increasingly the speaker's tone becomes plaintive as he meditates on lovers that cannot age, trees that will not shed their leaves, unheard melodies that, like unconsummated love, will never grow stale. He tries to persuade himself that these timeless and lifeless states are preferable to timebound human passion "That leaves a heart high-sorrowful and cloyed, / A burning forehead, and a parching tongue" (29–30). He seems to arrive at the weak conclusion that moments of true harmony and happiness are accessible only as "Cold pastoral" and that the only refuge from painful mortality lies in the silent immortality of the urn.

This conclusion is, however, open also to a stronger interpretation: that the speaker can bear the world "full of Misery and Heartbreak, Pain, Sickness and oppression" (*Letters* 1:281) as long as this world includes marble urns, artifices of eternity that order violent *and* tranquil, distressing *and* re-creative symbols into a *concordia discors*. Neither the pure harmony of pastoral inspiration nor the echoing green bower can, for this speaker, offer restorative spots of time. Only dissonant "Cold pastoral" can help the mind uncover moments of arresting beauty within the world of pain and flux. Keats concludes his unresolved contests between naive and sentimental modes of feeling, between plastic art and lyric poetry, between the stillness of pastoral joy and the bittersweet intensity of mutable existence, as the Pygmalion-like speaker gives life and voice to the urn. Generously and ironically, he lets the timeless piece of sculpture have the last word, addressed to timebound generations of men. With its commonplace epigram, the urn triumphs over the poet.[9] But since the whole debate has been a psychomachia, in which Keats brilliantly incorporated the motif of a pastoral contest with its prize cup, since he made the cup itself a participant in his contest, the poet-umpire has nothing to award to the victor. His Greek urn must be its own award.

Keats's debate with an imaginary urn may serve as a fit emblem for the Romantic poets' recuperation of pastoral motifs and perspectives. Like the urn, pastoral *topoi* are silent survivors from the past until poets endow them with new life by engaging them in dynamic debate, interrogating them, and assimilating them into their armory of the mind. But deploying them in forays into uncharted territories became increasingly problematical. Keats's odes point up the problem and suggest one solution for the modern poet: intensifying the dissonance between an ideal pastoral ethos and the alienating consciousness of the contemporary world. The poet then experiences the Wordsworthian double consciousness of the self as the speaking subject and of the earlier self as the subject about which the speaker speaks, but he can no longer trust that the traces of the earlier self,

> Those shadowy recollections,
> Which, be they what they may,
> Are yet the fountain light of all our day,
> Are yet a master light of all our seeing. . . .
> (*Intimations of Immortality* 150–53)

The Wordsworthian belief in an Arcadia of the soul whose emanations could permeate the fibers of adult life and change the fabric of society became a dubious ideology.

By the end of the nineteenth century, pastoral had become an endangered species in England. It is true that Yeats and Auden could still, at times, take their key from Keats's gently ironic tone, even as they intensified his consciousness of dissonance. Thus Yeats notes that Arcadian harmony and joy have been displaced by the "cracked tune that Chronos sings," even as he offers the anachronistic, romantic consolation that "Words alone are certain good" (*The Song of the Happy Shepherd* 9–10). And Auden shared Yeats's nostalgia for pastoral harmony without denying his consciousness of dissonant antipastoral reality:

> We, too, had known golden hours
> When body and soul were in tune,
> Had danced with our true loves
> By the light of a full moon. . . .

Such resonant song was soon displaced by a cacophonous din:

> All words like Peace and Love,
> All sane affirmative speech,
> Had been soiled, profaned, debased
> To a horrid mechanical screech.
> No civil style survived
> That pandaemonium
> But the wry, the sotto-voce,
> Ironic and monochrome:
> And where should we find shelter
> For joy or mere content
> When little was left standing
> But the suburb of dissent?
>   (*We Too Had Known Golden Hours* 1–4, 17–28)

Keats would have recognized the kindred spirit of a romantic classicist in Auden. He himself began to glimpse the abyss between an Arcadian past "when body and soul were in tune" and an ever more counterfactual Elysian future that had to assert itself against the "suburb of dissent." Looking back at the pastoral visions of Wordsworth and Keats from the perspective of Yeats and Auden, we can see how well founded were Schiller's doubts about the humanistic enterprise of restoring man's wholeness through the possible coalescence of naive and sentimental ways of feeling, seeing, and saying the ideal in the real and the real in the ideal.

NOTES

CHAPTER 1

1. See Congleton 75–114. For an excellent synopsis of the debate, see also Aubrey Williams's introduction to Pope's "A Discourse on Pastoral" (Pope 1:15–18).

2. Frequently this demand was based on the claim that Theocritus described the real rural life, real climate, and real valleys of Sicily. Cf., for example, Richard Polwhele's "Dissertation on Theocritus": "The pieces of Theocritus are the result of his own accurate observation. He described what he saw and felt. His characters, as well as his scenes, are the immediate transcript of nature. We may well imagine, that the shepherds and the herdsmen . . . piped before him the current ditties of their times; and that he was frequently a witness of their dialogues and contentions" (2:6). The claim that Theocritus accurately transcribed nature became commonplace among eighteenth-century critics from Joseph Warton to John Aiken.

3. An anonymous review in *The Literary Magazine and British Review* 2 (1789):244.

4. Coleridge offers this Rousseauistic description in *The Friend*, 26 October 1809: "What I dared not expect from constitutions of Government and whole Nations, I hoped from Religion and a small Company of chosen Individuals, and formed a plan, as harmless as it was extravagant, of trying the experiment of human Perfectibility on the banks of the *Susquehannah*; where our little Society, in its second Generation, was to have combined the innocence of the patriar-

chal Age with the knowledge and genuine refinements of European culture" (2:146).

5. Wordsworth's paradisal community again reminds us of that stage in man's development that, in his *Discourse on Inequality*, Rousseau calls the happiest epoch, just before the beginning of man's exploitation of nature and of man (72–73).

6. As R. F. Jones points out, the metaphor served both the ancients and the moderns, since the pygmy figure emphasizes civilization's decay while the improved perspective from the shoulders of the giants argues for modern superiority (280n12). For an excellent discussion of Schiller's relation to the battle between ancients and moderns, see Jauss, *Literaturgeschichte*, 67–105.

7. Schiller's three essays appeared as follows: "Über das Naive," in *Horen* 4: 11 (November 1795); "Die sentimentalischen Dichter," *Horen* 4: 12 (December 1795); "Beschluss der Abhandlung über naive und sentimentalische Dichter, nebst einigen Bemerkungen einen charakteristischen Unterschied den Menschen betreffend," *Horen* 5: 1 (January 1796). Besides making some cuts, Schiller made few revisions when he combined the three essays into a single treatise for his collection of *Kleinere prosaische Schriften*, Pt. 2 (1800). Information on the genesis of *Über naive und sentimentalische Dichtung* is conveniently brought together in *NA* 21:278–86.

8. Schiller's term *Empfindungsweise* is difficult to translate because in the eighteenth century *Empfindung* had a wide range of meaning that the word *feeling* does not adequately capture. As Wilkinson and Willoughby indicate in their Glossary (*AL* 307–8), for Schiller the terms *Empfindung* and *Gefühl* included a range of meanings from "sensation" to "felt thought." One of Coleridge's notebook entries throws further light on the problem by distinguishing feeling from sensation and perception:

> A SENSATION,—a Feeling referring to some *Thing*, and yet not *organized* into a definite *Object* nor separated from the sentient Being— or abstracted from a Perception, as we abstract matter from form.
>
> A Perception—sensations organized into an Object, and thus projected out of the sentient Being in real or in ideal Space.—
>
> A Feeling—an act of consciousness having itself for its only Object, and not a Symbol or representative of any thing else. Thus I have a *sensation* of Heat, a *Feeling* of Life.—We feel what *is* in us— we have a sensation of what we *find* in us—The Germans, the great

Nomenclators in all the Sciences, in psychology & metaphysics not less than in Minerology, express this in the verbs as well as substantives—*fühlen* und *empfinden* as well as *Gefühl* und *Empfindung*. (*CN* 3:3605 f118v)

Whereas *Empfindung*, this feeling of "what is in us," may be evanescent, *Empfindungsweise* or *Empfindungsart* denote more habitual modes, more lasting ways of feeling.

9. In his famous birthday letter of 23 August 1794, Schiller told Goethe that the "neulichen Unterhaltungen mit Ihnen haben meine ganze Ideenmasse in Bewegung gebracht" (*GA* 20:13).

10. See Schiller's letter to Goethe of 23 August 1794 (*GA* 20:15).

11. This passage occurs only in the first version published in the *Horen* and is reprinted in *NA* 21:288.

12. See the *Oxford English Dictionary* on *express* and *expression* and Adelung on *ausdrucken* and *Ausdruck*.

13. Schiller's insistence that the poet should express an ideal of humanity sharply differs from Kant's position. In the *Critique of Pure Reason* Kant discusses the ideal of humanity in the course of distinguishing between ideas and ideals of pure reason. He roundly condemns as impractical and absurd the attempt to realize the ideal either in an example or in a fictitious narrative (485–86).

14. Schiller cites Homer and Shakespeare as examples of such impersonal creation. It is interesting how frequently this *topos* of the poet who disappears behind his creation recurs in Romantic criticism, with Shakespeare cited as the prototypical "centrifugal" poet—to use Coleridge's term for the intelligence that "tends to *objectize* itself," as distinguished from the "centripetal" intelligence that tends to "*know* itself in the object" (*BL* 1:286). His distinction between Shakespeare and Milton is also relevant: Shakespeare "darts himself forth, and passes into all the forms of human character and passion, the one Proteus of the fire and flood; the other attracts all forms and things to himself, into the unity of his own IDEAL" (*BL* 2:27–28). The *topos* becomes a commonplace through Hazlitt and Keats down to T. S. Eliot's insistence on the poet's impersonality, a goal he cannot reach "without surrendering himself wholly to the work to be done " (*Selected Essays* 11). Significantly, Eliot, like Schiller, is developing his argument in the context of the modern poet's coming to terms with being judged by the standards of the past.

15. Schlegel uses the term *Transcendentalpoesie* in the context of a typology of poetry that owes a great deal to Schiller's *Naive and Sentimental Poetry*.

16. Cf. also Schiller's important discussion of poetics—the problem of the representation (*Darstellung*) of subject matter, as well as the problem of language as the poetic medium—in his *Kallias* letters (*Briefe* 3:291–99). For an illuminating commentary on Schiller's poetics, see Szondi.

17. Cf. also Schiller's criticism of Haller's didactic poetry (*NA* 20:453–54).

18. "... der Mensch wurde aus einem unschuldigen Geschöpf ein schuldiges, aus einem vollkommenen Zögling der Natur ein unvollkommenes moralisches Wesen, aus einem glücklichen Instrumente ein unglücklicher Künstler" (*NA* 17:400). Schiller acknowledges his debt to Kant's similar argument in his short essay "Mutmasslicher Anfang der Menschengeschichte."

19. Coleridge quotes these lines from Schiller's *Die Worte des Glaubens* in 1810 (*CN* 3:3814), having earlier entered in his notebooks the whole stanza in which these lines occur (1:1074 and 2:2431). Schiller's *Worte des Glaubens* testify to the speaker's faith in the immutable *inner* worth of the golden age, of freedom, virtue, and God, whereas the companion poem *Die Worte des Wahns* exposes as false the belief that the highest good exists in the *external* world.

20. See *Briefe* 3:294–99.

21. Adelung notes that the adjective *empfindsam* (which I have translated as *sentimental* in the quotation from Schiller) is a recent coinage that was gaining wide currency through Yorrick's sentimental journeys. Significantly, Schiller uses the term *sentimentalisch* (not *empfindsam*) when he is contrasting naive and sentimental modes of feeling (*Empfindungsweisen*). Adelung does not include *sentimentalisch* in his dictionary.

22. *Der spielende Knabe* (*NA* 1:233) may be paraphrased in prose as follows: "Play! lovely innocence! Arcadia yet surrounds you and you freely follow nature's joyous urge; exuberant power creates merely imaginary barriers and the willing spirit is as yet free from duty and purpose. Play! for soon toil will appear, haggard and grave, and imperious duty will lack inclination and spirit."

23. Cf. Schiller's address to a "sensitive friend of nature" (*NA* 20:428) and his seminal statement on the idyll (20:472).

24. It is worth noting that in his review of Bürger, in which

he discusses the fragmentation and dissociation that result from division of labor, Schiller uses Hebe as a symbol for poetry's power of rejuvenating the human spirit: "Aus noch so divergierenden Bahnen würde sich der Geist bei der Dichtkunst wieder zurechtfinden und in ihrem verjüngenden Licht der Erstarrung eines frühzeitigen Alters entgehen. Sie wäre die jugendlichblühende Hebe, welche in Jovis Saal die unsterblichen Götter bedient" (22:245–46).

25. In Walter Arndt's translation this passage is rendered as follows: "Alas! Do not excite my yearning. . . / Phoebus I never gazed upon, / Of Ares, Hermes saw no sign, / Then stood before my eyes the one / Whom men would worship as divine. / . . . No like of his will Earth engender, / Nor Hebe lift to Heaven's throne; / Here must the laboring lyre surrender, / In vain do they torment the stone" (186–187).

CHAPTER 2

1. "A Pastorall Aeglogue Upon the Death of Sir Phillip Sidney" (43).

2. On the interesting interrelation between pastoral and epic as exemplified by Virgil and Milton, see the studies by Coolidge and Martz.

3. I am borrowing the terms "norm-fulfilling" and "norm-breaking" from Jauss's "Levels of Identification" (295). Although I have greatly profited from his insights into the aesthetics of reception, both in this article and in his full-length study *Aesthetische Erfahrung*, my borrowing of terms does not mean that I subscribe to his rather rigid system of modalities of reader identification.

4. Cf. Hartman, *Wordsworth's Poetry*, 17–18.

5. Shelley's phrase from *To a Sky-Lark* (5) echoes Milton's "unpremeditated Verse" (*Paradise Lost* 9:24).

6. Nowottny shows that the "compelling syntactical relations" in such passages communicate to the reader both some specific information and, simultaneously, its significance. "The Genesis passage," she argues, "informs us of the fact that, and of the manner in which, God created light; the exact form in which this information is conveyed compels us to regard it as meaning, further, that what God willed was forthwith brought to pass exactly according to His word as

the consequence of that word; these significances proceed from the relations, apprehended in a flash by the reader's mind, between the parts of the command (and their organization) and the parts of the fulfilment (and their organization)" (10).

7. Parker (54–55) calls attention to the relevance to *This Lime-Tree Bower* of Coleridge's remarkable statement on the meditative process. The passage I have quoted comes from the second of two little-known letters "To a Junior Soph" that Coleridge contributed to *Blackwoods Magazine* in 1821.

8. See *CL* 1:334.

9. In his letter to Benjamin Bailey, 22 November 1817, Keats mentions a favorite speculation of his, "that we shall enjoy ourselves here after by having what we called happiness on Earth repeated in a finer tone" (*Letters* 1:185).

10. On Shelley's extensive use of pastoral conventions, see the two articles by George Norlin. For a theoretical discussion of the self-conscious use of convention in pastoral elegy, see Alpers's "Convening and Convention in Pastoral Poetry" (279–87).

11. Cf. Spenser's November Eclogue of the *Shepheardes Calender* for a similar lament over human life's and fame's exclusion from nature's cyclical rebirth:

> Whence is it that the flouret of the field doth fade,
> And lyeth buryed long in winter's bale:
> Yet soone as spring his mantle doth displaye,
> If floureth fresh, as it should never fayle?
> But thing on earth that is of most availe,
>   As vertues braunch and beauties budde,
>   Reliven not for any good.
>   O heavie herse!
> The braunch once dead, the budde eke needes must quaile.
>   O carefull verse!
>   (83–92)

12. "Der Ursprung des Kunstwerkes" (*Gesamtausgabe* 5:68): "Ist die Kunst noch eine wesentliche und eine notwendige Weise, in der für unser geschichtliches Dasein entscheidende Wahrheit geschieht, oder ist die Kunst es nicht mehr?"

13. Schiller draws this distinction between poetic and non-

poetic pathos in his discussion of satire, but it is a basic tenet of his po-
etics and applies to other genres and other modes of feeling.

14. Shelley deifies Keats-Adonais by the kind of negative
theology that Renaissance Platonists developed from the doctrines of
Dionysus the Areopagite. Cusanus, Pico, and Ficino all agreed with
the Areopagite that "the ineffable power of the One could be de-
scribed only by contradictory attributes, that is by negating those traits
which would render it finite and thereby accessible to the intellect"
(Wind 54).

15. Shelley's dismissal of Wordsworth's this-worldly faith oc-
curs in a letter of 10 April 1822, in a passage dealing with Goethe's
Faust, which Shelley had been reading and rereading. Despite his pact
with Mephistopheles, Faust appears to Shelley "less demoniacal" than
Wordsworth: "all discontent with the *less* (to use a Platonic sophism)
supposes the sense of a just claim to the *greater*, & that we admirers of
Faust are in the right road to Paradise.—Such a supposition is not
more absurd, and is certainly less demoniacal than that of Words-
worth—where he says—

> This earth,
> Which is the world of all of us, & where
> *We find our happiness or not at all.*"
> (*Letters* 2:406)

Shelley is apparently quoting Wordsworth from memory. He is mis-
quoting the concluding lines of "French Revolution as It Appeared
to Enthusiasts at Its Commencement," which first appeared in *The
Friend*, 26 October 1809, and was included in *Poems* (1815). Its earliest
version in *The Prelude* (1805) was, of course, unpublished during Shel-
ley's life.

16. Cf. *NA* 20:473.

17. Keats's letter to Shelley, 16 August 1820, deals with his
reaction to *The Cenci*. Keats writes: "You I am sure will forgive me for
sincerely remarking that you might curb your magnanimity and be
more of an artist, and 'load every rift' of your subject with ore. . . .
And is not this extraordina[r]y talk for the writer of Endymion?" (*Let-
ters* 2:323).

CHAPTER 3

1. In a letter to Lady Beaumont in July 1805, Dorothy Wordsworth quoted Coleridge's explanation that his ideas about the *Recluse* were "burnt as a Plague-Garment" (*EY* 607).

2. Wordsworth explained to Coleridge in his letter of 22 May 1815 that one of his principal aims in the *Excursion* was "to put the commonplace truths, of the human affections especially, in an interesting point of view; and rather to remind men of their knowledge as it lurks inoperative and unvalued in their own minds, than to attempt to convey recondite or refined truths" (*MY* 2:238). To which Coleridge replied, on 30 May 1815, by recapitulating his own high expectations for the whole *Recluse* and suggesting rather drily that Wordsworth had already dealt with commonplace truths in the *Lyrical Ballads*, as far as that was possible, "without an insight into the whole truth" (*CL* 4:576).

3. In July 1832, near the end of his life, Coleridge reportedly still spoke along similar lines of the plan for the *Recluse* (*Table Talk* 175).

4. Coleridge used "omniformity" to contrast with "uniformity" and "simplicity" in Appendix C to *The Statesman's Manual* (*Lay Sermons* 73).

5. For the tradition of the *beatus vir* figure, see Røstvig. The resemblances between St. Basil and Wordsworth are discussed by Butler (244–45).

6. Johnston has recently argued that in the whole *Recluse* project, from the early drafts of 1797 through the completed final books of the *Excursion* (1812–14), Wordsworth's process of composition shows a dialectical alternation between the *Recluse* and *Prelude* projects, between a pull toward the social theme and a recoil into the self ("Wordsworth and *The Recluse*").

7. In the Preface to the *Lyrical Ballads* Wordsworth speaks of the poet as being "in the situation of a translator" (*Prose* 1:139) and comments on the poet's language falling short of the words produced under the actual pressure of passions (1:138).

8. See Eliade's "Yearning for Paradise" (255–56).

9. Rudolf Otto characterizes the numinous as a state of mind *sui generis*, undefinable and inexpressible, an "unnamed Something" eluding "apprehension in terms of concepts" yet expressing a "clear overplus of meaning" (5–7).

10. Cooke comments illuminatingly on Wordsworth's rhetorical resources, including his use of the figure of litotes (197–98). For the best discussion of the ambiguities in Wordsworth's figurative language in *Home at Grasmere*, see Garber's comments on Wordsworth's difficulties in building a paradise in Grasmere (187–200).

11. Cf. Coleridge's letter to Thomas Poole, 14 October 1803, stating his concern over Wordsworth's tendency fo "Self-involution" and rejoicing that Wordsworth has at last turned to his "great work necessarily comprehending his attention & Feelings within the circle of great objects & elevated Conceptions" (*CL* 2:1013).

12. Lovejoy has claimed that one of the most momentous changes in the history of thought was from the Enlightenment's dominant commitment to "the simplification and standardization of thought and life" to the Romantic belief that "diversity itself is of the essence of excellence" (292–93). Recently Abrams has amended Lovejoy's formulation, adding that "what was most distinctive in Romantic thought was the normative emphasis not on plenitude as such, but on an organized unity in which all individuation and diversity survive. . . . The norm of the highest good was thus transferred from simple unity, not to sheer diversity as such but to the most inclusive integration" (*Natural Supernaturalism* 185–86). This is precisely the kind of inclusive integration that Schiller postulated as the aesthetic goal of the idyll and that White (36–38) sees exemplified in Romantic synecdoche.

13. In a curiously misguided final revision, Wordsworth transferred the experience to an unidentified "roving school-boy," only to reveal his identity suddenly in an awkward aside:

> Since that day forth the Place to him—*to me*
> (For I who live to register the truth
> Was that same young and happy Being) became
> As beautiful to thought as it had been
> When present to the bodily sense. . . .
> (MS D 46–50)

14. For the connection between death and Arcadia, see Panofsky's classic exposition in "Et in Arcadia Ego."

15. Wordsworth did not retain this passage in either the 1805 or the 1850 texts.

16. Kroeber discusses the parallels between Wordsworth's

poetry and Constable's landscapes, with some passing references to Turner.

17. I am quoting the translation of Wilkinson and Willoughby included in *Aesthetic Letters* (292–93n). As they point out in their note, Freud incorporated Schiller's letter into his second edition of the *Interpretation of Dreams*.

18. Wordsworth speaks of Coleridge as being no slave

> Of that false secondary power by which
> In weakness we create distinctions, then
> Believe our puny boundaries are things
> Which we perceive and not which we have made.
>
> (*1799 Prelude* 2:251–54)

CHAPTER 4

1. MS E, the final fair copy from which the 1850 text was printed, received its title after Wordsworth's death (*Prelude* xxiv). MS B of the 1805 text contains the following title, inscribed in ornate lettering: "Poem / Title not yet fixed upon / by / William Wordsworth / Addressed to / S. T. Coleridge." DeSelincourt reproduced this title page opposite the title page of the 1850 edition.

2. Isabella Fenwick note to the Immortality Ode, *PW* 4:464.

3. Heidegger's play on the word *Sprache* (language) is untranslatable: "In Erfahrungen, die wir *mit* der Sprache machen, bringt sich die Sprache selbst zur Sprache" (*Unterwegs zur Sprache* 161).

4. This wonderful phrase—"twilight of rememberable life"— occurs only in the *1799 Prelude*. When Wordsworth transposed the "spots of time" passage in which it occurs to Book 11 in the 1805 *Prelude*, he replaced it with the less felicitous phrase "As far as memory can look back" (11:278), which, in turn, in 1850 he reduced to the simple narrative statement "I remember well" (12:225), eliminating the psychological subtlety altogether. It is worth noting that other lines referring to experiences drawn from the threshold of consciousness, which I quote in the subsequent discussion from the 1805 *Prelude*, all survived with minimal revision from the 1799 version.

5. Translated into prose, this passage says: "If the eye were not sun-like, it never could perceive the sun; if divine power did not dwell in us, how could the divine enrapture us."

6. I borrow the term "root metaphor" from Stephen C. Pepper (ch. 5) although I do not subscribe to his theory of world hypotheses. The concept of a root metaphor is useful for denoting the dynamic process by which a powerful analogical hypothesis generates explanations about phenomena or experiences that fall outside the bounds of rational explanation—that are overdetermined, in Freud's sense of the term. It is close to Hayden White's concept of synecdoche, which incorporates Pepper's theory (13, 36). The term "root metaphor" is used not only by Pepper but also by Paul Ricoeur (*Rule of Metaphor* 244). Max Black draws on Pepper's concept to establish his own notion of "conceptual archetypes" (239–41). Victor Turner uses the term "root paradigm" to denote "irreducible life stances of individuals, passing beneath conscious prehension to a fiduciary hold on what they sense to be axiomatic values" (*Dramas* 64).

7. This is Victor Turner's formulation of what he calls Arnold van Gennep's "striking discovery" (*Dramas* 13).

8. For the dating of the fragment, see Stephen Parrish's introduction to the *1799 Prelude* (6).

9. The phrase "rushing power" occurs in an early MS fragment—"a storm not terrible but strong / with lights and shades and with a rushing power" (MS JJ, *1799 Prelude*, p. 123). The phrase clearly echoes the pentecostal storm: "And suddenly there came a sound from heaven as of a rushing mighty wind. . . . And they were all filled with the Holy Ghost, and began to speak with other tongues, as the Spirit gave them utterance" (Acts 2:2–4).

10. For other recent deconstructive interpretations of the dream, see the articles by Mary Jacobus and Cynthia Chase.

11. Steiner is here drawing on Heidegger's *Der Ursprung des Kunstwerkes*.

12. Wordsworth's designation of "general truths" as "Under-Powers" (1:163) anticipates Heidegger's insight, in *Der Ursprung des Kunstwerkes*, that the truth which art embodies and exhibits is itself at work in the realization of the work of art: "Das Wesen der Kunst, worin das Kunstwerk und der Künstler zumal beruhen, ist das Sich-ins-Werk-setzen der Wahrheit" (*Gesamtausgabe* 5:59).

13. A draft makes the explicit distinction between passionate

"desultory sound" and laborious "slow creation" (MS 33, *1799 Prelude*, p. 163).

14. The painting is in the Kunsthistorisches Museum of Vienna. Jean Leymarie suggests that "Vermeer is showing us the way he painted 'a Vermeer' " (192).

15. In an earlier remark on the same subject in a letter to Lady Beaumont, Wordsworth attributes the idea to Coleridge: "Never forget what I believe was observed to you by Coleridge, that every great and original writer, in proportion as he is great or original, must himself create the taste by which he is to be relished; he must teach the art by which he is to be seen" (*MY* 1:150).

16. Coleridge's comment about Wordsworth's egotistical sublime is apparently connected with his reading of *The Prelude*. In her comment on this notebook entry, Kathleen Coburn argues that Coleridge had with him in Malta the copy of Wordsworth's poems (MS M) prepared for him by Dorothy Wordsworth and Sara Hutchinson. The copy contained the *Prelude*, books 1–4, the *Ruined Cottage*, and some short poems. (See *CN* 2:2057n and 2092n.)

17. "Denn die sichtbaren empfindlichen Dinge sind ein Wesen des Unsichtbaren; von dem Unsichtlichen, Unbegreiflichen ist kommen das Sichtbare, Begreifliche: von dem Aussprechen oder Aushauchen der unsichtbaren Kraft ist worden das sichtbare Wesen; das unsichtbare geistliche Wort der göttlichen Kraft wirket mit und durch das sichtbare Wesen, wie die Seele mit und durch den Leib" (5:1).

18. Schiller's superbly formulated passage deserves to be quoted in full:

> Wenn der Schulverstand, immer vor Irrtum bange, seine Worte wie seine Begriffe an das Kreuz der Grammatik und Logik schlägt, hart und steif ist, um ja nicht unbestimmt zu sein, viele Worte macht, um ja nicht viel zu sagen, und dem Gedanken, damit er ja den Unvorsichtigen nicht schneide, lieber die Kraft und die Schärfe nimmt, so gibt das Genie dem seinigen mit einem einzigen glücklichen Pinselstrich einen ewig bestimmten, festen und dennoch ganz freien Umriss. Wenn dort das Zeichen dem Bezeichneten ewig heterogen und fremd bleibt, so springt hier wie durch innere Notwendigkeit die Sprache aus dem Gedanken hervor, und ist so sehr eins mit demselben, dass selbst unter der körperlichen Hülle der Geist wie entblösset erscheint. Eine solche Art des Aus-

drucks, wo das Zeichen ganz in dem Bezeichneten verschwindet, und wo die Sprache den Gedanken, den sie ausdrückt, noch gleichsam nackend lässt, da ihn die andre nie darstellen kann, ohne ihn zugleich zu verhüllen, ist es, was man in der Schreibart vorzugsweise genialisch und geistreich nennt (*NA* 20:426).

CHAPTER 5

1. In his Fenwick note to *Ode to Lycoris*, Wordsworth makes the point that the Virgilian name Lycoris might affect some readers as unnatural and thus "tend to unrealize the sentiment that pervades these verses." He charmingly argues that, having abstained from such classical allusions in his earlier poetry, surely he "may be allowed to retrace his steps in the regions of fancy which delighted him in his boyhood, when he first became acquainted with the Greek and Roman Poets" (*PW* 4:422). In *The Prelude*, however, he disparaged his training in "classic niceties" as that "overpriz'd / And dangerous craft of picking phrases out / From languages that want the living voice / To make of them a nature to the heart" (6:127, 129–32). Hazlitt attributed this dismissal of classic niceties to the Lake School's revolutionary ferment: "Nothing that was established was to be tolerated. All the commonplace figures of poetry, tropes, allegories, personifications, with the whole heathen mythology, were instantly discarded; a classical allusion was considered as a piece of antiquated foppery" (5:162).

2. Oral tradition replaced for Wordsworth not only mythological but also historical associations. In Book 8 of *The Prelude* he tells us that English history never delighted him since "high-wrought modern narratives / Stript of their harmonising soul, the life / Of manners and familiar incidents" (774–76). He owed his sense of place not to historical "records or traditions" (781) but to a present awareness of "what had been here done, and suffer'd here / Through ages, and was doing, suffering, still" (782–83). Moreover, his present observations of the place before his eyes were frequently so intensified and transformed by remembrances of his own past that they became "like vital functions of the soul" (789): "And out of what had been, what was, the place / Was throng'd with impregnations, like those wilds / In which my early feeling had been nurs'd" (8:789–91).

3. Soft and hard views of pastoral are well summed up by Frank Kermode in his introductory essay to *English Pastoral Poetry* (17–18).

4. John F. Lynen convincingly emphasizes the importance of the pastoral narrator's perspective: "Pastoral comes to life whenever the poet is able to adopt its special point of view—whenever he casts himself in the role of the country dweller and writes about life in terms of the contrast between the rural world with its rustic scenery and naive, humble folk, and the great outer world of the powerful, the wealthy, and the sophisticated" (9). Perceptive though his study is of Frost's pastoralism, Lynen's comments on Wordsworth are often inadequate, especially his claim that *Michael* is concerned with the processes of the poet's mind and not with the moral values shared by a local community (61).

5. For an excellent discussion of Wordsworth's use of the epitaph tradition, see Hartman's "Wordsworth, Inscriptions, and Romantic Nature Poetry."

6. See the Fenwick note (*PW* 2:478). The importance of realistic detail to authenticate veracity and sincerity in Wordsworth's poetry is fully discussed by Perkins (33–60).

7. In discussing this "defect" of Wordsworth's poetry (*BL* 2:126), Coleridge takes his example not from *Michael* but from *The Excursion*. Coleridge actually praises the character of Michael, along with the vicar and shepherd-mariner of *The Brothers*, as having "all the verisimilitude and representative quality, that the purposes of poetry can require" (*BL* 2:47). Elsewhere he similarly stresses Wordsworth's commendable verisimilitude, furnishing through the scenes and characters of *Michael* "important documents of the kindly ministrations of local attachment" prevailing in the Lake District (*CL* 2:664).

8. Roger Sharrock (68) contrasts these effective symbols with what he calls "abortive symbols" in Wordsworth's experimental ballads —e.g., the hooting owls in *The Idiot Boy*. It should be noted that Wordsworth originally attempted to compose *Michael* as an experimental, jocular ballad, as Stephen Parrish has shown (50–75).

9. In his Preface to *Lyrical Ballads* (1800), Wordsworth clearly diagnosed the deleterious effects of urbanization and mass media on the powers of the mind: "For a multitude of causes unknown to former times are now acting with a combined force to blunt the discriminating powers of the mind, and unfitting it for all voluntary exertion to reduce it to a state of almost savage torpor." He goes on to specify

that "the most effective of these causes are the great national events which are daily taking place, and the encreasing accumulation of men in cities, where the uniformity of their occupations produces a craving for extraordinary incident which the rapid communication of intelligence hourly gratifies." To counter these forces blunting the discriminating powers of the mind is, according to Wordsworth, "one of the best services in which, at any period, a Writer can be engaged, . . . especially so at the present day" (*Prose* 1:128). For Wordsworth's most direct protest against the dehumanization of a world dominated by machines, see *The Excursion*, Books 8 and 9.

   10. Potts quotes from the Celestial City in *Pilgrim's Progress*: "Whose Delectable Mountains are these? And whose be the sheep that feed upon them?—These mountains are Immanuel's Land. And they are within sight of his City; and the sheep also are his, and he laid down his life for them" (239).

   11. This landscape suggests the kind of pleasance described by Freud as the epitome of fantasy-making: "The creation of the mental realm [*des seelischen Reiches*] of phantasy finds a perfect parallel [*Gegenstück*] in the establishment of 'reservations' or 'nature reserves' [*Naturschutzparks*] in places where the requirements of agriculture, communications and industry threaten to bring about changes in the original face of the earth which will quickly make it unrecognizable. A nature reserve preserves its original state which everywhere else has to our regret been sacrificed to necessity. . . . The mental realm of phantasy is just such a reservation withdrawn from the reality principle" (11:387).

   12. On Claude Lorrain's landscapes, see Kenneth Clark (64). A good example of Claude's schematized pastoral is his *Landscape with the Flight into Egypt*, which Clark includes as an illustration (pl. 63). E. H. Gombrich's *Art and Illusion* provides the best commentary on the importance of schemata for the painter's representation of reality; see especially chapters 2 ("Truth and Stereotype"), 5 ("Formula and Experience"), and 11 ("From Representation to Expression").

   13. See especially lines 2, 16, 322, 482.

   14. On Wordsworth's sacramental naturalism, compare the following passage from *The Prelude*: "Oh! sorrow for the Youth who could have seen / Unchasten'd, unsubdu'd, unaw'd, unrais'd / To patriarchal dignity of mind, / And pure simplicity of wish and will, / Those sanctified abodes of peaceful Man" (6:441–45).

   15. Goethe's poem *Hegire* from *Der West-Östliche Divan* (*GA*

3:287–88) celebrates the Orient as a place where life is pure and good and as a time that allows the speaker to penetrate the mysteries of human origins, a time when man still received God's wisdom in earthly tongues: "Dort im Reinen und im Rechten / Will ich menschlichen Geschlechten / In des Ursprungs Tiefe dringen, / Wo sie noch von Gott empfingen / Himmelslehr in Erdesprachen" (7–11).

16. Insisting that the Hesiodic didactic strain is essentially hostile to Theocritean pastoral, Rosenmeyer excludes *Michael* from his pastoral canon (24). He overlooks Wordsworth's originality in fusing the Epicurean pleasure principle with the Protestant work ethic. Unlike our own culture, which assumes a dichotomy between the unpleasurable hours clocked by work and pleasurable leisure time, Wordsworth's evokes a unity in which work as much as leisure brings life-affirming joy.

17. In his *Guide Through the District of the Lakes*, Wordsworth similarly looked back from the England of 1810 to the more idyllic days of his youth—adjusting the dating on a sliding scale as his *Guide* went through later editions. In 1810 the happier time was forty years ago, then in 1820 it was fifty years ago, and in 1835 it was sixty years! In that happier time in the Lake District "was found a perfect Republic of Shepherds and Agriculturists, among whom the plough of each man was confined to the maintenance of his own family." It was "like an ideal society or an organized community, whose constitution had been imposed and regulated by the mountains which protected it" (*Prose* 2:206, 206n).

18. Wordsworth used these terms in the 1802 version of *Michael*: "let this sheep-fold be / Thy anchor and thy shield" (*PW* 2:92n).

19. In a notebook memorandum of April 1805, Coleridge speaks of the "beautiful passage" in *Michael* "respecting the forward-looking *Hope* inspired pre-eminently by the birth of a child." It confirmed his own sense of the "immense importance of young Children to the keeping up the stock of *Hope* in the human Species" (*CN* 2:2549).

20. Geoffrey Durrant offers a different interpretation, seeing in the oak "a reminder of the persistence with which life maintains itself," and in the remains of the sheepfold "a mute reminder of the inherent tendency of things to seek, as the scientists tell us they do, an ever greater degree of disorder" (51).

21. Cf. Schiller *NA* 20:469.

22. In his *Keywords* Raymond Williams illuminatingly traces

the changes in the meaning of *industry*, semantic changes that reflect significant socioeconomic shifts (137–39).

23. Cf. Wordsworth's efforts to arrive at a consoling ending for *The Ruined Cottage*, redrafting the Pedlar's concluding lines several times (*PW* 5:400–404). Bostetter provides a fine commentary on Wordsworth's efforts to transmute the tale's negations into affirmations (63–65).

24. On the relation of pastoral to heroic modes, see Coolidge (1–23) and Cullen (4–5).

25. In the MS ballad version of *Michael*, the poet has the whole story from Michael himself: "[An] hour will I spend to relate / What old Michael once told me while on a loose [stone]" (Parrish 72).

26. In her biography of Wordsworth, Mary Moorman reports that Wordsworth thought *Joanna* and *Nutting* showed the "greatest genius" of any poems added in the second edition of *Lyrical Ballads*, though he pointed to *Michael* as containing his most important "views" (506).

27. On Wordsworth's commitment to community, see Ahearn's article and the important full-length treatment of the subject by Friedman. McFarland trenchantly sums up the key features of Wordsworthian community: "the family as archetypal society; the small estate as extension of its owner's personality; and *lived-into* land as the arena of communal interaction" (174).

CHAPTER 6

1. Cf. also Rosenmeyer 41.

2. Wilkie compares Coleridge's role to that of Augustus for Virgil, the Duke of Ferrara for Tasso, and King Sebastian for Camoens, "each of whom is urged to maintain and project into the future the ideals celebrated in the poem" (109).

3. On dating Book 10 of the *Prelude*, see de Selincourt's introduction (liii) and Jonathan Wordsworth's, Abrams's, and Gill's discussion of the composition of the 1805 text (*Norton Prelude* 518–19). Coleridge actually left Sicily in November 1804, but posts were extremely slow and precarious, leaving Wordsworth often uncertain for months about Coleridge's whereabouts and well being.

4. For a provocative discussion of the story of Vaudracour and Julia, see Spivak 324–36.

5. On the *topos* of *Et in Arcadia ego* see Panofsky 223–54. I owe the description of Sicily as a political *memento mori* to Wilkie 109.

6. *Idyll* 7, on which Wordsworth draws in the remainder of his envoy to Book 10, also speaks of nature's sympathetic response to a suffering (rather than a dead) herdsman: "Tityrus shall sing how once Daphnis the neatherd loved Xenea, and how the hill was sorrowful about him and the oaktrees which grow upon the river Himeras' banks sang his dirge, when he was wasting like any snow under high Haemus or Athos or Rhodope or remotest Caucasus" (72–77). In *The Ruined Cottage* Wordsworth's Pedlar justifies this elegiac convention in memorable lines:

> The Poets in their elegies and songs
> Lamenting the departed call the groves,
> They call upon the hills and streams to mourn,
> And senseless rocks, nor idly; for they speak
> In these their invocations with a voice
> Obedient to the strong creative power
> Of human passion.
>   (MS D, 1:73–79)

7. In revising the 1805 text of Book 10, Wordsworth introduced Hyblean exhortations into his field of Enna—"Sunny lawns / Of fragrant Hybla offer to his lip / Your choicest sweets" (*apparatus criticus* p. 424). In further revision he deleted this reference, evidently not wishing to prescribe for Coleridge an overdose of honey.

8. Wordsworth may well have owed some details of his final tableau to the concluding scene of *Idyll* 7, a harvest festival celebrated in a pastoral grove containing Demeter's altar and a sacred spring. Theocritus links the present scene to mythic prototypes: "Nymphs of Castalia that haunt the steep of Parnassus, was it such a bowl as this that old Chiron served to Heracles in Pholus's rocky cave? Was it such nectar . . . as ye Nymphs mingled for us to drink that day by the altar of Demeter of the Threshing-floor?" (148–50, 154–55). Is this scene not a likely model for Wordsworth's Coleridge, whose inspired vision is "Worthy of poets who attuned their harps / In wood or echoing cave, for discipline / Of heroes" (1850, 11:457–59) and who lingers as a "gladsome Votary" near "pastoral Arethuse" (10:1034)?

CHAPTER 7

1. Clymene's experience interestingly parallels that of
Wordsworth's dreamer to whom a mysterious Arab offers a shell. He
instantly intuits the "unknown Tongue" in which he hears "articulate
sounds, / A loud prophetic blast of harmony" (*Prelude* 5:94–96).
Whereas the Arab's "prophetic blast" foretells ultimate destruction,
the strange melody that Clymene hears in her shell foretells a new
golden age.

2. Cf. also Wilkinson and Willoughby, "The Whole Man,"
194.

3. Two other Romantic island paradises are located in the
Aegean: Haidée's island in *Don Juan* is one of the "wild and smaller
Cyclades" (2.127:2), while the island Shelley's persona longs to share
with his beloved in *Epipsychidion* is an "isle under Ionian skies, / Beau-
tiful as a wreck of Paradise" (422–23). Herbert Lindenberger takes
the island as symbolic of all Romantic pastoral, which he sees as "an
isolated moment, a kind of island in time, and one which gains its
meaning and intensity through the tensions it creates with the histori-
cal world" ("The Idyllic Moment" 338).

4. See Sperry (187–89) for an insightful discussion of Apollo
as symbolizing Keats's poetic ideal. Cf. also Rajan: "Apollo stands as
the fictional surrogate for the poet who contemplates life without suf-
fering, while Hyperion is the troubled creation of a dreamer who is
unable to separate the dawn from the dusk, pleasure from pain"
(165).

5. See above, pp. 34–37, on the relation of the *Reich der
Schatten* to Schiller's projected idyll.

6. On Romantic foregrounding of subjective feeling, see
Coleridge's comments in his lecture on Dante that Ariosto's treatment
of the Diomede-Glaucus exchange of arms differs from Homer's by
Ariosto's introducing his own feelings. After quoting Ariosto, Cole-
ridge comments: "And here you will observe, that the reaction of
Ariosto's own feelings on the image or act is more fore-grounded (to
use a painter's phrase) than the image or act itself" (*Miscellaneous Criti-
cism* 149). Cf. also Coleridge's notes for this lecture, in which he uses
Ariosto as an example of how the "re-action of the Poet's general re-
flections on any Act or Image [becomes] more *fore-grounded* than the
act itself" (*CN* 3:4498f139). Coleridge borrowed his example from
Schiller's contrast between the truly self-effacing, naive treatment of

Homer and Ariosto's self-consciousness that betrays the influence of a more artificial age and a modern sensibility (*NA* 20:434–35). Schiller does not, however, use the term *foregrounded*.

7. Keats's description of the shrine and altar formed by nature's art can be instructively compared to a similar—though far more austere—natural sanctuary in *The Excursion*, which may have stirred Keats's imagination. (Keats wrote to Haydon that "there are three things to rejoice at in this Age—The Excursion Your Pictures, and Hazlitt's depth of Taste" [*Letters* 1:203].) The Wanderer and the Solitary discover in a "hidden nook" (*Excursion* 3:51) rocky pillars and other stones shaped like an altar, on which appears a tall, shiny holly (3:60–62). This scene then becomes the occasion for a long debate between the optimistic Wanderer and the disillusioned Solitary on whether there is a providential design revealed in nature or whether the rocks before their eyes "doubtless must be deemed / The sport of Nature, aided by blind Chance / Rudely to mock the works of toiling Man" (3:125–27). Keats's natural altar in the *Fall of Hyperion* is not the occasion for a comparable debate; only after he transforms his arboreal landscape into a stony temple does Keats introduce his debate on a more secular issue—the question of what a poet is and does.

8. In Arndt's translation the passage reads: "No cramping fortress would be rightful / Abode for you; in wiltless verdure set, / To make our residence delightful, / Arcadia encircles Sparta yet. / For refuge lured to smiling harbors, / You fled to fortune's blithest kiss! / These thrones are changing into arbors, / Arcadian-free shall be our bliss!"

9. Cf. especially Keats's letter to the George Keatses in Spring 1819 dealing with "Soul-making" (*Letters* 2:102–4).

10. Keats's "antechamber" calls to mind his image of the chambers of life, and particularly his description of how through the knowledge that the "World is full of Misery and Heartbreak, Pain, Sickness and oppression," the Chamber of Maiden Thought gradually darkens "and at the same time on all sides of it many doors are set open—but all dark—all leading to dark passages—We see not the ballance of good and evil" (*Letters* 1:281).

CHAPTER 8

1. Although the dating of all the odes, except *To Psyche*, is conjectural, a case can be made for placing the *Ode on Indolence* first in the sequence of odes of the spring of 1819. From Colvin to Bate, critics have argued for a late date, either the end of May or the first week of June. Others have proposed that the ode was second in the sequence and have dated it as early May. The inconclusive arguments for placing the ode either second or last have been conveniently summarized by Sperry (286–87n26). He thinks that the ode "appears to have been completed last, although in many ways it looks back to the beginning of the progression" (286). But why should it be regarded as looking back to the beginning or as echoing phrases and images from *Psyche, Nightingale,* and *Grecian Urn,* as Bate claims (*Keats* 528)? Since the "echoes" of *Ode on a Grecian Urn* are the most extensive yet appear already in Keats's journal-letter of 19 March 1819, more than a month before he began the *Grecian Urn,* surely it is more plausible that the *Ode on Indolence* created the kernel of the later odes, that it generated some of the lexicon—flowery grass, benumbing drowsiness, aching for wings, open casement, figures on a marble urn—that Keats imaginatively elaborated in the later odes. Although Vendler (20) similarly argues that *Indolence* is the seminal ode, she bases her claim merely on the *experience* of indolence described in the March journal entry and assigns a May date to Keats's reimagining the March experience and writing the ode. But all we know for a fact is that Keats conceived of the ode on or before 19 March and that he completed it some time before 9 June 1819, when he mentions it in a letter to Sarah Jeffrey (*Letters* 2:116).

2. In her headnote to the *Ode on Indolence,* Allott concludes that Keats probably reread this journal entry in May before mailing the whole journal to the George Keatses. This conjecture is supposed to support a May date for the ode (541).

3. Ian Jack says that Poussin's painting was highly suggestive for Keats's portrayal of Apollo in the minor poems as well as in *Endymion* and *Hyperion* (181–82). He does not, however, mention it in connection with the *Ode on Indolence,* identifying its visual source as a Greek vase and Poussin's *The Realm of Flora* (245–46).

4. Ian Jack, to whom I owe the reference to Hazlitt, thinks that Keats must have known engravings of Raphael's Farnesina cycle and that "although Raphael has nothing corresponding to the central

group in the Ode the voluptuous quality of his painting may well have influenced the poem" (210–11).

5. Keats may be remembering that Apuleius tells early in his narrative that Psyche's matchless beauty inspired so much homage that people began to neglect Venus's shrines. Keats reinterprets the situation: Venus neglected and Psyche honored becomes Psyche neglected but newly honored by Keats himself.

6. Among other literary echoes, Keats's "gardener Fancy" recalls Spenser's Garden of Adonis, where "all that Nature did omit, / Art, playing second Natures part, supplyed it" (*Fairie Queen* 4.10.21:8–9). Cf. also Spenser's *Hymne in Honour of Love* 254–55 and the *locus classicus* on producing an unnatural variety of flowers through art, the *Winter's Tale* 4.4.90–97.

7. See Jack 215–21 for a full discussion of Keats's visual sources.

8. See Rosenmeyer 305–6n54 for references to the wide-ranging adaptations of the *topos* of the prize cup.

9. After reviewing the principal divergent judgments of Keats's famous apothegm, Sperry concludes that "what it offers us is a sublime commonplace" (278). I think it offers just a commonplace.

WORKS CITED

Abrams, M. H. "The Correspondent Breeze: A Romantic Metaphor."
In *English Romantic Poets: Modern Essays in Criticism*, edited by M. H.
Abrams, 37–54. New York: Oxford University Press, 1960.
_____. *Natural Supernaturalism: Tradition and Revolution in Romantic
Literature*. New York: Norton, 1971.
_____. "Structure and Style in the Greater Romantic Lyric." In *From
Sensibility to Romanticism: Essays Presented to Frederick A. Pottle*, edited
by Frederick W. Hilles and Harold Bloom, 527–60. New York: Ox-
ford University Press, 1965.
Adelung, Johann Christoph. *Versuch eines vollständigen grammatisch-
kritischen Wörterbuches der hochdeutschen Mundart*. 5 parts. Leipzig:
Breitkopf, 1774–86.
Ahearn, Edward J. "The Search for Community: The City in Hölder-
lin, Wordsworth, and Baudelaire." *Texas Studies in Literature and Lan-
guage* 13 (1971): 71–89.
Alpers, Paul. "Convening and Convention in Pastoral Poetry." *New Lit-
erary History* 14 (1983): 277–304.
_____. *The Singer of the "Eclogues": A Study of Virgilian Pastoral*. With a
new translation of the *Eclogues*. Berkeley: University of California
Press, 1979.
_____. "What Is Pastoral?" *Critical Inquiry* 8 (1982): 437–60.
Aquinas, Saint Thomas. *The Basic Writings*. Edited by Anton C. Pegis.
2 vols. New York: Random House, [1945].
Arendt, Hannah. *The Human Condition*. 1958. Reprint, Garden City:
Doubleday, 1959.

Auden, W. H. *Collected Poems*. Edited by Edward Mendelson. London: Faber and Faber, 1976.

Bate, Walter Jackson. *From Classic to Romantic: Premises of Taste in Eighteenth-Century England*. Cambridge: Harvard University Press, 1946.

———. *John Keats*. Cambridge: Harvard University Press, 1963.

Black, Max. *Models and Metaphors: Studies in Language and Philosophy*. Ithaca: Cornell University Press, 1962.

Blake, William. *The Poetry and Prose*. Edited by David V. Erdman. Commentary by Harold Bloom. Garden City: Doubleday, 1965.

Bloch, Ernst. *Das Prinzip Hoffnung*. 2 vols. Frankfurt am Main: Suhrkamp, 1959.

Boehme, Jakob. *Sämmtliche Werke*. Edited by K. W. Schiebler. 7 vols. in 5. Leipzig: Johann Barth, 1831–60.

Bostetter, Edward E. *The Romantic Ventriloquists: Wordsworth, Coleridge, Keats, Shelley, Byron*. Seattle: University of Washington Press, 1963.

Bradley, A. C. *Oxford Lectures on Poetry*. London: Macmillan, 1909.

Bunn, James H. "Keats's *Ode to Psyche* and the Transformation of Mental Landscape." *English Literary History* 37 (1970): 581–94.

Butler, James A. "Wordsworth's *Tuft of Primroses*: 'An Unrelenting Doom.'" *Studies in Romanticism* 14 (1975): 237–48.

Byron, George Gordon. *Childe Harold's Pilgrimage and Other Romantic Poems*. Edited by Samuel C. Chew. New York: Odyssey Press, 1936.

———. *Don Juan and Other Satirical Poems*. Edited by Louis I. Bredvold. New York: Odyssey Press, 1935.

Carlyle, Thomas. *Sartor Resartus*. London: Chapman & Hall, 1897.

Cassirer, Ernst; Kristeller, Paul Oskar; Randall, John Herman, Jr., editors. *The Renaissance Philosophy of Man*. Chicago: University of Chicago Press, 1948.

Chase, Cynthia. "The Accidents of Disfiguration: Limits to Literal and Rhetorical Reading in Book V of *The Prelude*." *Studies in Romanticism* 18 (1979): 546–65.

Clark, Kenneth. *Landscape into Art*. 1949. Reprint, Boston: Beacon Press, 1961.

Cody, Richard. *The Landscape of the Mind: Pastoralism and Platonic Theory in Tasso's "Aminta" and Shakespeare's Early Comedies*. Oxford: Clarendon Press, 1969.

Coleridge, Samuel Taylor. *Biographia Literaria*. Edited by James Engell and W. Jackson Bate. Vol. 7 (in 2 parts) of *The Collected Works*. Edited by Kathleen Coburn. London: Routledge & Kegan Paul; Princeton: Princeton University Press, 1983.

————. *Biographia Literaria*. Edited with his Aesthetical Essays by John Shawcross. 2 vols. Oxford: Oxford University Press, 1907.

————. *Collected Letters*. Edited by Earl Leslie Griggs. 6 vols. Oxford: Clarendon Press, 1956–71.

————. *The Complete Poetical Works*. Edited by Ernest Hartley Coleridge. 2 vols. Oxford: Clarendon Press, 1912.

————. *The Complete Works*. Edited by W. G. T. Shedd. 7 vols. New York: Harper, 1853.

————. *The Friend*. Edited by Barbara E. Rooke. Vol. 4 (in 2 parts) of *The Collected Works*. Edited by Kathleen Coburn. London: Routledge & Kegan Paul; Princeton: Princeton University Press, 1969.

————. *Lay Sermons*. Edited by R. J. White. Vol. 6 of *The Collected Works*. Edited by Kathleen Coburn. London: Routledge & Kegan Paul; Princeton: Princeton University Press, 1972.

————. *Miscellaneous Criticism*. Edited by Thomas Middleton Raysor. Cambridge: Harvard University Press, 1936.

————. *The Notebooks*. Edited by Kathleen Coburn. 3 vols. to date. London: Routledge & Kegan Paul, 1957-.

————. *The Philosophical Lectures*. Edited by Kathleen Coburn. London: Routledge & Kegan Paul, 1949.

————. *Shakespearean Criticism*. Edited by Thomas Middleton Raysor. 2 vols. 1907. Reprint, London: J. M. Dent, 1960.

————. *Specimens of Table Talk*. Edited by H. N. Coleridge. 2nd ed. London: Murray, 1836.

Colie, Rosalie L. *Paradoxia Epidemica: The Renaissance Tradition of Paradox*. Princeton: Princeton University Press, 1966.

————. "The Rhetoric of Transcendence." *Philological Quarterly* 43 (1964): 145–70.

Congleton, J. E. *Theories of Pastoral Poetry in England, 1684–1798*. Gainesville: University of Florida Press, 1952.

Cooke, Michael G. *Acts of Inclusion: Studies Bearing on an Elementary Theory of Romanticism*. New Haven: Yale University Press, 1979.

Coolidge, John S. "Great Things and Small: The Virgilian Progression." *Comparative Literature* 17 (1965): 1–23.

Cullen, Patrick. *Spenser, Marvell, and Renaissance Pastoral*. Cambridge: Harvard University Press, 1970.

Curtius, Ernst Robert. *European Literature and the Latin Middle Ages*. Translated by Willard R. Trask. 1953. Reprint, New York: Harper and Row, 1963.

Damon, Phillip. *Modes of Analogy in Ancient and Medieval Verse*. Berkeley: University of California Press, 1973.

Drake, Nathan. *Literary Hours, or, Sketches Critical and Narrative.* London: n.p., 1798.

Durrant, Geoffrey. *Wordsworth and the Great System: A Study of Wordsworth's Poetic Universe.* London: Cambridge University Press, 1970.

Eliade, Mircea. *Cosmos and History: The Myth of the Eternal Return.* Translated by Willard R. Trask. 1954. Reprint, New York: Harper & Row, 1959.

————. *Patterns in Comparative Religion.* Translated by Rosemary Sheed. 1958. Reprint, Cleveland: World Meridian Books, 1963.

————. "The Yearning for Paradise in Primitive Tradition." *Daedalus* 88 (1959): 255–67.

Eliot, T. S. *Four Quartets.* New York: Harcourt, Brace & Company, 1943.

————. *Selected Essays 1917–1932.* New York: Harcourt, Brace & Company, 1932.

Empson, William. *Some Versions of Pastoral.* Norfolk: New Directions, 1960.

Freud, Sigmund. *Gesammelte Werke.* Edited by Anna Freud with the collaboration of Marie Bonaparte. 18 vols. Vols. 1–17, London: Imago, 1942–52; Vol. 18, Frankfurt am Main: S. Fischer, 1968.

Friedman, Michael H. *The Making of a Tory Humanist: William Wordsworth and the Idea of Community.* New York: Columbia University Press, 1979.

Garber, Frederick. *The Autonomy of the Self from Richardson to Huysmans.* Princeton: Princeton University Press, 1982.

Gilbert, Allan H., editor. *Literary Criticism: Plato to Dryden.* 1940. Reprint, Detroit: Wayne State University Press, 1962.

Gleckner, Robert F. *The Piper and the Bard: A Study of William Blake.* Detroit: Wayne State University Press, 1959.

Goethe, Johann Wolfgang. *Faust: Backgrounds and Sources.* Translated by Walter Arendt. Edited by Cyrus Hamlin. New York: Norton, 1976.

————. *Gedenkausgabe der Werke, Briefe und Gespräche.* Edited by Ernst Beutler. 27 vols. Zürich: Artemis Verlag, 1948–71.

Gombrich, Ernst H. *Art and Illusion: A Study in the Psychology of Pictorial Representation.* London: Phaidon Press, 1960.

Guillén, Claudio. *Literature as System: Essays toward the Theory of Literary History.* Princeton: Princeton University Press, 1971.

Hagstrum, Jean H. *The Sister Arts: The Tradition of Literary Pictorialism and English Poetry from Dryden to Gray.* Chicago: University of Chicago Press, 1958.

Hartman, Geoffrey H. "Wordsworth, Inscriptions, and Romantic Nature Poetry." In *From Sensibility to Romanticism: Essays Presented to Frederick A. Pottle,* edited by Frederick W. Hilles and Harold Bloom, 389–413. New York: Oxford University Press, 1965.

———. *Wordsworth's Poetry, 1787–1814.* New Haven: Yale University Press, 1964.

Hazlitt, William. *The Complete Works.* Edited by P.P. Howe. 21 vols. London: J. M. Dent, 1930–34.

Hegel, Georg Wilhelm Friedrich. *Sämtliche Werke.* Edited by Hermann Glockner. 3rd ed. 26 vols. Stuttgart: Fromanns, 1949–59.

Heidegger, Martin. *Gesamtausgabe.* 18 vols. to date. Frankfurt am Main: Klostermann, 1976–

———. *Unterwegs zur Sprache.* Pfullingen: Neske, 1959.

Herder, Johann Gottfried. *Sprachphilosophische Schriften.* Edited by Erich Heintel. Hamburg: Meiner, 1960.

Hesiod. *The Homeric Hymns and Homerica.* With an English translation by Hugh G. Evelyn-White. Loeb Classics. Cambridge: Harvard University Press, 1959.

Hobsbawm, E. J. *Industry and Empire: An Economic History of Britain Since 1750.* London: Weidenfeld and Nicolson, 1968.

Huizinga, Johan. *Men and Ideas: Essays on History, the Middle Ages, the Renaissance.* Translated by James S. Holmes and Hans van Marle. 1959. Reprint, New York: Harper & Row, 1970.

Jack, Ian. *Keats and the Mirror of Art.* Oxford: Clarendon Press, 1967.

Jacobus, Mary. "Wordsworth and the Language of the Dream." *English Literary History* 46 (1979): 618–44.

James, William. *The Principles of Psychology.* 2 vols. 1890. Reprint, [New York:] Dover Publications, 1950.

Jauss, Hans Robert. *Aesthetische Erfahrung und literarische Hermeneutik.* München: Fink, 1977.

———. "Levels of Identification of Hero and Audience." *New Literary History* 5 (1974): 283–317.

———. *Literaturgeschichte als Provokation.* Frankfurt am Main: Suhrkamp, 1974.

Johnston, Kenneth R. "'Home at Grasmere': Reclusive Song." *Studies in Romanticism* 14 (1975): 1–28.

———. "Wordsworth and *The Recluse*: The University of Imagination." *PMLA* 97 (1982): 60–82.

Jones, Richard Forster. *Ancients and Moderns: A Study of the Rise of the Scientific Movement in Seventeenth-Century England.* 2nd ed. St. Louis: Washington University Press, 1961.

Kahler, Erich. *The Tower and the Abyss: An Inquiry into the Transformation of Man.* 1957. Reprint, New York: Viking, 1967.

Kant, Immanuel. *Critique of Judgement.* Translated by J. H. Bernard. 1914. Reprint, New York: Hafner, 1951.

―――. *Critique of Pure Reason.* Translated by Norman Kemp Smith. 1929. Reprint, New York: St. Martin's Press, 1965.

Keats, John. *The Letters of John Keats, 1814–1821.* Edited by Hyder Edward Rollins. 2 vols. Cambridge: Harvard University Press, 1958.

―――. *The Poems.* Edited by Miriam Allott. London: Longman, 1970.

―――. *The Poetical Works and Other Writings.* Edited by H. Buxton Forman. Revised by M. Buxton Forman. 8 vols. Hampstead Edition, 1938–39. Reprint, New York: Phaeton Press, 1970.

Keith, W. J. *The Poetry of Nature: Rural Perspectives in Poetry from Wordsworth to the Present.* Toronto: University of Toronto Press, 1980.

Kermode, Frank, editor. *English Pastoral Poetry: From the Beginnings to Marvell.* London: Harrap, 1952.

―――. *The Sense of an Ending: Studies in the Theory of Fiction.* London: Oxford University Press, 1968.

Kroeber, Karl. *Romantic Landscape Vision: Constable and Wordsworth.* Madison: University of Wisconsin Press, 1975.

Lawall, Gilbert. *Theocritus' Coan Pastorals: A Poetry Book.* Washington, D.C.: Center for Hellenic Studies; Cambridge: Harvard University Press, 1967.

Lewalski, Barbara K. "Innocence and Experience in Milton's Eden." In *New Essays on Paradise Lost*, edited by Thomas Kranides, 86–117. Berkeley: University of California Press, 1971.

Leymarie, Jean. *Dutch Painting.* Translated by Stuart Gilbert. [New York:] Skira, 1956.

Lindenberger, Herbert. "The Idyllic Moment: On Pastoral and Romanticism." *College English* 34 (1972): 335–51.

―――. *On Wordsworth's Prelude.* Princeton: Princeton University Press, 1963.

Lovejoy, Arthur O. *The Great Chain of Being: A Study of the History of an Idea.* Cambridge: Harvard University Press, 1936.

Lukács, Georg. *Goethe and His Age.* Translated by Robert Anchor. London: Merlin Press, 1968.

―――. *Probleme der Ästhetik.* Neuwied & Berlin: Luchterhand, 1969.

_____. *Studies in European Realism.* New York: Grosset & Dunlap, 1964.

Lynen, John F. *The Pastoral Art of Robert Frost.* New Haven: Yale University Press, 1960.

Mack, Maynard. *The Garden and the City: Retirement and Politics in the Later Poetry of Pope, 1731–1743.* Toronto: University of Toronto Press, 1969.

Makkreel, Rudolf A. *Dilthey: Philosopher of the Human Studies.* Princeton: Princeton University Press, 1975.

Mann, Thomas. *Versuch über Schiller.* Berlin & Frankfurt am Main: S. Fischer, 1955.

Martz, Louis L. "The Rising Poet, 1645." In *The Lyric and Dramatic Milton,* edited by Joseph H. Summers, 3–33. New York: Columbia University Press, 1965.

Marvell, Andrew. *The Poems.* Edited by Hugh MacDonald. Cambridge: Harvard University Press, 1952.

Marx, Karl. *The Marx-Engels Reader.* Edited by Robert C. Tucker. New York: Norton, 1972.

McFarland, Thomas. *Romanticism and the Forms of Ruin: Wordsworth, Coleridge, and Modalities of Fragmentation.* Princeton: Princeton University Press, 1981.

McGuire, Mary Ann C. "The Cavalier Country-House Poem: Mutations on a Jonsonian Tradition." *Studies in English Literature* 19 (1979): 93–108.

Miller, J. Hillis. "The Still Heart: Poetic Form in Wordsworth." *New Literary History* 2 (1971): 297–310.

_____. "The Stone and the Shell: The Problem of Poetic Form in Wordsworth's Dream of the Arab." In *Mouvements premiers: études critiques offertes à Georges Poulet,* 125–147. Paris: Librairie José Corti, 1972.

Milton, John. *Paradise Lost.* Edited by Merritt Y. Hughes. New York: Odyssey Press, 1935.

_____. *Paradise Regained, The Minor Poems and Samson Agonistes.* Edited by Merritt Y. Hughes. New York: Odyssey Press, 1937.

Moorman, Mary. *William Wordsworth: A Biography. The Early Years, 1770–1803.* Oxford, Clarendon Press, 1957.

Murray, Roger N. *Wordsworth's Style: Figures and Themes in the Lyrical Ballads of 1800.* Lincoln: University of Nebraska Press, 1967.

Norlin, George. "The Conventions of the Pastoral Elegy," *American Journal of Philosophy* 32 (1911): 294–312.

_____. "Greek Sources of Shelley's Adonais." *University of Colorado Studies* 1 (1904): 305–21.

Nowottny, Winifred. *The Language Poets Use*. New York: Oxford University Press, 1962.

Otto, Rudolf. *The Idea of the Holy*. Translated by John W. Harvey. 1923. Reprint, London: Oxford University Press, 1968.

Ovid. *Metamorphoses*. Translated by Rolfe Humphries. Bloomington: Indiana University Press, 1955.

Panofsky, Erwin. "Et in Arcadia Ego: On the Conception of Transience in Poussin and Watteau." In *Philosophy and History: Essays Presented to Ernst Cassirer*, edited by Raymond Klibansky and H. J. Platon, 223–54. New York: Harper & Row, 1963.

Parker, Reeve. *Coleridge's Meditative Art*. Ithaca: Cornell University Press, 1975.

Parrish, Stephen. "*Michael* and the Pastoral Ballad." In *Bicentenary Wordsworth Studies in Memory of John Alban Finch*, edited by Jonathan Wordsworth, 50–75. Ithaca: Cornell University Press, 1970.

Peacock, Thomas Love. "The Four Ages of Poetry." In *Shelley's Critical Prose*, edited by Bruce R. McElderry, Jr., Appendix B. Lincoln: University of Nebraska Press, 1967.

Pepper, Stephen C. *World Hypotheses: A Study in Evidence*. Berkeley: University of California Press, 1966.

Perkins, David. *Wordsworth and the Poetry of Sincerity*. Cambridge: Belknap Press of Harvard University Press, 1964.

Pindar. *The Odes*. Translated by Richmond Lattimore. 4th ed. Chicago: University of Chicago Press, 1976.

Plato. *The Collected Dialogues*. Edited by Edith Hamilton and Huntington Cairns. Princeton: Princeton University Press, 1961.

Poggioli, Renato. *The Oaten Flute: Essays on Pastoral Poetry and the Pastoral Ideal*. Cambridge: Harvard University Press, 1975.

Polwhele, Richard, translator. *The Idyllia, Epigrams, and Fragments of Theocritus, Bion, and Moschus, with the Elegies of Tyrtaeus*. With Dissertations and Notes. 2 vols. Bath: Cruttwell, 1792.

Pope, Alexander. *Pastoral Poetry and an Essay on Criticism*. Edited by E. Audra and Aubrey Williams. Vol. 1 of *The Twickenham Edition of the Poems*. Edited by John Butt. London: Methuen, 1961.

Potts, Abbie. *Wordsworth's "Prelude": A Study of Its Literary Form*. 1953. Reprint, New York: Octagon Books, 1966.

Putnam, Michael C. J. *Virgil's Pastoral Art: Studies in the Eclogues*. Princeton: Princeton University Press, 1970.

Rad, Gerhard von. *Old Testament Theology.* Translated by D. M. G. Stalker. 2 vols. Edinburgh: Oliver & Boyd, 1963–65.

Raine, Kathleen. *Blake and Tradition.* 2 vols. London: Routledge & Kegan Paul, 1968.

Rajan, Tilottama. *Dark Interpreter: The Discourse of Romanticism.* Ithaca: Cornell University Press, 1980.

Ricoeur, Paul. *Freud and Philosophy: An Essay on Interpretation.* Translated by Denis Savage. New Haven: Yale University Press, 1970.

————. *The Philosophy of Paul Ricoeur: An Anthology of His Work.* Edited by Charles E. Reagan and David Stewart. Boston: Beacon Press, 1978.

————. *The Rule of Metaphor: Multi-Disciplinary Studies of the Creation of Meaning in Language.* Translated by Robert Czerny; with Kathleen McLaughlin and John Costello. Toronto: University of Toronto Press, 1977.

Rilke, Rainer Maria. *Ausgewählte Werke.* 2 vols. N.p.: Insel-Verlag, 1951.

Rosenmeyer, Thomas G. *The Green Cabinet: Theocritus and the European Pastoral Lyric.* Berkeley: University of California Press, 1969.

Røstvig, Maren-Sofie. *The Happy Man: Studies in the Metamorphoses of a Classical Ideal.* 2 vols. Oslo Studies in English 2, 7. Oslo: Akademisk Forlag, 1954, 1958.

Rousseau, Jean-Jacques. *Du Contrat social ou principes du droit politique. Discours sur les sciences et les arts. Discours sur l'origine de l'inégalité parmi les hommes. . . .* Paris: Editions Garnier Frères, 1962.

Sartre, Jean-Paul. *What Is Literature?* Translated by Bernard Frechtman. New York: Philosophical Library, 1949.

Schiller, Friedrich. *Briefe. Kritische Gesamtausgabe.* Edited by Fritz Jonas. 7 vols. Stuttgart: Deutsche Verlagsanstalt, 1892–96.

————. *On the Aesthetic Education of Man, in a Series of Letters.* Edited and translated with an introduction, commentary and glossary of terms by Elizabeth M. Wilkinson and Leonard A. Willoughby. Oxford: Clarendon Press, 1967.

————. *Werke. Nationalausgabe.* Edited by Julius Petersen, Gerhard Fricke, Lieselotte Blumenthal, and Benno von Wiese. 17 vols. to date. Weimar: Hermann Böhlaus Nachfolger, 1943–.

Schlegel, Friedrich. *Kritische Friedrich-Schlegel-Ausgabe.* Edited by Ernst Behler. 35 vols. to date. München: F. Schöningh, 1958–.

Sharrock, Roger. "Wordsworth's Revolt Against Literature." In *Wordsworth's Mind and Art,* edited by A. W. Thomson, 56–72. Edinburgh:

Oliver and Boyd, 1969.

Shelley, Percy Bysshe. *Critical Prose*. Edited by Bruce R. McElderry, Jr. Lincoln: University of Nebraska Press, 1967.

———. *The Letters*. Edited by Frederick L. Jones. 2 vols. Oxford: Clarendon Press, 1964.

———. *Poetical Works*. Edited by Thomas Hutchinson. London: Oxford University Press, 1967.

———. *Poetry and Prose: Authoritative Texts and Criticism*. Edited by Donald H. Reiman and Sharon B. Powers. New York: Norton, 1977.

Southey, Robert. *Poems*. Edited by Maurice H. Fitzgerald. London: Oxford University Press, 1909.

Spenser, Edmund. *The Complete Poetical Works*. Edited by R. E. Neil Dodge. Cambridge Edition. Boston: Houghton Mifflin, 1936.

Sperry, Stuart M. *Keats the Poet*. Princeton: Princeton University Press, 1973.

Spivak, Gayatri Chakravorty. "Sex and History in *The Prelude* (1805): Books Nine to Thirteen." *Texas Studies in Literature and Language* 23 (1981): 324–60.

Staiger, Emil. *Friedrich Schiller*. Zürich: Atlantis Verlag, 1967.

Steiner, George. *After Babel: Aspects of Language and Translation*. London: Oxford University Press, 1975.

———. *Heidegger*. [London:] Harvester Press, 1978.

Stevens, Wallace. *Opus Posthumous*. Edited by Samuel French Morse. New York: Knopf, 1957.

Strich, Fritz. *Deutsche Klassik und Romantik, oder Vollendung und Unendlichkeit: ein Vergleich*. 1928. Reprint, Bern: Francke, 1962.

Szondi, Peter. "Poetik und Geschichtsphilosophie: zu Schillers Abhandlung über naive und sentimentalische Dichtung." In *Geschichte: Ereignis und Erzählung*, edited by Reinhart Koselleck and Wolf-Dieter Stempel, 377–410. München: Wilhelm Fink, 1973.

Taylor, Thomas. *Selected Writings*. Edited by Kathleen Raine and George Mills Harper. Princeton: Princeton University Press, 1969.

Theocritus. *Theocritus*. Edited with a translation and commentary by A. S. F. Gow. 2 vols. Cambridge: Cambridge University Press, 1950.

Thomson, James. *The Castle of Indolence and Other Poems*. Edited by Alan Dugald McKillop. Lawrence: University of Kansas Press, 1961.

Thompson, E. P. *The Making of the English Working Class*. London: Victor Gollancz, 1964.

Turner, Victor. *Dramas, Fields, and Metaphors: Symbolic Action in Human Society*. Ithaca: Cornell University Press, 1974.

————. "Social Dramas and Stories about Them." *Critical Inquiry* 7 (1980): 141–68.

Valéry, Paul. *The Collected Works.* Edited by Jackson Matthews. 15 vols. to date. New York: Pantheon Books, 1956–.

Van Ghent, Dorothy. *Keats: The Myth of the Hero.* Revised and edited by Jeffrey Cane Robinson. Princeton: Princeton University Press, 1983.

Vendler, Helen. *The Odes of John Keats.* Cambridge: Belknap Press of Harvard University Press, 1983.

Vico, Giambattista. *The New Science.* Abridged translation of the 3rd edition by Thomas Goddard Bergin and Max Harold Fisch. Ithaca: Cornell University Press, 1970.

Virgil. *Eclogues.* With a New Translation by Paul Alpers. In *The Singer of the Eclogues: A Study of Virgilian Pastoral,* 10–63. Berkeley: University of California Press, 1979.

Wagenknecht, David. *Blake's Night: William Blake and the Idea of Pastoral.* Cambridge: Belknap Press of Harvard University Press, 1973.

Wasserman, Earl R. *Shelley: A Critical Reading.* Baltimore: Johns Hopkins University Press, 1971.

White, Hayden. *Metahistory: The Historical Imagination in Nineteenth-Century Europe.* Baltimore: Johns Hopkins University Press, 1973.

Wilkie, Brian. *Romantic Poets and Epic Tradition.* Madison: University of Wisconsin Press, 1965.

Wilkinson, Elizabeth M., and Willoughby, Leonard A. "'The Whole Man' in Schiller's Theory of Culture and Society: On the Virtue of a Plurality of Models." In *Essays in German Language, Culture and Society,* edited by Siegbert S. Prawer, R. Hinton Thomas, and Leonard Forster, 177–210. London: University of London Institute of Germanic Studies, 1969.

Williams, Raymond. *The Country and the City.* New York: Oxford University Press, 1973.

————. *Keywords: A Vocabulary of Culture and Society.* New York: Oxford University Press, 1976.

Wimsatt, William K., and Brooks, Cleanth. *Literary Criticism: A Short History.* New York: Knopf, 1965.

Winckelmann, Johann Joachim. *Sämtliche Werke.* Edited by Joseph Eiselein. 12 vols. Donauöschingen: Verlag deutscher Klassiker, 1825–29.

Wind, Edgar. *Pagan Mysteries in the Renaissance.* New York: Norton, 1968.

Wordsworth, William. *Home at Grasmere.* Edited by Beth Darlington.

The Cornell Wordsworth. Edited by Stephen Parrish. Ithaca: Cornell University Press, 1977.

_____. *Letters of William and Dorothy Wordsworth: The Early Years, 1787–1805.* Edited by Ernest de Selincourt. 2nd edition revised by Chester L. Shaver. Oxford: Clarendon Press, 1967.

_____. *The Letters of William and Dorothy Wordsworth: The Middle Years, Part 1, 1806–1811.* Edited by Ernest de Selincourt. 2nd edition revised by Mary Moorman. Oxford: Clarendon Press, 1969.

_____. *The Letters of William and Dorothy Wordsworth: The Middle Years, Part 2, 1812–1820.* Edited by Ernest de Selincourt. 2nd edition revised by Mary Moorman and Alan G. Hill. Oxford: Clarendon Press, 1970.

_____. *The Poetical Works.* Edited by Ernest de Selincourt and Helen Darbishire. 5 vols. Oxford: Clarendon Press, 1940–49.

_____. *The Prelude.* Edited by Ernest de Selincourt. 2nd edition revised by Helen Darbishire. Oxford: Clarendon Press, 1959.

_____. *The Prelude, 1798–1799.* Edited by Stephen Parrish. *The Cornell Wordsworth.* Edited by Stephen Parrish. Ithaca: Cornell University Press, 1977.

_____. *The Prelude, 1799, 1805, 1850.* Edited by Jonathan Wordsworth, M. H. Abrams, and Stephen Gill. New York: Norton, 1979.

_____. *The Prose Works.* Edited by W. J. B. Owen and Jane Worthington Smyser. 3 vols. Oxford: Clarendon Press, 1974.

_____. *The Ruined Cottage and the Pedlar.* Edited by James Butler. *The Cornell Wordsworth.* Edited by Stephen Parrish. Ithaca: Cornell University Press, 1979.

Yeats, William Butler. *The Variorum Edition of the Poems of W. B. Yeats.* Edited by Peter Allt and Russell K. Alspach. New York: Macmillan, 1965.

INDEX